CROSSING BAR LINES

CROSSING BAR LINES

THE POLITICS AND PRACTICES OF BLACK MUSICAL SPACE

JAMES GORDON WILLIAMS

FOREWORD BY
ROBIN D. G. KELLEY

University Press of Mississippi / Jackson

The University Press of Mississippi is the scholarly publishing agency of
the Mississippi Institutions of Higher Learning: Alcorn State University,
Delta State University, Jackson State University, Mississippi State University,
Mississippi University for Women, Mississippi Valley State University,
University of Mississippi, and University of Southern Mississippi.

www.upress.state.ms.us

The University Press of Mississippi is a member
of the Association of University Presses.

First printing 2021
∞

Library of Congress Cataloging-in-Publication Data

Names: Williams, James Gordon, 1970– author. | Kelley, Robin D. G., writer
of foreword.
Title: Crossing bar lines : the politics and practices of black musical
space / James Gordon Williams; foreword by Robin D. G. Kelley.
Description: Jackson : University Press of Mississippi, 2021. | Includes
bibliographical references and index.
Identifiers: LCCN 2020042481 (print) | LCCN 2020042482 (ebook) | ISBN
9781496832108 (hardback) | ISBN 9781496832115 (trade paperback) | ISBN
9781496832122 (epub) | ISBN 9781496832139 (epub) | ISBN 9781496832146
(pdf) | ISBN 9781496832092 (pdf)
Subjects: LCSH: Jazz—2001–2010—History and criticism. |
Jazz—2011–2020—History and criticism. | Jazz—Political
aspects—United States—History—21st century. | African
Americans—Music—21st century—History and criticism.
Classification: LCC ML3508 .W545 2021 (print) | LCC ML3508 (ebook) | DDC
781.65/0973—dc23
LC record available at https://lccn.loc.gov/2020042481
LC ebook record available at https://lccn.loc.gov/2020042482

British Library Cataloging-in-Publication Data available

CONTENTS

FOREWORD

Through all the sorrow of the Sorrow Songs there breathes a hope—a
faith in the ultimate justice of things. The minor cadences of despair
change often to triumph and calm confidence. Sometimes it is faith in
life, sometimes a faith in death, sometimes assurance of boundless justice
in some fair world beyond.
—W. E. B. Du Bois, *The Souls of Black Folk*

Du Bois's words can be read as a distillation of what James Gordon Williams calls Black musical space. Sorrow/joy, hope/despair, life/death are not
merely opposites held in dialectical tension but coexist in Black music and,
by extension, in the totality of Black life—past, present, and future. Elaborating on Du Bois's profound insights, Williams reveals the inseparability of
Black music from Black affirmations of life, resistance to premature death,
and an imperative to constantly create from a place of deep memory and
forgetting, experimentation and collaboration, tradition and indeterminancy, dissonance and inclusion. A brilliant pianist and composer steeped
in Black Studies, critical theory, and an interdisciplinary approach to art,
Williams understands music as more than formal markers of pitch, timbre,
melody, rhythm, and notation. While he does not ignore these elements, he
nevertheless insists that we pay attention to the social, political, cultural,
emotional, and psychic worlds that animate Blackness, for these domains

are the foundations of Black musical space, what he calls "the luminescence of blackness manifested in the improvised expression of humanity."

Crossing Bar Lines examines the work of three generations of Black musicians: pianist Andrew Hill and drummer Billy Higgins, both born in the 1930s; Terri Lyne Carrington and Terence Blanchard, born in the 1960s; and trumpeter Ambrose Akinmusire, born in 1982. But the book was written during a particular historical moment characterized by a wave of state-sanctioned and vigilante murders of Black people, resulting in a wave of opposition from groups such as Hands Up United, Lost Voices, Organization for Black Struggle, the Dream Defenders, We Charge Genocide, the Black Youth Project 100, the Community Rights Campaign, and the Movement for Black Lives. Williams researched and wrote much of this book as Trayvon Martin's murderer was exonerated by a Florida jury; Jordan Davis was gunned down by a white man annoyed by his music; Eric Garner was choked to death by New York City's finest for selling loose cigarettes and breaking up a fight; Michael Brown was fatally shot by a Ferguson, Missouri, officer for walking in the middle of the street; twelve-year-old Tamir Rice was killed by a Cleveland cop for running around in a park brandishing a toy gun he got from Walmart; nine Black congregants of Charleston's Emmanuel AME Church were brutally murdered by a twenty-one-year-old white supremacist. The bodies continued to pile up: Walter Scott, Ezell Ford, John Crawford II, Rekia Boyd, Darrien Hunt, Tanisha Anderson, Aura Rain Rosser, Aiyana Stanley Jones, Miriam Carey, Roshad McIntosh, Akai Gurley, Sandra Bland, Freddie Gray, Alton Sterling, Shantel Davis, Same Dubose, Darnisha Harris, Philando Castile, Terence Crutcher, to name a few. Williams began researching and thinking about *Crossing Bar Lines* before there was a Trump presidency, as African Americans confronted voter suppression and other strategies of disfranchisement, unbridled corporate power, growing poverty and inequality, a tidal wave of home foreclosures, an expansion of police powers, wars in the Middle East, wars on trade unions, wars on women, two-and-a-half-million people living in cages, and a climate catastrophe threatening to end all life on this planet.

Williams discovered in contemporary Black musical space a powerful force against catastrophe. And he *heard* it, not only from those included here but in the audacious music of William Parker, James Brandon Lewis, Nicole Mitchell, Heroes Are Gang Leaders, Tomeka Reid, Kamasi Washington, Esperanza Spalding, Christian Scott aTunde Adjuah, Samora Pinderhughes, Kenyon Harrold, Jon Jang, Jamire Williams, Kris Bowers, and Ben Williams, to name but a few. In many ways, this soundtrack of refusal and regeneration shaped the tenor and sense of urgency that runs through the book. Williams's

own intellectual audacity matches that of the music. He jumps headlong
into the eye of a very contested storm and wrestles with a very old and yet
unresolved problem: what is Black music and what does it mean under the
conditions of modern white supremacy? What are its aesthetic principles?
How do we understand the broader context, the social, political, and cultural
events that swirl around these artists? How do we weigh social and religious
movements, family life, systems of policing and criminal justice, historical
memory, and other cultural and artistic developments against recordings
and notated music?

Just as Du Bois recognized how the "Sorrow Songs" breathed "hope"
and possibility into choking realities of dark times, Williams understands
Black musical space as a kind of breathing space. Breath is fundamental
to *Crossing Bar Lines*, not just as a trope or metaphor but as a basic activ-
ity of music-making. From trumpeter/composer Terence Blanchard's
powerful work "Breathless," dedicated to the slain Eric Garner, to drummer Billy Higgins's breathing as critical dimension of ensemble work
and community building. Breath gives life; the absence of breath spells
death. But breath is also rhythm. Runners, singers, and instrumentalists
invariably link breath to rhythm, pace, tempo. Breath, in the astute words
of Ashon T. Crawley, is also a "performative act" that, for Black people
whose very survival in this so-called New World depends on a fugitive
existence, is "constitutive for flight, for movement, for performance."[1]
Consider the sacred dimensions of breath in all sorts of ancient and indigenous musics—from the trained circular breathing required to play the
Aboriginal digeridoo to the human heartbeat itself, which percussionist,
scientist, acupuncturist, herbalist, and scholar Milford Graves identifies
as the common denominator of all music.

In other words, if we understand breath as the animating force of Black
music, then Williams is absolutely right to refuse to treat Black musical space
as merely a response to the dehumanizing forces of anti-Blackness. Black
musical space certainly acknowledges and accounts for the horrors of slavery, white supremacy, and colonial violence, but it is not defined by, nor is
it a reaction to, these historical and ongoing oppressions. It is a space of joy
and beauty that celebrates Black life, Black imagination, Black subjectivity,
and Black triumph over adversity. It is also a contingent and contested space,
constantly evolving as contradictions are revealed and resolved. Williams
examines the most enduring form of exclusion within Black musical space—
gender—in his chapter on Terri Lyne Carrington. Acclaimed as one of the
greatest drummers of her generation, bandleader, composer, and educator,
the Grammy award–winning Carrington is also the founding director of

the Institute for Jazz and Gender Justice at the Berklee School of Music. It's slogan "Jazz without Patriarchy" envisions a transformation of Black musical space based on "a faith in the ultimate justice of things" and the breath of those historically excluded—women, LGBTQIA, and gender non-conforming folks. Thus, the Institute exists not outside of Black musical space, not as a body demanding entry into a boys' club. Rather, it *is* Black musical space, as it embodies an authentic commitment to inclusion based on shared principles of creativity and liberation. Williams writes, "Though Black musical space extends from Black life, it has the potential to be an inclusive space for all humanity. . . . Black musical space is not about ownership but about freedom. It comes from people who have been enslaved, marginalized, and murdered and who therefore understand the importance of love over property. It extends from Black life but does not belong to any race, gender, religion, or creed."

But this elusive freedom is not a given. It demands an obligation to struggle, a commitment to a boundless imagination, and an abiding respect for Black life. Turn the page. Enter. Inhale.

Robin D. G. Kelley
Los Angeles, October 2019

CROSSING BAR LINES

INTRODUCTION

Entering a Theory
of Black Musical Space

We as black people still have the power to shift spaces.[1]
—Amy Sherald

Spaces can be real and imagined. Spaces can tell stories and untold histories. Spaces can be interrupted, appropriated and transformed through artistic and literary practice.[2]
—bell hooks

Black music, like other forms of black artistic and cultural expression, opens a space for reflection, a meditative space that bears critically on the precarious and predatory world in which its auditors and its producers find themselves.[3]
—Nathaniel Mackey

Crossing Bar Lines grew from my interest in how African American composers and improvisers use musical expression to articulate what it means to be Black in an often hostile world. Consequently, this book is about how Black musical space is created by, and represented in, the work of five African American improvisers. Black musical space is not expressed only in creative improvisation and composition; but the scope of this book is limited to African American artists whose musical language is creative improvisation and composition. There is no separation between how an African American musician creates and how he or she ontologically expresses what it means to be Black in the world. The life and politics of African American improvisational culture are reflected in how improvising musicians create their own Black music space in which to articulate their humanity.

I explore how these five African American improvisers use their improvisation as a platform to do the cultural work of addressing social inequalities while affirming their humanity. Readers can use this book as a tool for exploring these improvisers' polychromatic approaches to Black musical expression and its relationship to space-making. Some improvisers, such as trumpeters Terence Blanchard and Ambrose Akinmusire use their improvised music to make commentary on systemic and structural racism expressed in police brutality. Whereas drummer Terri Lyne Carrington, in a more intersectional approach, addresses racism and gender inequity simultaneously through her collective approach to social science music. These artists explicitly take part in current political discourses on the systemic marginalization that contributes to social inequality and Black social death. In contrast, for improvisers pianist Andrew Hill and drummer Billy Higgins performances of cultural work and resistance is not as explicit or openly political. My goal is not to compare the effectiveness of the cultural work among these musicians. This book examines why and how these improvisers do this work. My larger argument concerns how African American improvised music culture illustrates the political stakes involved in living between social life and death through space-making performances. Understanding how African American improviser-philosophers approach improvisation by creating their own musical and political space is as important now in the twenty-first century as it was in the 1960s and generations before. To that extent, some chapters of this book focus on the cultural work improvisers are doing in relation to contemporary social movements, while never forgetting that they stand on the shoulders of cultural workers and improvisers in the past.

I have structured this book on the architecture of five case studies, so that each musician's work is connected through common cultural characteristics across space and time and not the era in which they did their work. Think of these chapters as a "flow of paths," since "evil travels in straight lines."[4] While I have read A. B. Spellman's *Four Lives in the Bebop Business* (1966) and Robin D. G. Kelley's *Africa Speaks, America Answers: Modern Jazz in Revolutionary Times* (2012), their excellent work on improvised music and jazz culture was not a consciously chosen model for this book. Yet my work connects to Spellman's *Four Lives* in how I also ignore whether the improviser is considered a mainstream or an avant-garde jazz artist. Such distinctions between musicians are even less relevant today, when improvisers are creating even more interdisciplinary musical texts that incorporate not only a panoply of improvisational languages and music cultures but also recorded video and audio. As a musician, I have never limited myself to genre classifications or thinking in a style. As a pianist I have worked with both the late saxophonist Joseph Jarman, known for his membership in the Art Ensemble of Chicago and the Association for the Advancement of Creative Musicians (AACM), and jazz vocalist Gregory Porter. In that sense the way I have approached writing this book is a reflection of my own experience as an African American improviser. While that experience informs every word in this book, my personal experience as a musician will not be as explicit as David Toop's is in *Into the Maelstrom: Music Improvisation, and the Dream of Freedom: Before 1970* (2016). I privilege the improvisers' voices through interviews in this text when possible. Those readers who do not read music or understand music analysis should not feel alienated by the critical musicology frame I deploy in this book. Readers will be able to gain insight on these improvisers' cultural work through the other theoretical lenses I use.

I chose these five African American improvisers because their musical work demonstrates complex relationships within notions of Blackness, gender, and a Black sense of place. While all of their work is political, the politics are expressed differently. In many ways their work is a backlash and a repudiation against common notions of African American improvisation reflected in jazz pedagogical and performance practice orthodoxy. I have put these artists in conversation with each other because their work represents the practice of place-making in defiance of codified aesthetics that reflect the social constraints of structural and institutional racism. Their music and the instruments they play are a reflection of their minds.[5] These African American improvisers articulate Black musical space in different but ontologically related ways. They are masters of improvisation and compositional forms but are never limited by the musical forms that they innovate. But the central theme of this book is how these featured musicians reveal in their work the politics, struggle, and joy in the practice of Black musical space-making.

Improvised Music as the Practice of Respatialization

Improvisation by African American musicians is an articulation of Black humanity that happens within spaces and transforms those very spaces.

Black musical space is ontological, imaginary as well as a reflection of social and cultural geography. Black musical space is rooted in the materiality of Black people's lived experiences, a sociality with surprising permutations in what Patricia Hill Collins calls Black Civil Society.[6] In this text I lay out how African American improvisers produce musical space in response to social inequality faced in quotidian life but also create sonic narratives about love, laughter, and liminality in Black life. African American improvisation is understood here as a musical practice rooted in critiquing the social systems that have marginalized musicians and their communities. But it is also understood as a practice of producing space that reflects the radical imagination for a better future.

Improvisation is the practice of cartography in real time. Thinking about African American improvisation practices through Katherine McKittrick's theory of Black Geographies has been helpful in theorizing Black musical space. I theorize African American improvisers as cartographers of alternative musical maps that demonstrate musical and ontological place-making. This musical place-making is necessary because the "structural workings of racism kept Black cultures in place and tagged them as placeless."[7] Colonial logic, which forms the philosophical basis for plantocracy and defines humanity within terms of owning Black people as property, has never fully accorded Black people the sign of the human.[8] For McKittrick, who builds on Sylvia Wynter's formulation, the social alienation that comes from displacing Black people inspires their subversive creative acts and represents a reinvention of Black life in contradistinction to the colonial logic of white supremacy. I contend that Black creativity represented in improvisation is the practice of spatial insubordination that highlights the value of Black humanity while refuting the belief system(s) that consistently invalidate Black humanity. Black musical space reflects experiences on the ground and also the spatial imagination. Building on Wynter and McKittrick, I contend that African American improvised music is a practice of "living geography,"[9] a practice of sonically improvised space-making that contests and disrupts the marginalization that buttresses the falsely imagined neutral and transparent spaces we share.

While the practice of Black musical space comes from imagining Black subjectivity in radically new ways and then transforming that imagination into radical musical practices, this space is not magical, essentialized, or about separatism. As indicated in the epigraph, Black feminist theorist bell hooks asserts that space is both tangible and a reflection of the Black imaginary. Spaces are potential locations for storytelling and revealing hidden histories. Hegemonic spaces that have displaced Black people can be changed when interventions through creative practices happen. hooks argues that when Black people change their orientation or positions in order to write their own worlds, "radical creative space" can be made for affirming Black subjectivity.[10] This idea of space that hooks constructs and critiques is located in both the creative imagination and the physical margins of civil society. She calls this space "a profound edge"[11] where Black people find a non-monolithic community of resistance to anti-Blackness. This space is also an aperture where the language of love, light, and life is cultivated, crafted, and deployed. hooks explains, "For me this space of radical openness is a margin—a profound edge. Locating oneself there is difficult yet necessary. It is not a 'safe' place. One is always at risk. One needs a community of resistance."[12] I contend that the risk hooks discusses here is embodied in the various improvisational and compositional strategies and theoretical critiques of the musicians featured in the chapters of this book. The cultural work these African American improvisers deploy is never about artistic risk taking for risk's sake. It takes improvisation and imagination for African American people to survive in this world, and those peculiar tactics and strategies were a part of building up a Black civil society long before the word "jazz" existed. This idea is characterized by a statement Cornel West made in an interview with trumpeter Terence Blanchard in a postlude to Blanchard's composition "Winding Roads" (2009). West states: "I can't conceive of a great musician who has not explored the highest levels of courageous engagement in their craft . . . at the level of form and content . . . at the level of style and substance . . . that's what greatness is: it's a courage to go to the edge of life's abyss, to step out on nothing and still think you gon' land on something."[13] While musical expression is only one representational arena where Afro-diasporic cultural strategies of improvisation are shown, for our purposes here I focus on how improvisation is ontological place-making. This book serves to document and analyze this production of musical space that extends from the social margins.

Black musical space extends from concrete, quotidian experiences in African American life, experiences that connect to the geography of transatlantic slavery, an institution built on the belief system that Black people are less than human. Space is often theorized as detached from human geographies in the analysis of Black art.[14] Improvisation is theorized here as a production of space in real time from an African American improviser's sense of place, or sense of "placelessness." The concept of Black Geographies argues that Black life is spatial life and connects the spatiality of imagination and the practice of space-making in physical places. Black Geographies posits that "all social relations are grounded in spatial relations and "privileges Black world-making practices in all of their multiplicities."[15] Both violence and resistance to violence takes place in spaces. McKittrick calls this resistance "respatializations," which is rooted in "alternative geographic formulations" and are important interventions and survival strategies.[16] McKittrick explains, "I want to stress that if practices of subjugation are also spatial acts, then the ways in which Black women think, write, and negotiate their surroundings are intermingled with place based critiques, or, respatializations."[17] McKittrick has argued that a Black sense of place is linked to a history of racial violence on many registers, but especially the structural and the epistemic. She positions the plantation as the locus of modernity and a structural template for how Black bodies can be disciplined within space and time zones.[18] Moreover, the spatialized violence of the slave ship, the plantation, the auction block all represent spatialized violence that has worked to erase what a "black sense of place."[19] My central concern is how this Black sense of place is reflected in African American improvisation and composition.

How do African American practices of improvisation become respatializations? How do African American musicians create a sense of place through critiquing the spaces of racial and sexual violence and gender inequality, but also the spaces of joy, love, and hope? How does improvisation represent a mapping that reflects an alternative space that is both real and imaginary, interior and exterior? I argue that the practice of Black musical place-making is about creating a sense of place that reflects the interiority of the Black radical imagination and the interfacing with physical spaces. This improvised musical place-making represents not only how spatial domination affects Black people's lives but also how they create alternative spaces of affirmation in response to the historical relegation of Black people to placelessness. That placelessness, which is built up by the structure and logic of racism and shaped by the history of dehumanization, colonialism, and geographical displacement, informs what a "black sense of place" is.[20] As McKittrick argues, this displacement of Black people occurred within the geography of the plantation economy "which tagged them as placeless."[21] Yet these structures that forcibly facilitated the collective sense of placelessness did not foreclose the possibility of improvising new cartographies outside of the maps drawn up by domination and white supremacy. African American improvisatory and compositional practices, which operates on the outskirts of colonial logic, is an expression of the diverse and unpredictable permutations of the lived experiences of Black people. Much of how McKittrick defines a Black sense of place is reflected in the indeterminate nature of African American improvisation. She writes that "a black sense of place is not a steady, focused, and homogeneous way of seeing and being in place, but rather a set of changing and differential perspectives that are illustrative of, and therefore remark upon, legacies of normalized racial violence that calcify, but do not guarantee, the denigration of black geographies and their inhabitants."[22] The social practice of improvisation by the African American musicians documented in these case studies represent practices of non-monolithic cartography; place-making practices that reveal philosophical ideas, and critiques that morph into exciting and vital improvisatory and compositional strategies.

I view African American improvisation as a deployment of oppositional spatial knowledge that reflects the material conditions and imaginations that shape Black lives on a daily basis. Examples of critiques that are mapped include the effects of white supremacy, sexism, violence, patriarchy, and the physical displacement of Black lives. Theorizing through the lives of Black women across the African diaspora, Katherine McKittrick argues that Black women create cultural landscapes, both real and imaginary, that reflect transatlantic slavery, the domination of settler colonialism, and the geographies of racial difference. Arguing that "black matters are spatial matters," Black people are understood as politically and culturally invested in producing space because, from the point of view of white supremacy, they have been understood as occupying placelessness. African American improvisers, and Black subjects in general, are committed to producing space because, viewed through the prism of white supremacy, they are not seen as occupying geography but as displaced racial and sexual beings.[23]

What are the parameters of Black musical space? This question cannot be answered without considering the parameters of inequality and social domination. If African American improvised music is about place-making through exploding the systemic constraints that have shaped Black musicians' lives, then there can be no end, no confinement to improvised respatialization in a society permeated by white supremacy. After all, what are the parameters of white supremacy and its impact on Black lives? Where does it begin and where does it end? The mechanisms of white supremacy seek not to restrain themselves but to continually displace the marginalized. While this book is African Americanist, the physical places where Black musical space is practiced and created are anywhere these improvisers and composers socially produce musical space as a critique of the world. Consequently, the production of space happens on the storied bandstands in the jazz clubs across America as well as festival stages around the world. It also happens in social movements and collectives. Black musical collectives such as the Association for the Advancement of Creative Musicians (AACM) and Union of God's Musicians and Artists Ascension (UGMAA), have shown us that producing Black musical space happens in parks, elite performance institutions, community centers and churches. These collectives are just two examples of artists producing alternative musical geographies within the south side of Chicago and Black cultural enclaves such as Leimert Park in Los Angeles respectively.[24] In rare circumstances, Black musical space is created in college music programs through institution building for gender quality while attacking the patriarchal culture of the music.

To Improvise Is to Theorize

Improvisation in this book is defined as producing creative space outside of the colonial logic that has defined what it means to be both human and less than human in this world. The practice of improvisation is a way of theorizing about society, which engenders a sense of the physical and imaginary, visible and invisible space. Arguing that "our picture of the world cannot be complete" without understanding the way musical practices construct a "sense of space," geographer Susan J. Smith contends the practice of music can be read as a form of theorizing society, which includes theories of space.[25] For Smith, musical spaces produced through musical practices are effected by the political economy, technology, constructs about high and low art, and the tension between religious ideology and the secular state.[26] All of these factors, Smith argues, influence how musicians are positioned in society as well as where performances take place. More relevant to my argument is how Smith asserts that music, which has "the most transgressive potential," is where formations of identity can be affirmed, that musical practice has the potential for creating "*a flexible space in which identities can be lived, experienced, shaped and altered* [my emphasis]. Crucially, it is a form through which those whose condition a wider society tries its best not to see have a way to make themselves heard."[27] Echoing what many Black scholars have argued for generations,[28] Smith contends that Black music articulates the marginalized positionality of Black people in relation to white civil society while shaping the identities of the people located in those spaces.[29] Similar to Frank Kofsky,[30] Smith argues that Black musicians seek to create Black musical spaces where their music could be practiced and not commodified, explaining: ". . . black musicians have always striven for a space of creativity which whites could not occupy. Jazz artists did this in a quest for virtuosity, seeking to develop a music so difficult that whites could not steal it."[31] Smith also explains, "music is a way of articulating the conditions of existence. It is a way of telling stories, of expressing the way lives are lived and of charting the geography of inequality."[32] Yet, Black musical space represented in improvised cartographies is not only about charting the geography of inequality but charting all aspects of Black life.

African American improvisation does not solely represent the legacy of forced placelessness or an articulation of rebellion against white supremacist systems and institutions that deny Black people a sense of place in society. African American improvisers are agents whose experiences expressed through music should not be read through the lens of trauma. They should be envisioned as space creators. As Robin D. G. Kelley argues, "reading black experience through trauma can easily slip into thinking of ourselves as victims and objects rather than agents. . . ."[33] Clyde Woods argues that blues music is a philosophical method of map construction that locates Black experiences in the historical, imagined, and physical institutions that reflect our time. For Woods, blues creates a space for critiquing systemic, social inequality while also focusing on "the utopian vision of the dispossessed."[34] Indeed, improvisation is a practice of creating an alternative sense of place of belonging that affirms the value of Black life. Building on the work of Sylvia Wynter's "Black Metamorphosis," McKittrick theorizes listening to Black popular music as a force for binding community and creating a space of intellectual engagement and love outside of hegemonic ideas of intellectualism and loving. The rhythmic grooves in Black popular music can be a political intervention while engendering affirming qualities of space-making. McKittrick writes, "one grooves *out* of the logics of antiblackness and *into* black life."[35] While McKittrick locates these subversive qualities in Black popular music, the regenerative qualities of Black music are genreless. Genre, a form of aesthetic segregation, is gleefully obliterated and transgressed by the improvisers I write about in this book. The musical inventions of the improvisers discussed in this book also work to subvert and expose white supremacy, strive to address social inequality, and boldly affirm the value of Black social life.

In theorizing through the concept of Black musical space, I do not measure the spatio-temporal strategies in improvisation as a one-to-one reflection of ontological Blackness. Musical information—relative to performance, composition, and improvisation—is an open form of symbolism, and the interpretation of musical events depends on who is doing the work of analytical listening.[36] Musicologist David Ake writes that listeners often project their own meanings onto jazz improvisation, generating narratives based on the assumption of what Nina Sun Eidsheim and Jennifer Stoever both posit as an assumed interiority apprehended by the listener.[37] He argues that sound on the level of rhythm, harmony, melody, or other aspects "cannot 'contain' morality or any other human quality. Neither can form, nor

melody, nor groove. People bestow meanings on music. . . . [T]hese meanings [may be] shaped . . . by timbre and other formalistic details but also
by an array of other aspects. In other words, it's never 'all in the music.'"[38]
This book is not about measuring an exact form of Blackness expressed in
improvised music because I do not believe that an exact measurement of
Blackness is possible. Scholar and performance artist E. Patrick Johnson
argues that policing Black authenticity through constructing exact definitions leaves out other possibilities of what it means to be Black in the world.
He claims the qualities of Black music cannot be restricted to an essentialist/
antiessentialist assessment or analytical framework, writing, "When blacks
attempt to define what it means to be black, they delimit the possibilities
of what blackness can be."[39] Composer and multi-instrumentalist Henry
Threadgill does not believe that the sound of music can communicate
definite meanings to the lay listener or the critical musicologist. Music
does not function like literature, which often indicates explicit meanings.
Threadgill explains: "It [music] won't give you any literary things. If it does,
the next person next to you will say, 'It doesn't say that to me.'"[40] When I
told Threadgill some scholars such as Frank Kofsky have argued that the
African American postwar modernistic music called bebop was created as
a form of resistance to white improvisers who stole and profited off their
musical ideas, Threadgill immediately disagreed:

> I don't accept that premise. They [Black bebop musicians] didn't create music
> for that. They created music because that is what came out of them; it had
> nothing to do with anything. You can't decide you are going to be greater than
> midgets, white people, or fat people. You either have that [musical] imagination
> or you don't. And when it [the creative music] is time to rise up in your system,
> it will come out. It's from a higher spirituality and is above all of the triviality
> of life's circumstances.[41]

Improviser, theorist, and chronicler of the Association for the Advancement of Creative Musicians (AACM) George E. Lewis has argued that
improvisation is a site of fluid meaning and should not be attached by
default to oppositional discourses. Improvisation can reflect politics but
the practice of improvised music need not pledge allegiance to a particular
stance because "improvisation is more fundamental than music."[42] Lewis
continues, "Not all improvisation deals with trauma . . . improvisation is
about infinite deferral; suspending, bracketing, deferring, never reaching
the end. It's a joyful forgetting."[43] The musical space of indeterminacy that
Lewis describes is not in contradistinction to the idea that a Black sense of

place can be produced through improvisation. It is important to reserve judgment about what improvising one's humanity in Black musical space might mean. Improvised music here is theorized as the practice of being open to a set of possibilities or conditions that musically reflects one's humanity. As improviser Douglas Ewart states, "You don't have a product but a set of conditions."[44] Black musical placemaking is not about ownership but about freedom. It comes from people who have been enslaved, marginalized, and systematically murdered and who therefore understand the importance of love over property. It extends from Black life but does not belong to any race, gender, religion, or creed. This is why Threadgill disavows racial constructs and passionately argues for the importance of being open to all music cultures, to experiencing the interrelated art cultures of the world beyond one's initial experience in one's community. For Threadgill, Black music culture is not something to be owned but information to be shared:

> You are born into the human family and then you go down into some racial or ethnic group. The first thing one learns in their first community is made up of things that you become aware of immediately around you. Some people just stay right there. All the music in the world and all the art, all the information is out there for me to learn, so things are stacked on top of that. Everything I learned in the first community is there as the first foundation. Cuba, China, Europe gets stacked and stacked. I'm not playing out of any racial or ethnic experience at all then. You ever hear that song by Abbey Lincoln, "I Got Some People in Me"? That's what we got.[45]

Black Sound and the Performance of Black Musical Space

Musicologist Nina Sun Eidsheim has argued that listening to music is political because it is a practice that is culturally and socially constructed within a community. The feedback loop between the musical gestures of a performer and a community's affirming response to that performance is proof that the shared musical information within a community is aurally processed as "rigged evidence," evidence mistaken for an innate musical style.[46] Consequently, Eidsheim's approach to musical analysis eschews achieving the most accurate interpretation of a vocal performance, or what she calls "fidelity."[47] For Eidsheim, focusing on style, technique, and the details of the vibrational performance is more important than symbolic naming. While I find value in Eidsheim's analytical approach, I argue that it is still important to name and theorize Black musical space because Black people's sense of place, and the music that extends from that place, has been subject to discursive forces of eradication. In other words, it is important to name the political practice of space-making by the African American improvisers in this text because much of that practice has been subject to abuse and erasure in the political economy of jazz.[48] Moreover, naming musical space does not negate the multiplicities of Black agency that constitutes the space.

The African American improvisers I write about in this book have all subverted the white imaginary that informs white audience sonic expectations of how Black improvised music should sound. Through compositional and improvised performance practices, these improvisers have long subverted what Jennifer Stoever calls the "sonic color line,"[49] as a discriminatory barrier that racializes sound through constructed definitions of sonic whiteness and Blackness. Stoever investigates how white people have learned how to recognize and label sound as Black, arguing that "racialized listening" has relegated Black voices to a set of sonic archetypes. The sonic color line requires conformity to racialized sonic norms; this becomes hegemonic in our understanding, rendering sounds produced by white bodies as superior and those of Black bodies as inferior. While sound has been used to ghettoize Black people in social spaces, Black people have responded to this spatial marginalization with a "long history of black agency, resistance, and activism in the face of such silencing."[50] The sonic color line has existed in jazz criticism for years. Using the framework of Henry Louis Gates Jr.'s "signifyin(g)" theory, Robert Walser argues that the white modernist criticism of Miles Davis's performance techniques suggests that critics did not understand that Davis never aimed to achieve what theorist George E. Lewis defines as "Eurological" standards of improvised music performance.[51] Davis was articulating regenerative, cyclic Black musical space when he improvised on the chord changes of "My Funny Valentine" with his bandmates in that storied 1964 benefit concert at Lincoln Center. Trumpeter, composer, and theorist Wadada Leo Smith understood how the sonic color line worked, which is why he argued for Black self-determination. Smith notes that the creative practice of Blacks is open to misunderstanding, so Black artists must take charge of how their creative practice and art is represented in the world: "We do not need our creations dissected by others who cannot know what they see. We must not wait for others to document their own distortions of that which we can say rightly for ourselves. So I am self-conscious, and I want every black person to become self-conscious."[52]

Black musical space is the non-cadencing and anti-perfection core of the subjectivity mode of Black improvisation. Pianist Thelonious Monk encapsulated Black musical space when he told vocalist Abbey Lincoln, who was recording his composition "Blue Monk": "Don't be so perfect."[53] Perfection as defined by Eurological values has no place in Black musical space. Fred Moten asserts that there is a peculiar ontological essence in the Black sound that is the path to a new kind of world where "the universal" is legitimately inclusive of all people: the Black diasporic ontological sphere; the "space-time of an improvisation," which he describes as "liberatory" in nature; an "erotics of the cut," blurry, improvised, liberatory, politically obsessed with freedom and the product of damaged love.[54] Moten goes further: "Your ass is what you sing."[55] He theorizes Black improvisation in relation to his definition of universality, which views the Black aesthetic as birthed within a counterhegemonic spatialized break.[56] Moten's theory of rupture also positions improvised music as producing space of infinite deferrals: "And how should we listen to music that refuses to 'coalesce,' that has a 'differential resistance to enclosure'?"[57] Fumi Okiji asks the same question differently when she writes, "Could it be that jazz takes advantage of the inevitability of failure encoded in artistic pursuit?"[58] The affirmation of Black value is anchored in the joyous process of deferring meaning and the generation of spatialized, balanced asymmetry, which animates the contours of musical risk and produces the purpose for crossing bar lines.

Crossing Bar Lines

Musical space as an aesthetic idea, like the discipline of geography, has been perceived as invisibly and universally white. That invisible whiteness has shaped how we understand music, and musical space in general. Sara Ahmed explains that spaces are oriented around whiteness, which makes nonwhite people have a heightened awareness of how they are often unwelcome in white civil society: "Spaces are orientated 'around' whiteness, insofar as whiteness is not seen. We do not face whiteness; it 'trails behind' bodies, as what is assumed to be given. The effect of this 'around whiteness' is the institutionalization of a certain 'likeness' which makes non-white bodies feel uncomfortable, exposed, visible, different, when they take up this space."[59] The evidence of orientation around whiteness is clear in my past, institutionalized musical training, where I was required to read *The History of Western Music* by Donald Jay Grout and not Amiri Baraka's *Blues People*.[60] Where, I wondered but was not sophisticated enough to articulate at that juncture, was the love for Black theoretical frameworks in music programs that could not exist without the musical labor of Black bodies over generations? Indeed, there is a systemic erasure in some college and conservatory curricula of historical contributions by Black "jazz" improvisers and composers, in an effort to whitewash those contributions—or at least smother them under kumbaya multiculturalism and bastardized versions of Du Bois's double consciousness. A misguided desire to create parity in the discourse between Black and white contributions to this quintessentially American-rooted but global music is one factor fueling this erasure. Another is the paucity of Black musicians and scholars in college and conservatory music programs whose experiences would diversify and make the jazz discourse more inclusive. These factors motivate the following questions: What happens in African American improvisers' lived experiences? How do their experiences in a world that continues to deny them full humanity shape their creative practices? How do African American improvisers suggest a Black sense of space, a kind of spatial politics, with musical gestures such as a note, phrase, or compositional structures? How do they spatially articulate their humanity by musically rewriting the world through improvisation and composition? Place-making by African American improvisers critiques and challenges this field of whiteness that permeates the world through its various institutions and is the residue of both colonialism and institutional slavery. Black musical space is a ceaselessly productive space of a lived asymmetry with Western notions of progress, finality, or aesthetic greatness.

Crossing bar lines is a theoretical phrase I have redefined to describe the metaphorical connection between African American musicians' use of unconventional and "experimental" music strategies and their articulation of Black musical space—as well as their improvised musical performance of social action in that space.[61] The traditional understanding of the phrase suggests the idea of musical notation; two rhythms of any value, for example, tied together across a bar line on sheet music. However, I use "crossing bar lines" as a metaphor for Black performative insurgency in sound for the purpose of expressing Black humanity. I remix the term past its traditional, purely notational meaning to redefine it within Black musical space, where Black music explodes hegemonic theoretical constraints and opens up new interdisciplinary pathways and types of alternative knowledge that elucidate African American improvisatory and musical practices. I don't use "crossing bar lines" to privilege any single musical feature or gesture in African diasporic musical practices.

Bar lines in this study serve as a spatial metaphor for transgressing social constraints connected to white supremacy. Crossing them applies not only to experimental Black music but to how African Americans improvisers have had to cross structural barriers to fight the social injustices that obstruct their way of life. Although their musical resistance is one of the most vital ways to understand what is at stake for African American cultural workers in their continual battle for social justice, the artistic articulation of Black humanity occurs on many different registers beyond resistance. For example, "crossing bar lines" also describes African Americans' unwillingness to assimilate to white spaces that dictate the dominant way of life.[62]

I want to understand what sound tells us about Black humanity, so I study how Black music is performed in the service of articulating everyday Black life. My "crossing bar lines" hermeneutic represents how Black musicians tell the complex story of how Black people live in, and imagine, spaces.

My theory of "Black musical space" relative to my definition of crossing bar lines is developed in order to break from the teleological narratives prominent in the jazz discourse and to achieve a greater understanding of how African American improvisers as cultural workers produce Black musical space. This approach takes into consideration the lived experience of African American improvisers, composers, and performers who produce musical space that explodes the social constraints of institutional and structural racism, establishing new narratives of what it means to be Black in the world. The African American improvisers in this book have been inculcated with, and in most cases have mastered, Western music theory. Yet African American improvisers work to create musical space within dominant culture to provide what philosopher Charles Mills calls a "(partially) internalist critique of the dominant culture by those who accept many of the culture's principles but are excluded by them."[63]

The notion of musical multiculturalism has led to the redefining of Du Bois's theory of double consciousness to create nonincendiary theoretical frameworks, which offend and check dominant sensibilities in the jazz discourse. Fumi Okiji identified this rewriting of Duboisian double consciousness in the work of some critical improvisation scholars when she wrote, "It is, perhaps, nostalgia, fueled by this 'gumbo' narrative, that has led to cursory renderings of double consciousness that fuse it to a nebulous multiculturalism, defusing the specificity of the modern narrative that Du Bois was carefully reconstructing in his constellation of ideas."[64] The double consciousness embodied in African American produced musical space cannot be mapped onto white lives because Black musical space arises out of

Black lived experience—lived experience that reflects how Black people are spatially relegated to the outskirts of civil society.

Improvising on the Axes of Social Life and Social Death

Since Black musical space is a cultural theory rooted in the analysis of social structures that privilege white space, Afro-pessimism has been an important theoretical framework for understanding social constraints that oppress marginalized peoples. Afropessimism theory engages systemic racism rooted in the history of transatlantic slavery. Its core concept is that Black people—not just African Americans but others of African descent—live in a type of social death.[65]

Afropessimist Frank Wilderson criticizes humanities scholars who have constructed "a causal link between the performance of Black art and the emancipation of the Black people who produce and consumed it—as though art is the very essence of, rather than an accompaniment to, structural change."[66] He asserts that Black Studies programs, whose theoretical foundations are anchored in the imagination of a unified African diaspora, have promoted the idea of a direct link between Black creativity and social change. Yet the Afropessimist framework denies Black people agency and self-definition.

If I were to accept the notion, as I have written in the past, that Black people are ontologically positioned outside the scope of humanity, and therefore that Black musicians create improvised music and compositions that reflect and articulate social death, I would be unable to reconcile that pessimist belief with the clear evidence of Black musicians who live to express the beauty of Black life and freedom by producing musical space. I would have to ignore the life-affirming cultural impact Black music has had, and continues to have, on the world. As a theory, "Black musical space" is not rooted in the idea that African American artists transform society through performance. However, improvised music is important in the creation of musical spaces that articulate and affirm Black sociality in an environment that is structurally hostile to Blackness. The Afropessimist argument, as I understand it, highlights a false binary between social life and social death. Black musicians have taught us a fundamental fact of African American life: Black music expresses and articulates the complexity of both of these conditions.

In discussing aesthetics of the Black radical tradition, Fred Moten writes about a different kind of space that exists "in the break"; one that avoids the common discourse that reduces Black life to associations with the "tragic" and the "elegiac."[67] For Moten "the break" is an imagined space that existed before the "spatio-temporal discontinuity."[68] Within this musical space there is the possibility of reaching a generative and creative Black ontology outside of the common epistemology that has shaped the understanding of Black life. This creative Black space does not negate the tragic experiences of African Americans. It is a space of social identity and resistive potentiality represented in improvised music and other forms of art. Twentieth-century composer and pianist Thelonious Monk, who danced in circles in his own version of the ring shout, spun on the axis of social life and social death. His orchestrated revolutions, simultaneously steeped in adversity and joy, were defined by the monumental issues with which he had to deal as a Black man in America.[69] His music and dancing represented that marginalized, but regenerative, space that he produced between the notes and in the break. Black life is lived between the well-tempered tones of the hegemonic clavier, a life representing the *illified* sounds of the ill-tempered clavier. Improvised Black musical space is the ontologically unfixed assemblage of Black tonal indeterminacy, a repository of oppositional dissonance, the spatial luminescence of Blackness manifested in the improvised expression of humanity. While Black musical space extends from Black lived experiences, it is not about exclusion.

Black Musical Space, Improvisation, and Inclusiveness

Though Black musical space extends from Black life, it has the potential to be an inclusive space for all humanity. Like the Black civil society rent parties with multiracial clientele that pianist Mary Lou Williams attended as a girl while learning the language of music, or the Black "all-girl bands" who welcomed Native American, Asian, and white female musicians into their space, Black musical space cannot abide segregation. African American improvisers understand how structural racism has shaped Black lives, then and now. Black musical spaces do require, however, that white musicians disavow racism, perform music on a level that meets the defined high standards of Black aesthetic excellence, and embrace the perpetual exploration of the musical mind. The space produced by African American improvisers has also been a space of patriarchy and homophobia. While Black musical space has the potential to be inclusive, that inclusiveness has not always been generative of gender equity and the acceptance of the LGBTQIA community. The fight for inclusivity in Black musical space is unfinished.

Producing Black musical space, at its root, is about the cultural memory
and quotidian life of Black people, forged in diverse identity formations in
the world. African American improvisers often strive for exercising non-
separatist, utopian values in this space, striving for open musical dialogue
and the active denunciation of aesthetic demagoguery. Black musical space
is created in response to the placelessness shaped by historical human degradation; it is also about joy and human potentiality in all of its artistic and
unexpected realizations through the sonic arts. The word *music* has at times
itself been a restrictive signifier, a type of conceptual encasement that cannot
quell this Black human and sonic expression.

Over the past several generations, scholars of Black music have categorized Black musical characteristics to create alternative pedagogies. The late
musicologist Samuel Floyd documented the "multifarious African and Africa-
derived traits" of Black music.[70] Floyd's "Call/Response" framework includes
"calls, cries, and hollers; call-and-response devices; additive rhythms and
polyrhythms; heterophony, pendular thirds, blue notes, bent notes, and eli-
sions; hums, moans, grunts, vocables, and other rhythmic-oral declamations,
interjections, and punctuations; off-beat melodic phrasings and parallel
intervals . . ."[71] Ethnomusicologist Portia Maultsby has argued that Africanisms in African American music are evidence of a cultural retention of an
African consciousness rooted in the African diasporic worldview. Laying
out Black musical features in categories called "delivery style, sound quality,
and mechanics of delivery," Maultsby has organized a list of key features
of Black music social codes and concepts.[72] The groundbreaking works of
scholars like Floyd and Maultsby, to name just two scholars, have created an
invaluable foundation on which I build. I understand the important need
for Black scholars to create their own canons of Black musical brilliance,
especially since those contributions to global music culture have historically
been erased or relegated to the margins by musical research institutions.
That fight is not over. Yet the cultural production of Black musical space is
beyond canonization and cannot be reduced to taxonomies or lists of musical
gestures. Black creative musicians who improvise musical space continue to
revise and innovate musical forms in our time. Black music culture is mal-
leable, embracing any and all forms of music. Aimé Césaire wrote "poetic
knowledge is born in the great silence of scientific knowledge."[73] Theorizing
through Black musical space does not reject the importance of evidence
that supports claims. Yet the poetics of this musical space, rooted in the
lived experience of African Americans, cannot be defined in a way that fits
within the Eurological positivist framework at the basis of our institutions
of higher learning.

It should come as no surprise that my writing and research would be influenced by the Black Lives Matter movement. After all, I am an African American musician who has been policed in various urban cities throughout my life.[74] Sherrie Tucker's definition of policing is useful here: "by *police* I mean everyone who acts on the social or institutional power to police other people, not just the official police."[75] This policing and harassment affects my analysis of music and has given me an affinity for improvised music that creates critical commentary on the continuing legacy of violence and anti-Blackness in our time. African American improvisers have a long history of critiquing inhumane treatment of Black people through documented performances at least since 1958 with saxophonist Sonny Rollins's *Freedom Suite*.[76] Rollins's comments ring true today: "America is deeply rooted in Negro culture: its colloquialisms, its humor, its music. How ironic that the Negro, who more than any other people can claim America's culture as his own, is being persecuted and repressed, that the Negro, who has exemplified the humanities in his very existence, is being rewarded with inhumanity."[77]

To my knowledge, this is the first book that considers how African American improvisers respond to the Black Lives Matter movement. Books like Orejuela and Shonekan's *Black Lives Matter & Music* situate their analysis within the context of protest popular music in places like Detroit and Washington, DC.[78] For the Black Lives Matter movement, the motivation for the work is not new but its expression is innovative. Following generations of cultural work of African American improvisers, Black Lives Matter is as much about music as it is about boots on the ground.

The first chapter focuses on trumpeter Terence Blanchard's composition "Breathless" (2015) as a critique of the July 17, 2014, killing of Eric Garner by members of the police on Staten Island. Blanchard's "Breathless," performed by his electric band E-Collective, features the sustained sound of male and female musical breathing as a compositional device. Through the displacement of breath rhythm, Blanchard takes us past the musical articulation of despair, and beyond the systemic chokehold on desire for Black freedom and into the crossroads of Black spirituality, a spirituality informed by his connection to the Black church and Buddhism. I analyze how he sonically indicates breathlessness harmonically, rhythmically, and melodically. Moreover, his orchestration of reverbed male and female sounds of exhalation—in harmony with the spoken-word lyrics of JRei Oliver—creates a social critique of systemic violence. Blanchard's composition is in conversation not only with the Black Lives Matter movement but with the archives and repositories of social justice music by past African American improvisers who have historically created a sense of place through musical practices.

Chapter 2 presents an analysis of the late drummer and community leader Billy Higgins's improvised brushwork and breathing strategies in his performance of Hoagy Carmichael's "Georgia on My Mind" on his frequent collaborator's Charles Lloyd's recording *The Water Is Wide* (2000). I listen to Higgins in an unconventional way, focusing on his breathing as he improvised. When Higgins states, "I try to get a little 'air' with the instrument,"[79] he is referring to the way he shaped the musical environment through his concept of air and breathing. His approach to breath and phrasing was integral to his understanding of Black musical space. I view Higgins's breathing as a form of spiritual, improvised respatialization, and argue that his breathing strategies were a way to enhance and inspire his risk-taking in improvisation. Behind Higgins's breath is not only a lifetime of musical experiences on the most important stages, but also his community organizing in the Leimert Park section of Los Angeles, which has been referred to as the epicenter of Black Los Angeles. Higgins served his community by creating (with poet Kamau Daáood) the World Stage in Leimert Park, which fostered community through music. Connecting with the broader theme of the politics and cultural work of creating Black physical and musical space, I use Ashon Crawley's "black pneuma" hermeneutic to position Higgins's breathing strategies as an orchestration of individual and community sound, and argue that it represents his denial of ego for the benefit of the group sound and the larger social movement of Leimert Park.[80] Breathing during improvisation for Higgins was a way to access all the colors of the human condition, a way to cross bar lines, while remaining connected to his sense of Blackness.

In chapter 3 I explore the music, life, and institutional work of drummer Terri Lyne Carrington. Through Carrington's cultural work I examine how Black musical space remains a less inclusive space for women improvisers. I write about how Carrington uses Black feminist, intersectional thought to expose the irony that jazz culture is one of the most aesthetically and culturally democratic forms and musical spaces of human expression while one of the most isolating for women improvisers who are often discouraged from playing instruments and becoming jazz improvisers from an early age. Carrington has been inspired by some of the leading Black feminists, which has helped shape the way she thinks about her music projects and her institutional mandate. I analyze Carrington's musical arrangement of Bernice Johnson Reagon's composition "Echo" for Sweet Honey in the Rock originally featured on *Breathless* (1998) and explain the intertextual relationship between Johnson's original version and Carrington's arrangement of "Echo" on her first iteration of *The Mosaic Project* (2011). I also analyze several compositions on Carrington's recent project, *Terri Lyne Carrington and Social Science* (2019), and argue that her definition of social science music is an intersectional analysis of racism, gay conversion therapy, Black feminism, and gender inequity represented in "Bells (Ring Loudly)," "Pray the Gay Away," "Anthem," and "Purple Mountains." This chapter also examines how Carrington attacks patriarchy in jazz culture through her leadership as artistic director and founder of the Berklee Institute of Jazz and Gender Justice founded in 2018. She uses her influence as a professor and platform as a multi-Grammy–winning artist to create a musical space rooted in resistance to racial and sexual hierarchies. This musical space is not only for women improvisers who have been historically isolated due to the patriarchal culture in Black musical space, but for members of the improvisation community who identify as lesbian, gay, or gender dysphoric. Carrington's practice of Black feminist coalition politics is not only represented in her institutional projects but also in the collective sound she envisions as exemplified in her *Mosaic Project* and her ensemble Social Science.

Chapter 4 addresses trumpeter Ambrose Akinmusire's use of unconventional music strategies to create innovative commentaries on police brutality. His compositions "My Name Is Oscar" (2011) and "Rollcall for Those Absent" (2014), among others, are analyzed to understand how they articulate his Black political thought on systemic police violence toward African Americans. Akinmusire's improvisation on his instrumental composition "Confessions to My Unborn Daughter" (2011) is also analyzed relative to how his improvised note choices represent a Black sense of musical space. Part of this Black sense of space is revealed in his philosophical approach to music. That is, Akinmusire has committed himself to a sonic approach that enunciates through improvisation a raw and glistening artistic honesty. His sonic art is a spatial art, an art of collage that exploits and explores musical textures. His musical approach is not a rebellion toward what some critics would consider jazz orthodoxy but a dedication to rekindling ancestral substance rooted in the musical space and language of his ancestors. In his compositions and performances, Akinmusire articulates the complex ranges of Black life on the social life/social death axis.

Chapter 5 focuses on a different kind of improvised respatialization in the work of the late pianist Andrew Hill, who refused to conform to archetypes of the jazz musician throughout his musical career. Central to this chapter is the examination of what Hill called a "street approach to jazz improvisation." This approach lays out what appears to be his unfinished theory of musical acculturation, which grew from his experiences as a young musician in the musical spaces of the Black South Side Chicago jazz clubs. Hill's street theory is grounded in his belief in musical intuition, an aesthetic feeling formed in the sociality of his early musical experiences. He wanted the institutional music curriculum to acculturate to the methods and ways of learning that had shaped his musical approaches throughout his life. In contrast to the Blanchard, Carrington, and Akinmusire chapters, in which these improvisers overtly interact with contemporary social movements, the chapter on Hill demonstrates that Black political thought expressed in music is not always explicit and does not always register in the public consciousness. Other musicians' creative work in this study may be better known because of the level of jazz industry press coverage it received, or its identifiable ties to social movements. Hill, however, chose the anti-genre path of no musical style; shunned any discussion of his placement by critics and historians in jazz historiography; and refused to acquiesce to the common narrative imposed on his iconoclastic creative output by music critics. I argue that the reason musicology scholarship on Hill's work has largely focused on analyzing his musical approaches to composition and improvisation is due to his resistance to being pigeonholed in the jazz discourse. I hope to make an intervention in the discourse on Hill by contextualizing his creative practice within Black political thought. I analyze Hill's crafting of melodic space in composing the melody for "Malachi" (2006), as well as his improvising a Black spatio-temporality that reflects his choice of creativity over style, nonconformity over conformity, and an "apolitical" stance that, politically, has resisted Black nationalism.

1

Terence Blanchard and the Politics of Breathing

Black music says, as does an allied, radically pneumatic poetics, that breath, especially imperiled breath, matters. It insists that we can, for a time at least, breathe, that what we do with breath, from which, to belabor the obvious, animacy, agency and all possibility of action arise, matters most. This is the innate, implicit activism of the music . . . It says that black breath matters, black lives matter, at risk in multiple ways on a crowded, conflictual planet on which, though everyone is at risk and yes, all lives matter, blackness is the sign and the symbol of risk in a scapegoating, sacrificial world order for which black is the color of precarity itself.
—Nathaniel Mackey[1]

The sigh is the pathway to breath; it allows breathing. That's just self-preservation. No one fabricates that. You sit down, you sigh. You stand up, you sigh. The sighing is a worrying exhale of an ache. You wouldn't call it an illness; still it is not the iteration of a free being.
—Claudia Rankine[2]

Born March 13, 1962, in New Orleans, trumpeter and composer Terence Blanchard is a prominent African American musician who has created scores for several Spike Lee films. The *Malcolm X Jazz Suite* (1993) and *A Tale of*

God's Will (A Requiem for Katrina) (2007)[3] are two examples of Blanchard's compositions with political themes that address structural and geographic racism. In the wake of the Eric Garner incident, between late 2014 and early 2015, Blanchard felt a responsibility to make a political statement through his E-Collective band about the African American experience with police brutality.

Terence Blanchard's composition "Breathless" (2015) represents the production of Black musical space-making while representing the humanity of Eric Garner, who violated what was an increasingly gentrified space and was killed by members of the Staten Island police in the mid-summer of 2014. Blanchard's work features compositional, improvisational, and studio production techniques that feature male and female sung breathing drones that allude to the humanity of Black people while critiquing the violence that has partially shaped their lives. Blanchard's composition is a commentary on the systemic harassment that he and his son have personally faced. His definition of Black musical space is informed by his experiences in the Black church as a place for communal reflection, and this in turn informs his understanding of the power of improvised music and composition as a place for contemplating such issues as how Black "citizens" are policed, and the often tragic results of that policing.

For Blanchard, Black space-making through improvisation is a reflection of how a musician processes the events of life. The production of musical space is a sonic narrative rooted in improvised musical contemplation in real time. Blanchard reflects, "The wonderful thing about being human is that we are all given the ability to sit down and process the events of life. We may come out with different results at the end of the process, but the opportunity to process those events is what is important. That's the powerful thing about any great music."[4] He locates this process of life represented in Black musical space-making in the improvisational sonic sculptures of Miles Davis, stating, "Miles Davis was the king of that shit. Miles Davis could play one note, let it sit there for a minute, and you would go, 'damn!' (laughter)."[5]

Blanchard understands that improvisation as respatialization is rooted in collectively reflecting on the absurdity of violence: "The space comes from needing to take a breath, you know, needing to reflect, so I can do something productive with it. It's a moment of reflection. The moment of musical space is different for all of us due to how we may react to things."[6] Those moments of reflection, connected to the way Blanchard thinks about improvisational space, comes out of his growing up in the Black church. For Blanchard, the way preachers preach is directly related to the way people play music and it all relates to contemplation: "It comes down to my experiences growing up in church, like when a minister is giving a sermon and if there is something he wants you to reflect on. He'll (the minister) say it and let it [his words] hang for a second so the words can seep in. So, to me, that's where it [the sense of Black musical spatiality] comes from. It comes from that idea of saying, 'You know what? I want you guys to really reflect on this message, so I'm just going to let it hang for a second.'"[7] This kind of spatial connection is clear when viewing the way Aretha Franklin manipulates musical space during her improvised singing at the New Temple Missionary Baptist Church in Watts, Los Angeles, and then viewing how her father, the Reverend C. L. Franklin, uses space when he makes comments about Aretha Franklin being a "stone cold singer."[8]

Blanchard cites the tearful speech Barack Obama gave on December 14, 2012, in the wake of the Sandy Hook Elementary School shooting in Newtown, Connecticut.[9] For Blanchard the pauses Obama made in his sermonic statement connect to a Black sense of musical space in church. He believes there is no disconnect between the rhetorical strategies of Black preachers and those people, such as Obama, who have modeled their public speaking on those exemplars. Blanchard asserts, "It's one of the things that drew us to Obama . . . he has that pace in his tone and in his presentations."[10] When Obama made the statement, "The majority of those who died today were children . . . beautiful little kids between the ages of five and ten years old," Blanchard believes that, apart from his emotional distress, Obama wanted America to meditate on the absurdity of violence in the space of that pause; he claims, "the exact same thing happens in music, bruh, the exact same thing."[11]

Hope, despair, anger, and most of all frustration motivated the then-fifty-six-year-old innovator to make a statement on the Garner killing and the Black Lives Matter (BLM) movement that continues to sprout urgent commentary about how Black people are unwanted in certain spaces. The frequent killing of Black men and women by the police compels Black people to live in and through that carousel of emotions on a daily basis, even if they want to get off that circular ride. Though Blanchard is acclaimed in the music world, that acclaim does not give him the option of cavalierly strolling through a society with a police culture that views him as a Black suspect. And though he rightfully focuses his musical attention on the profiling and killing of young African American males, Black woman have also ended up dead on the other side of an interaction gone haywire due to their assumed criminality. Blanchard explains:

"See Me as I Am," to me, is a very strong statement about young African American males because people don't see them for who they truly are. They see them

for what they think they are, or this image that's been portrayed about who young
Black men are . . . it's unbelievable to think that, in this country, young Black men,
it's hard for them to walk down the street, just from point A to point B.[12]

Blanchard's comments on his motivation for writing the instrumental "See
Me as I Am" (2015) shows how he perceives what it means to be a Black male,
vulnerable to the whims of fear and prejudice. He has personally experienced
this stigma when communicating in person with people in the music business who have little experience with Black folk. He explains how his partners
have been initially afraid of him until they get to know him as the human
being that he is: "You can see in their eyes exactly when their minds change
about who you are. Yet they should have given me that benefit of the doubt at
the beginning of the conversation."[13] Blanchard's statement about "See Me as I
Am," which confronts the subject of young Black male identity, also connects
to the February 26, 2012, killing of Trayvon Martin, where the assumption
of his criminality led to death. "See Me as I Am," an instrumental, medium-
tempo blues/funk composition based on rhythmic riffs of perfect fifth power
chords, may help those on the outskirts of this harrowing experience develop
an appreciation of this marginalized space since Blanchard has explained
the narrative behind the composition.

African Americans are incarcerated and killed by the police at a tremen-
dously higher rate than whites, given the disparity in the overall population.
This is the backdrop against which Blanchard composed "Breathless" as a
response to the social conditions that led to the death of Eric Garner. The "We
can't breathe" chant that became part of the international BLM movement
is shortened by Blanchard to one word that encapsulates, not only the tragic
events around Garner's death, but the metaphorical systemic chokehold, in all
of its permutations, which prevents African American citizens from breathing
freely. Two years after Martin's death, the killing of an unwelcomed purveyor
of loosies in a gentrifying Staten Island would spark more public outrage.

Garner's Life on Bay Street

Eric Garner (1970–2014) was a city-employed horticulturist, former drug
dealer, and seller of unlicensed individual cigarettes, or "loosies," in front of
a beauty parlor on 202 Bay Street in Staten Island. He was part of a cast of
colorful characters who worked across the street from Tompkinsville Park.
Because new real estate developments were being built across the street from
where he plied his black-market cigarette trade, police surveillance increased

on the street where Garner lived and worked. Though whites purchased Garner's loosies regularly, they had no desire to see, speak, or live next to people like him. The nobility of liberal politics is often outweighed by property values that guarantee a segregated existence.[14] And Garner's reported slovenly appearance was incompatible with the social and aesthetic values developers wanted in the neighborhood, where they were trying to attract new clientele to their developing projects. According to the white American journalist Matt Taibbi, Garner's excessive weight, his oversized diabetic feet that spilled out of his shoes, his pants with holes, and his constantly running nose, which he wiped with his hands, made him persona non grata. Arrested and imprisoned several times, Garner was already known to police and constantly under police surveillance.

Millions have seen the July 17, 2014, the various YouTube videos of Eric Garner being choked to death by New York City police officer Daniel Pantaleo, with the literal weight of Pantaleo and other members of the police on Garner's back.[15] The Ramsey Orta cell phone video of Garner's tackling and subsequent strangulation showed that once the machinery of the police state begins its arrest cycle, death is inevitable for too many Black citizens.[16] The routine theatricality of it all, the specter of public murder followed by a deliberate lack of medical care for Garner's dying body, should be bizarre, but it has been increasingly spun and normalized in the public's conscious. Like so many Black men in the world—whose situations cut across class, educational levels, and regions of the United States and the larger Black diaspora—I imagined being in Garner's position.

While Garner could not breathe and likely died on the Bay Street sidewalk, the artifice of the police and EMS charade, urging his lifeless body to comply with their orders, is evidence that it was a macabre performance art for the gathered crowd—and for Orta's phone camera. The police and EMS likely understood that this video was going to be broadcast around the world. Black people have a collective breath connected to a Black sense of place informed and shaped by the history of brutality, slavery, and Jim Crow discrimination, old and new. Stories like Garner's are in danger of being ignored by media outlets distracted by the onslaught of relentless dysfunction of the White House administration. With the almost quotidian scandals coming from the Oval Office and beyond, with the attacks on democratic norms filtering through the American government bubbling up daily in the American collective consciousness, we hear less about the progress of social movements against police brutality and other forms of social inequality. There appears to be less space for these serious issues in our newspapers' pages. As Taibbi writes, "The Trump story captivated the world and dominated the Internet and social media, obliterating everything else."[17] Our current president relishes dominating all media apparatuses with antics and policies that relegate social movements to the back of the nation's consciousness. Yet the Black Lives Matter movement has not receded into a place of lesser importance in the lives of people who face violence on a daily basis. Moreover, it is not a separatist movement and does not have the exclusionary politics of white ethnonationalism.[18]

Matt Taibbi wrote that he had to face the limitations of his experience when writing about the events surrounding Garner's death. Garner's experience of being harassed by the police, being thrown in jail, and living in poverty was foreign to Taibbi, who remarks, "As a white man I was poorly equipped to even guess what he [Garner] might have thought or felt about any of this, and I knew that any story I tried to tell about Garner would therefore be lacking in important ways. All I could do was try to describe the incredible breadth of the institutional response to his life and death."[19] For many of us, these tragedies are lived experiences beyond the visceral line of palpability.[20]

The stop-and-frisk lawsuit filed by civil rights groups against the New York Police Department (NYPD) proved there was a policy fueled by the assumption of Black and brown criminality. This ingrained racism was enough for probable cause despite the fact that the majority of people stopped were not found to have committed any crime.[21] The leadership of the NYPD enforced a policy that emphasized arrests and summonses while suppressing reports of felonies in order to feign institutional progress.[22] The NYPD followed a mandate of preventing crime but were also required to report how well they achieved their crime-prevention goals. This created a clear conflict of interest, one that relegated the welfare of the public good to the bottom of the list.

Young Black and Latino men were (and are) considered "raw materials" for getting the arrest count up and giving out summonses. The Garner incident took place during the era when the NYPD used a "broken-windows" policy.[23] NYPD cops have an expression for how they treat Black and Latino men, which reveals their awareness of how these marginalized men are burdened with an assumed criminality. This term is "socially raping," which describes the methodology of stripping these men naked in plain view of the community during a mass search. These are the words of one Bronx police officer that Taibbi quotes: "Sometimes they'd yank a guy's pants down in the precinct, but other times they'd do it in the open air, right on the sidewalk. . . . 'I've seen a guy's penis, I've seen his ass, you can't believe what's going on here.'"[24] Police officers often make the victims of strip searches thank them for their humiliating experience. There is a whole generation of Black and

Latino men trained to "assume the position" when a cop pulls them over; the officer would then simply check off boxes on their standard "Stop, Question and Frisk Report Worksheet," or UF-250, which conveniently lists justifications. The most common checkboxes on the form include "suspicious bulge," "furtive movements," "actions indicative of engaging in violent crimes," and inappropriate attire ("wearing clothes/disguises commonly used in commission of crime").[25]

We Are All Human

Music is a reflection of the artist's mind, the carrier of dreams, hopes, and ambitions—a reflection of belief systems that encompass untold versions of spirituality and mysticism. And since there is culture and humanity in sound, musical elements such as color, chords, notes, phrases, fermatas, repeat signs, tempos, and dynamics are not just musical gestures but also signs that can prompt our critical intellectual faculties into new areas and move us to action. Blanchard's music is a reflection of his politics and his experience as an African American who has traveled the world as a global citizen. He composed "Breathless" in response to the slogan "We can't breathe," which echoed Eric Garner's last eleven cries of "I can't breathe." He describes his rationale here: "When I did that album [*Breathless*, 2015], I didn't want to sit down and point my fingers and make white people defensive. I was trying to go in the opposite direction and open a window for dialogue."[26] Blanchard understands the healing power of music, its ability to distract from the pain of life. But he believes it's more important to face the stark issues that shape Black lives through music. He explains, "What we [the musicians in the band] are trying to say is that we are all human."[27] Part of the process for Blanchard is commenting on the insanity of people who defend the violent actions of state actors and white supremacists who condone and participate in systemic violence on Black bodies. He explains that it is "the absurdity of not seeing that we bleed, and die, and suffer, and rejoice, and love and laugh like anybody else."[28] Ashon Crawley communicates a similar sentiment when he writes: "'I can't breathe' charges us to do something, to perform, to produce otherwise than what we have. We are charged to end, to produce abolition against, the episteme that produced for us current iterations of categorical designations of racial hierarchies, class stratifications, gender binaries, mind–body splits."[29] Nothing communicates the fierce urgency of now more clearly than a Black man struggling to breathe, face down on the pavement. "Breathless" is now a part of the repository of musically expressed BLM statements on the humanitarian crisis of racist policing. Blanchard's musical and production choices reflect his connection to the history of African American musicians who combined their improvisations and compositions with a radical political stance.

Blanchard's "Breathless" has been described as "biting" and "politically charged."[30] Despite America's long history of Black protest music, the notion that Black musicians, and musicians in general, should leave politics aside and solely entertain is still alive. Perhaps it is just a different version of what a conservative commentator told basketball player LeBron James and other Black athletes who dare to have a political stance on police brutality: "shut up and dribble."[31] Historically, music critics have often categorized a musical work composed by an African American musician as radical. Experimental musician and scholar George E. Lewis argues that improvisation should not be burdened with the discourse of Black nationalism, that making Black political music is "a necessary way station. It's kind of like what I heard Gayatri Spivak call something like strategic essentialism. It's a bit like that. But you have to move past that at some point."[32] Lewis's critique is not a formalist one. He understands that Black nationalism influences criticism of improvisation because Black musicians are socially marginalized. In fact, Lewis has composed a number of socially conscious works. Although improvisation is a global phenomenon with productive intercultural manifestations, African American musicians still have important things to say musically about their own lived experiences in a world that does not treat them as equal human beings. To suggest that African American musicians no longer need to make this type of musical critique alludes to a postracial stance, a stance that I am sure that Lewis does not have. Having lived through much of the racism that many readers can experience only in books, he is understandably weary of the way the discourse on the political economy of jazz has pigeonholed Black improvisers and rightfully wishes to be free to write music as an artist. African American artist David Hammonds reminds us that when Black artists create, the art that is being made has no politics, because it is not defined, and may never be defined. Political positioning of an artefact, or a recorded or live improvisation, happens after the artefact has been created:

> They call my art what it is. A lot of times I don't know what it is because I'm so close to it. I'm just in the process of trying to complete it. I think someone said all work is political the moment that last brushstroke is put on it. Then it's political, but before that it's alive and it's being made. You don't know what it is until it's arrived, then you can make all these political decisions about it.[33]

Without lyrics, a title, or the composer telling the audience what he or she is trying to do compositionally, music is information without any particular stance. I would not have known that "Breathless" was about Blanchard's frustration with police brutality until I read interviews, interviewed him myself, and listened to the lyrics. Blanchard's son and collaborator JRei Oliver contributes lyrics that contextualize the music and give us a broader understanding of the composer's intentions.

Though Blanchard ultimately approved the spoken word text to be used in the song, it is not clear how he envisioned the text aligning with the music. Blanchard admits in one interview that his primary purpose for composing the album *Breathless* was not to be political but to show young improvisers musical possibilities. "We were surprised, because it had a very strong impact on the community. It had a strong impact on young musicians, for musical reasons, which is one reason we did it. But the social justice piece is something I hadn't anticipated to the level of which it was received."[34] Though an artist may have a general idea of a political statement he or she would like to make, the composer first starts with sound; the true political meaning is added to the piece later. Music is a way of thinking through problems, and composers, like writers, cannot know what they think until they compose their ideas out. Creating a recording of compositions to show young musicians possibilities for making improvised music is not out of sync with having a political theme attached to the project. And Blanchard did discuss with drummer Oscar Seaton a musical response to the BLM movement several years prior to recording the album.

Analyzing the Musical Representation of Breathlessness

"Breathless" is performed by Terence Blanchard's E-Collective. The letter E in the name refers to the sole use of electric instruments in the performance, as opposed to traditional acoustic instruments unconnected to electricity. The compositional form of "Breathless" comprises three sections of eight bars each, for a total of twenty-four bars. I refer to the first eight bars as section A, the second eight as section B, and the third eight as section C. Sections A and B have repeated two-bar phrases that rhythmically cross bar lines. I have labeled these sections based on the repetition of harmonic material, in which there are clear demarcations of where one section begins and ends. On a sonic level, there are several musical gestures at play that connect the music to the idea of breathlessness.

When I asked Blanchard about specific musical strategies he used to create the sonic element of breathlessness in "Breathless" (2015), he initially seemed reluctant to discuss that aspect of his creative process and pivoted to an important story about how his thirty-one-year old son has been harassed by the police. Whether it was a move to protect the intricacies of his creative process relative to the studio production techniques he used, he did not answer that technical question. He asserted, earlier in our conversation, "For me, the music has to touch that core and not be an intellectual exercise."[35] This statement by Blanchard represents what has long been a false binary in the thinking of musicians and those who write about the music as well. Ingrid Monson has argued that statements like Blanchard's may support the historical belief system that African Americans have less intellectual engagement with the music.[36] Yet the brain and heart are not compartmentalized; both work together to facilitate a deep connection with the sonic arts. He recounted a conversation he had with his mentor and former bandleader, drummer Art Blakey, who told him: "Being an artist is always a struggle between your brain and your heart."[37] Indeed, Blanchard does not want to over intellectualize his musical process, stating that his struggle with finding a balance between his mind and his heart continues to this day.

Blanchard creates a sound of mixed-gender exhalation as a central theme in the music. He achieves this by applying reverb to the trumpet, to the male and female voices, and to the synthesizer, piano, and guitar. Adding reverb to a recording manipulates the sound of space and is commonly used to lend a sonic fullness to a recording. However, the way Blanchard uses reverb in "Breathless" reminds me of Black liminality, the living on the threshold between life and death.[38] Blanchard improvisations are drenched in liquid reverb that blurs his phrases and makes each note bleed into each other in aqueous sound. Because of this, when he plays fast eighth notes and sixteenth notes, a sonic imbrication occurs: the sound of Blanchard's improvised notes catches up to itself in its own wake, like asymmetrical ghost notes. Religious and African American Studies scholar Ashon Crawley argues that whooping in the Black Pentecostal church is a "double gesture of inhalation and exhalation" between the preacher and the congregation, an exchange of oxygenated sociality he calls "Black pneuma."[39] Crawley believes there is momentary power in Black Pentecostal breath because it is a social expression, beyond theology and gender, that shows resistance to the violence that often marks Black existence. Blanchard's positioning of breath in "Breathless" is also a double gesture. First, his use of droned breath to underscore his music expresses the humanity and despair of Garner and the collective humanity of Black people. Second, however, Blanchard's composition—rather than demonstrating the power of Black pneuma—laments breath as a lost human right in a repeated, unresolved one-way gesture of male and female exhalation.

In her book *Citizen: An American Lyric*—quoted in the epigraph to this chapter—Claudia Rankine talks about sighing as a route to breathing again when one feels one cannot breathe. She describes sighing as an involuntary, honest reaction to the quotidian onslaught of oppressive behavior. The sigh Rankine refers to is not a universal sigh, but a sigh recognized by those who understand the historical weight of placelessness behind the exhalation. Blanchard's foregrounding of breath in the mix of "Breathless" reminds me of this individual and collective sigh. He marks the strain on Black humanity by sonically articulating the sound of the crossroads. Blanchard's reverbed sound enhances the often hidden breath and embouchure buzzing that goes into playing his three-valve machine. As he articulates that space between inspiration and respiration, Blanchard's reverbed trumpet improvising adds more drama to the breathless theme in the final minutes and seconds of the song, when he improvises in the high register of his trumpet.

The melody of "Breathless" has few notes, to allow space for the spoken-word component of the piece. As a seasoned film composer, he understands how not to distract from, while sonically enhancing, the primary message of a musical work. Except for a few large intervals, the melody can be sung quite easily. Whereas the simplicity of the melody allows access to vocality, the rhythm crosses bar lines in complex ways. The melodic rhythm of the piece is designed to give a floating feeling of breath through continual displacement on the offbeat, never giving the listener a feeling of resolution. Ultimately, Blanchard designed the melody to resemble the spiritual chanting that helps one internalize a crucial tenet. In this sense, he is influenced by his experience in the Black church but primarily by the Buddhist chanting he practices. He explains, "That comes from the whole notion of chanting; that melody. I became a Buddhist years ago and the chanting is no different than a preacher's speech or the religious orders that use rhythmic chanting to facilitate the internalization of a religious idea. The whole idea is to draw you into what we are doing so you can listen to the words that are being spoken. The melody is chantlike to create that type of mythic vibe."[40]

Musical example 1.1. The chanting melodic line and underlying harmony in the A section of Terence Blanchard's composition "Breathless."

The asymmetrical displacement of rhythm allows the listener to be transported into the nature of Blackness through the imagination of breath. The study and performance of improvised music has taught me that part of the Black aesthetic is about the musical play of finding and maintaining an asymmetrical equilibrium, a Black time at odds with the larger society that encourages cultural assimilation to the common time of white supremacy. Improvisation in the Black tradition is not about playing it safe but embracing uncertainty to discover something new on the other side. What is viewed as off kilter in Black music is actually Black equilibrium, Black time. This angular way of life is our saving grace, and this musical interaction with the world is informed by African cultural memory. As I mentioned in the introduction, in the Mande tradition, straight lines in textiles were considered evil, which is why it was important to "randomize the flow of paths" in their work.[41] This randomization is a core part of improvisation. In the tradition of Afrodiasporic art, dealing with stark issues indirectly is a way of dealing with those issues directly. This randomized Black aesthetic happens for example in the echoed, ghostly reverb fragments of Jamaican dub music, where the art is what happens not on the beat but in the wake of that initial beat.

The late musicologist Samuel Floyd believed that cultural memory is a living tradition.[42] African American improvisational and compositional forms articulate African cultural memory. Cultural memory should not be seen only as a list of musical techniques but as a worldview. Bringing attention to social issues is an extension of Black cultural memory manifested in an intellectual and artistic tradition. The musical strategies in "Breathless" are acts of political speech that critique violence without being separatist and promote inclusivity, dialogue, and love in the face of hate. James Baldwin wrote "the idea of speaking only to Black people seems unnecessary. No one in love or trouble or at the point of death is only a recognizable colour. What he is at that moment is his experience. It is himself."[43] And it is clear that Blanchard is not articulating only Black despair but the experience of many who are oppressed and relate to this continuing historical and structural siege of Black bodies.

The composition rests on a number of breathing pedal points strategically voiced in the lower harmonic register of the piece. The female and male breathing sounds are masterfully orchestrated to compositionally emphasize the breathlessness. The breath is a kind of continuous drone. There is a grain to this composition's polyphonic breathing, a texture that is smooth but rubs against the organ of Corti just below the surface of irritation. The gradation of breathing crescendos as the song moves forward in time. In the last eight bars of section C, the grainy drone of male and female breath vocals anchors the composition in phrases that are exhaled and sung continuously across bar lines. These long breathing phrases focus on the note E, underpinning the compositional structure and adding color while reminding the listener of the human breath theme. By orchestrating male and female drones of breath as a key feature of his composition, Blanchard draws my attention away from the virtuosity of his trumpet improvisations and toward the primary message of his musical work. The composition is innovative, yet innovation is not Blanchard's priority. His focus on Black ontological breath annihilates the idea of music as entertainment and causes me to imagine the radical politics of breath and the radical politics of love. Breath functions in a peculiar way in this piece. Breath is foregrounded through the doubling of the pitches of the melody but it also functions on a subliminal level, through the use of long breathing phrases of breath drones on key pitch colors of the harmony. The fragility of breath is a strong message in this piece. Who has the power to breathe freely in this world, and who fights to breathe? I hear only exhalation in these breath drones, which makes the experience of listening to "Breathless" disconcerting. As I listen, I realize that the song does not encourage me to inhale. The sound of inhalation, or inspiration, is minimal or nonexistent.

The constant sound of corporeal exhalation, of breath leaving these male and female bodies, means there is no recuperation. The reverb acts as a form of sonic enclosure, not just of the instruments and the male and female voices, but of our consciousness. I believe Blanchard uses these effects because he wants the listener to feel submerged in the sonic experience of breathlessness, with no escape from the sound of the systemic chokehold around the symbolic necks of the marginalized. The reverb masks the breathing process, making the sound of breathing less visceral. The physicality of Blackness sounds like phantom breath, a sonic blanket of air. Removed from the visceral identification of breath, the listener is asked to identify with Black social death.

This use of breath differs from the breathwork of Billy Higgins discussed in Chapter 2. Higgins used drumming to spread the breath of Black social life around the bandstand and audience. These respatializations of sonic breath have different but connected functionalities. While these examples of breath in the Higgins recording of "Georgia on My Mind" and Blanchard's "Breathless" are both modified by recording techniques, Higgins's breath has an immediacy because the recording is less produced and not treated with a heavy dose of reverb. With Higgins, I do not hear long phrases of continuous exhalation; I can hear spurts of breath and groans of inhalation and exhalation. Nevertheless, breath as used by both Higgins and Blanchard marks a Black musical space. Breathing strategies are used not through but in spite of compositional forms. Blanchard's project creates the sound of breath as an "earspectacle," drawing the listeners' attention to systemic violence toward Black people. Billy Higgins's use of breath is a ritual of improvised performance, an exercise in spirituality. Both expressions of breath say something remarkable about Black life. Black life is neither fully social death nor fully social life; it exists on the axis between the two. As African Americans go through their daily lives, they embody both Black social life and Black social death, spinning on the ontological axis of life.

Melodic Breathlessness

The melody of "Breathless" is played by guitar and trumpet and doubled by wordless vocals. The instrumental melodic line and the breathing vocal lines are in unison with the instrumental line of the guitar. Since the melodic material is repetitious, space is left for lyrical contrast. In addition to hearing breath phrased through the trumpet and guitar, I can also hear the breath of the voice strategically assigned a register lower in the recorded mix. Blanchard's goal is to signify a texture that flows like respiration. A skilled film composer, Blanchard creates a texture of sparse melody, easily sung, designed to accentuate the message of the spoken word. The melody is designed to leave space at the end of the phrase, perhaps as a release of tension, but more likely as a way to leave space for the lyrics. Despite the relative intervallic simplicity of the melody, the rhythm crosses bar lines in complex ways. Melodically constructed on the strength of two-bar phrases (see musical examples 1.1 and 1.2), the second phrase is the extension of the first melodic idea but moves into a different color by landing on a B major seventh chord. There are several melodies in this piece, making it a polyphonic composition about breathing. "Breathless" could symbolize the multiplicity of agency, that humans breathe polyphonically and in unison.

Harmonizing Breathlessness

The harmonies a composer uses can symbolize a deeper theme or subject. Imagining a post-apartheid South Africa, composer and pianist Abdullah Ibrahim used chord progressions that recalled the structure and harmony of church hymns to create a sonic environment of collective memory that signified congregational singing, family histories, and community rituals. The politics in Ibrahim's performance of these chord progressions is located in how he supplanted the original significations in the English, Dutch, or German hymn chords and infused his own cultural meanings.[44] The social and geographical backdrop behind Ibrahim's and Blanchard's musical strategies are not the same, but they both use music to forge community and bring awareness to a human rights crisis. The always palpable theatre of violence is not confined to a historical period but is relived in all human space-times. Blanchard's harmonic scheme signifies the feeling of breathlessness from frustration felt by the Black community.

Functional progressions in the traditional Western sense of the music theory term—that is, chords that move around in a hierarchical way—would not have been appropriate to express this tragic aspect of Black life. Instead, Blanchard organizes his offbeat, reverbed chords to frame the spoken lyrics while bringing the listening audience into meditation on the subject of the song. The harmony of this piece does most of the coloring work. Blanchard does not think of chords as progressions but as colors for creating an unpredictable, but relatable, emotional experience: "I try to have the harmonic colors move in a way that really grabs the listener's attention. For me, color is vibration; color is a thing that you feel. And by manipulating those colors with the repetitive melodic thing on top, it can create a very emotional experience . . . so the particular progressions themselves are only important because I am putting harmonic colors that a listener would not expect to be there."[45] the melody note E♭ is repeated through the entire section, whereas the underlying harmonies of D♭ major seventh, E major seventh, and F minor seventh shift under the repeating E♭ melody, giving the note three different harmonic colorings:

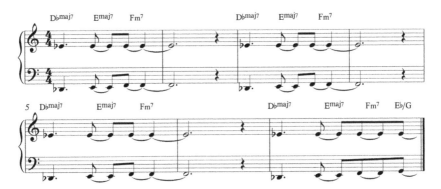

Musical example 1.2. An example of Blanchard's strategy of repetitive melody and shifting harmony in section B of "Breathless."

The rhythm of the shifting harmonies aligns with the rhythm of the single-note E♭ melody as the phrase crosses bar lines, landing on the second eighth note of the third beat of Fm7 and continuing through the entire fourth beat of the first bar. This continues for two to three beats of the second bar. "Breathless" has a harmonic structure that aligns with the two-bar phrase melodic structure through the entire piece, perhaps representing the cycle of exhaling and implied inhaling through the repetition of harmony. These repeating two-bar melodic phrases contrast with the orchestration of human exhale drones—a strategic way of representing frustration with the constant threat of police brutality. During the statement of the theme or head of the piece, section C of the compositional form is left open for Blanchard's reverbed improvisations. Unlike in sections A and B, he has not written melodic material in section C to play. Blanchard improvises over the oscillating chords that go from the E♭/G to F♯ major chord and from F♯ major to E♭/G. The E♭/G chord is typically described as a *pseudochord*, because it is not based on the root E♭ of the E♭ major chord, making its harmonic function unclear. Yet Blanchard is not trying to articulate music that validates Eurological aesthetic values by working within traditional theories of tonality. This composition does not adhere to forms of development found in European classical compositional forms. It is not goal-oriented in the sense of reaching a grand cadence, because infinite deferrals are preferred over resolution in the Black music imagination. The bass note of the E♭/G chord descends a half step down to F♯ major and then returns to G of the E♭ chord in the bass, reflecting a subtle change of harmonic color through half-step motions. Perhaps this half-step oscillation between the pseudochord of E♭/G and the "legitimate chord" of F♯ major also reflects the breathing process of exhaling and inhaling.

Lyrical Narrative in "Breathless"

So far, I have analyzed how Blanchard orchestrated the sound of breathlessness to bring the listener into a deep awareness of the Garner tragedy and the issue of violence in general. What is equally important is the verbal narrative spoken by JRei Oliver as a Black male character. The first words Oliver recites in "Breathless" tells us he is too tired to go on; he desires an escape to the land of Aceldama, which stands in for Africa, a land "soiled by the blood of brutality."[46] It isn't clear whose voice Oliver is speaking in or who he might be portraying. Initially I believed he was speaking in Garner's voice in the same way Ambrose Akinmusire (see Chapter 4) speaks in the voice of Oscar

Grant. On the whole, Oliver's text indicates that he is speaking from his own point of view. However, his lyrics transcend his personal testimony to give voice to Black men and women who share his experience and general sense of despair in relation to social surveillance. JRei Oliver's words represent not the individual experience but the shared Black experience: the reaction to systemic violence and the collective feeling of being under constant patrol.

In the second stanza Oliver speaks of planting a "mustard seed of faith" into soil that is by nature wicked, garnering only "fruits of hatred, degradation, and death." Oliver suggests the only way to escape this wicked land is to die a human death. His lyrics indicate that in the world of spirits below the Kalunga line, Black people can escape the deceit of the dominant race, which obscures Black reality through various types of misrepresentation.[47] Oliver can "fly through the clouds of judgment" that judge him for his defiant tone—the same tone that Sandra Bland had as she questioned the tactics of the police officer who subsequently hauled her off to jail, where she died. Oliver recites this spoken word from personal experience. He was arrested by several police officers in front of his fellow students at Dillard University. Fortunately, at the frightful scene, Oliver was known by one of the police officers as Terence Blanchard's son. The elder Blanchard explains that his son's soft-spoken nature, which masks his strong will, saved him from a worse fate: "Do you know how wrong that could have gone?"[48] For centuries defiance has often meant death for Black people. But African Americans refuse to bow their heads. The metaphor of flying that Oliver uses is a powerful one in Afro-Atlantic culture. The tropology of the Flying Africans tale continues to be a model for African Americans today and is instrumental in imagining Black existence in other space-times.[49] In the lyrics Oliver uses the image of flight to sing of how he flies past deceit, past the need to be cleared of suspicion of criminality. He flies past metaphorical trees of hope that are dried like the desert winds of the Sahara. But he does not escape death. Now metaphorically dead, Oliver speaks of roaming the earth as a form of freedom. In African belief systems, roaming spirits do not represent freedom but are considered punishment. In enslaved Black communities, the King Buzzard folk tale was a warning to other Africans not to betray the group; otherwise they were endlessly to roam as a restless spirit.[50] From this point of view, roaming is not desirable, and there is no freedom in death.

The third stanza is anchored by a series of rhetorical questions, and the drama of these questions is enforced by a chord sequence transposition of one whole step up, where the chord cycle now begins on G minor seventh. This transposition provides a different color scheme to frame Oliver's ontological questions. In the wake of so many police brutality deaths, Oliver asks

if he is wrong for wanting a better life. He asks is he wrong for believing in
Dr. Martin Luther King's dream of social equality, suggesting that King's
dream has not yet been realized. Oliver does not directly name Dr. King,
but it is clear that his use of the phrase "King's dream" refers to the slain
civil rights leader. Further on in the same stanza, Oliver describes Black
people as Black roses that grow from cracked pavements. That these Black
roses barely rise from cracks speaks to marginalization. These Black roses
are watered not with waters of hope but with "tears of the voiceless." I am
not sure why Oliver describes Black subjects as voiceless. Even in the most
dreadful of situations, Black people have made sure they have had a voice
through art, politics, and social movements. Perhaps Oliver is referring to
the murdered that will not make the headlines, the deceased whose last cries
will not become movement chants. His last line before the chant "We can't
breathe" is "as we lament a muted scream to the heavens." With this phrase,
Oliver references Garner's muted screams of "I can't breathe" as he struggled
within the officer's chokehold, gasping for breath due to compression on his
chest while straddled by peace officers.

Initially it was difficult for me to reconcile the spirit of the spoken word
with Blanchard's orchestration of the electronic instruments and his cutting-edge improvisations. I wanted the music to echo signs of hope for
marginalized life. Even while I initially projected my beliefs onto the song, I
knew in my core that "Breathless" is a cry for justice but also an expression
of frustration and despair. The nature of the lyrics is aligned with the sonic
nature of the song, saturated in semiotics of breathlessness. The exhaling of
female and male breath, the opaque, enveloping articulation of Black sound
swimming in a pool of aestheticized reverb—these create a sonic narrative
of Black frustration and weariness with the injustice of the criminal justice
system. Blanchard admits that "Breathless" was composed not to inspire hope
but to communicate through his experimental music "the pure exhaustion of
having to deal with this damn issue. It's tiring."[51] Blanchard is not interested
in having further debates about correcting the justice system and stopping
the racial profiling. He wants justice now. He wants to see badge-wearing
perpetrators prosecuted and jailed: "I don't want to create debate. We've been
debating this for generations. We need legislation. We need people to go to
jail. Debate doesn't seem to be curing this. What's insidious is that these guys
really think they can get away with it."[52] "Breathless," then, is a song of anger
and frustration stemming from dissatisfaction with the policing system that
has oppressed black citizens across generations, from public lynchings to
getting shot in the back while running away from police officers. "Breathless," then, is a composition in the tradition of Billie Holiday's improvisatory

performance of "Strange Fruit." Holiday's message is not about maintaining an attitude of hope in the face of racial violence; rather, she voiced the metaphorical narrative of Black death, boldly singing the truth through her innovative, musical phrasing about what can often be a violent reality for Black people.

"Breathless" is not upbeat. The lyrics are not about perseverance in the face of adversity. Yet "Breathless" resonates with many listeners. Historian Robert Farris Thompson stated that "Black culture marches on" in spite of all of the trials and tribulations that Black people face, and "gestures are culture and culture is forever."[53] The musical gestures of Black culture, which express both social death and social life, are valid because these musical gestures reflect distinct but always conjoined sides of the Black ontological coin.

Terence Blanchard recalled meeting Eric Garner's family after one of his concerts—in Staten Island, near where Garner was killed—and feeling overwhelmed by the audience response. Blanchard told his audience, "Love wins out every time, man."[54] Blanchard was not stating a cliché but describing how Black people's love for humanity has helped them survive in the face of anti-Blackness and the systemic enforcement of social inequality over centuries. Blanchard was speaking about love as a form of Black radical politics. Black people survived slavery and the residue of that system that remains at the heart of our institutions. Black humanity thrives even when racist institutions continue to deny Black people dignity. When Blanchard said love wins every time, he was talking about the miracle of Black social life fighting back in the nexus of social systems that promote Black social death. As George Lipsitz has written, "Time and time again, Black people have countered vicious dehumanization with determined and successful rehumanization."[55] This was Blanchard's motivation for writing "Breathless." His composition is part of an act of rehumanizing Garner as society becomes more desensitized to these killings.

The analysis of African American improvised music still yields fresh perspectives on cultural politics. African American improvisers continue to contribute critical commentary on social issues like police brutality, and their voices are as vital now as they ever were, because Black people are still fighting for civil rights. "Breathless" responds to collective despair, but it also resonates hope by helping create a continuing conversation about how we can *all* breathe equally and freely in our society. Black Studies scholar Keeanga-Yamahtta Taylor has defined Black liberation as a peaceful existence in which Black lives are valued: "Black people can live in peace, without the constant threat of the social, economic, and political woes of a society that places almost no value on the vast majority of Black lives. It would mean living in a world where Black lives matter. . . . Black liberation is bound up with the project of human liberation and social transformation."[56] The existence of socioeconomic woes in our society is critiqued in creative ways by improvisers who draw attention to these vital issues. Yet this is only part of the process: the responsibility for real change must be shared by those willing and able to change the status quo that protects white privilege. Until that time comes, African American improvisers/composers will continue to cross bar lines in order to delineate the imperatives of our time.

2

Billy Higgins in the Zone: Brushwork, Breath, and Imagination

the idea of race as a misnomer
the world is One
divided into many
the breath and the landscape of possibilities
the cleansing thought of circles
our seamless existence, cause and effect
—Kamau Daáood[1]

Drummer and composer Billy Higgins, whose Muslim name is Hassan Ahmed Abdul Karim reflecting his embrace of Islam in 1977, was a master drummer and the most recorded drummer in the history of jazz. Higgins crossed bar lines and created Black musical space through his spiritual breathing strategies, which were extended through the sound of his drums. Higgins's breath is a useful analytical frame expressing the uncontainable nature of Blackness. Blackness, in this construct, cannot be neatly apprehended. As Ashon Crawley writes, "The blues is a gathering of the materiality of vibration and announced as enunciation, announced as the displacement of air, announced—that is—as sound. What does this mean for an analytics, a theory, that thinks blackness, Black flesh, the blueness of blackness as a drive that is never meant to be contained, never meant to reach some there?"[2] The nature of Blackness that Crawley theorizes in relation to the blues and the Black Pentecostal church connects with my thesis regarding how Black musical space-making is created through breath by African American improvisers.

Although Higgins was not making explicit political commentary through his performances—unlike Terence Blanchard in his composition "Breathless" (2015), where his orchestrated breathing textures suggested Black humanity discarded by the perpetual violence of state actors (see Chapter 1)—Higgins's space-making was political nonetheless for how it communicated ideas about the Black community and the broader human condition. The first musical resonance (from the Latin *resonantia*, echo) we encounter as human beings is the rhythm and resonance of our own breath. Improvisation is the echo of the musician's conception, the echo of the improviser's breath. Breathing facilitates the courage to take a chance, to articulate unconventional music techniques. Breath control is not confined to vocalists and wind players; yet how often do we think about the breathing techniques of non–wind instrument improvisers–who also rely on breathing to improvise a musical idea in the moment? Higgins's improvised performances show us that breathing is a way to access all colors of humanity across the spectrum while being grounded in the cultural traits and musical traditions of one's own community.

Focusing on Higgins's performance of improvisation and accompaniment on "Georgia" on the Charles Lloyd album *The Water Is Wide* (2000),[3] I discuss how Higgins's use of breath in relation to his creative imagination influenced his improvisational risk taking; reflected his musical inventiveness and his vision of the Black community on the World Stage in Leimert Park; and articulated his improvised meditations in the final days of his life. Breathing is linked with the execution of creative ideas and the producing of Black musical space. Within that space improvisation is the evidence and manifestation of Black social life.

When thinking critically about improvised music performances, I have often focused on the instrumental sound the performer creates. Phrasing, intonation, diction, finger technique, proper embouchure: these are a few techniques on the grand list of performance practices to which musicians and musicologists pay attention. There is another repertoire that I have heard in these performances but often relegated to the corner of my mind: the repertoire of physicality, sounds that are not deliberately amplified but still come out in the mix. These sounds that we listeners digest subconsciously are as integral to the improviser's performance as is the cardiopulmonary system that sustains him or her in the process of making music, yet they are rarely addressed. Using the creak sound on Miles Davis's recording of "Old

Folks," jazz pianist and musicologist David Ake invites other scholars to "expand that musicological toolbox a bit" by exploring unintentional sounds made during a jazz recording.[4] Ake argues that, if musicologists explore the unintentional sounds made by the performing body during the artistic labor of improvisation, this critical exploration could redefine the meaning of art and create a more holistic music analysis. This type of music criticism would no longer negate the presence of the body on the recording:

> When all is said and done, how we conceive of jazz is as much about the body as it is about the "soul." As one small step toward reclaiming the centrality of the performing musician, I want also to reclaim the meaning of "the work of art." I do not mean that much-bandied phrase as it is typically understood: a noun, a thing, to be observed, contemplated, or admired . . . Here, the work of art refers to the physical (and also mental) effort necessary to create the sounds we hear as music.[5]

Where my analysis differs from Ake is that my goal is to assess not the unintentional sounds but the intentional sounds of improvisation and respatialization on this recording. In particular, I posit that the sound of breathing is a sonic sign of Black musical space.

Breathing is often the audible sound that improvisers make during a performance when they expend effort in the service of expressing a musical idea. Those of us who have listened to improvisers perform on digital compact discs over the past generation have become accustomed to hearing more clearly what have been considered extramusical sounds. Of course, any lay listener can hear pianist Keith Jarrett singing and breathing while improvising, even if that performance was on vinyl or tape cassette. What I am addressing here is more subtle. Higgins's breathing during his improvisation on "Georgia" reveals the permeable and human connections he had with the other musicians in the process of performing and recording the piece. His unpredictable breathing patterns are associated with crossing bar lines, an audible trace of his Black humanity. Jean-Christophe Bailly argues that humans in general recognize respiration cycles in each other and can analyze them and connect them to emotional states:

> One sees respiration outside of oneself in others' bodies and in the bodies of creatures. One sees it just as easily when they stir slowly in the most profound sleep as when they are running and out of breath from something that caused them to panic. And yet we are used to the range of breath—from a prolonged, even dilation to gasping and panting, and from joy to suffocation. It is the animal form of being in life, the space of our most proper emotion, and the

fundamental rhythm through which we identify life and the living. And it is even the sign of life that persists and resists.[6]

Though string and wind chamber musicians use breathing for sectional cues and phrasing, I am not talking about the Eurological tradition of breath control.[7] I am discussing the use of breath as a spiritual and musical dialogue that cuts across all space-times.[8] British saxophonist Evan Parker, known for his circular breathing techniques that manipulate his inhalation-exhalation cycles to create a continuous sound, has described free improvisation with other improvisers as a way of transporting oneself to a utopian space: "When I close my eyes and I am just playing with other people in a free situation, where we can all do what we want, I am in a utopian space. And I have been very lucky to spend a huge amount of my life in that utopian space."[9] Billy Higgins, as we'll see, used breathing in improvisation to produce Black musical space that could never be utopian in the way that Parker has suggested. Higgins's idea of utopia would have been built on that *memory of* freedom[10] bequeathed to him by his ancestors—who were not mere fungible property in a perpetual state of trauma but creative, radical shapers of their own sociality.

"He's a Watts Boy"

Born in the Watts section of Los Angeles in 1936, Billy Higgins began playing the drums at five years of age.[11] For Higgins, drumming was not a job but a vocation. When observers of the young Higgins did not understand his calling to play the drums, he had to step out of their ideological space-times and into his own. Higgins recalled an early episode of dealing with other people's doubt about his musical calling: "People used to ask me, say, 'Little boy, what do you want to be?' And I said, 'I want to play the drums,' you know? 'But no,' they'd say, 'But no, what do you really want to be?' I'd say, 'I want to play the drums.'"[12] He followed that initial sound he heard in South Park on 51st and Avalon in Los Angeles to a creative life playing the drums around the world. As a teenager, he worked alongside trumpeter Don Cherry in the *Jazz Messiahs*. While working as a stock clerk at the University of California, Los Angeles, he began to play with rhythm and blues bands that included musicians like singer and guitarist Bo Diddley and singer Jimmy Witherspoon. He began working with saxophonist and composer Ornette Coleman in 1956 and recorded *The Shape of Jazz to Come* (1959) and *Change of the Century* (1960). Higgins was never chained to a particular style of playing the drums, as is revealed by his colorful list of collaborators. Working with all these different musicians cultivated in him a stylistic malleability that prepared him to play with anyone. Creative musicians like Higgins did not draw an aesthetic line in the improvisational sand between playing "free" and playing the American Songbook standards. Whereas conservatory or college jazz programs might foster stylistic cliques, with the "advanced" free players socially ostracizing the bebop or straight-ahead players, in the real music world creative African American musicians play a multiplicity of music styles to survive—and to express tireless creativity. Higgins worked with pianist and composers Cecil Taylor and Thelonious Monk, trumpeter Lee Morgan, and saxophonists David Murray and Charles Lloyd, as well as with many other icons of improvisation.

Having been addicted to heroin by the age of eighteen, Higgins was arrested several times on narcotics charges in the 1950s and had his cabaret card revoked—as did many of his colleagues for various reasons. The loss of that card—the permit allowing performers to work in venues that served alcohol—meant he had to quit saxophonist Ornette Coleman's band. Higgins was house drummer for Blue Note Records for several years in the 1960s, which accounts for his being one of the most recorded drummers in the history of jazz. Higgins briefly retired in 1995 after a liver transplant but began performing music again in 1997. His transplanted liver began to fail in 2000, and he passed away in Inglewood, California, in 2001.

Black Musical Space and the World Stage

Since this book considers the intersection of space creation in the Black imaginary and the physical spaces where improvised music is performed, it is important to understand how Higgins's spirituality and cultural work connected with his creation of Black musical space during improvisation.

Higgins's belief in service is why he created the World Stage in 1989 with poet and friend community arts activist Kamau Daáood in the historic Leimert Park Village section of Los Angeles. The World Stage, which is still a thriving Black cultural space, was conceived as an oasis from the pressures and lunacy of wider Los Angeles and the world. The World Stage is a multidisciplinary Black space that features drum, vocal, and writing workshops. There are jazz performances and poetry readings that feature internationally renowned artists. Musicologist Guthrie Ramsey defines spaces like the World Stage as "community theatres."[13] These communal spaces, or "sites of cultural memory,"[14] are where Black music is defined or where musical meaning is generated in a kind of feedback loop. These theatres are not just about Black music but every expression of Black life. Initially restricted to Black Angelenos through housing covenants, Leimert Park Village is now known as the center of Black Los Angeles.[15] Leimert Park represents geographical Black self-determination with its panoply of Black-owned businesses, including the World Stage.

Daáood, who knew Higgins as well as anyone over several decades, explained the depth of Higgins's generosity relative to his co-creation of performance gallery: "Billy, he could have spent the rest of his life making money, moving around the world. But he chose to be in community, giving even to the detriment of himself."[16] Though musicians in the community viewed him as a sage, Higgins refused to embrace the sagacity ascribed to him. Claiming expertise in any kind of music would lock him into a reified parody of himself, truncating the potential of his future growth as an improviser and a Muslim. His improvised performances indicate that he understood the air he was breathing was on loan so that he could serve a larger purpose beyond his own self-importance. As pianist and composer Randy Weston observed, "The music that we tend to take as ours is really coming from the Creator, and it comes at certain points and through certain artists to give people inspiration, to set a tone for certain serious things that are happening and going to transpire in world history."[17] And so it was with Higgins who derived gratification from witnessing how people were changed by the complex beauty of the improvised music he performed alone and with others, explaining: "I've seen so many people transformed, I know how important the music is. I've seen people in there come out of the place beaming. You see something like that, and if you've got any kind of empathy in your heart, it starts to be what you're doing that is supposed to be done, and you're affiliated with this."[18] The radiant faces he saw in the course of his career were evidence that he was fulfilling the core mission of his art: he wanted people to experience light through revolutionary sound.[19] The experience of that light through sound was rooted in a spiritual worldview that connected to Higgins's belief in strengthening the Black community.

"Seeking Light through Sound": Islam and Black Musical Space

Though raised in the Black Holiness church, Higgins converted to Islam in 1977. African American improvisers had been converting to Islam since the mid-twentieth century, and approximately two hundred had joined the Muslim Brotherhood by 1953.[20] By the time Higgins converted to Islam, such African American improvisers as drummers Art Blakey and Kenny Clarke, as well as pianist Ahmad Jamal, had laid down this conversion template for a generation of Black musicians, turning to Islam "'not only as a rejection of the 'white man's religion' but also as a means to bring a moral structure to a world suffused with drugs, alcohol, and sex.'"[21]

Higgins's embrace of Islam manifested in such acts as co-founding the World Stage in Leimert Park so that musicians could study and practice improvisation in the Black community. His mission statement for the World Stage, concise and inspirational, was "Seeking light through sound."[22] For Higgins, the attraction to Islam was about more than being dissatisfied with Christianity: "I needed something very strong to get out of the situation I was in. It helped me straighten the whole thing out. If you do it like it's supposed to be done, it's on the money. And it's structural. Without structure, it's over. You're just like paper in the wind."[23] Kamau Daáood shared a story Higgins had told him about his challenges in the early stages of his musical life:

> Billy was in the streets, and he went through a lot of stuff that cats went through very heavily. He [Higgins] told me a story about returning to Rudy Van Gelder's recording studio, where they used to have the recordings, and there was a bathroom there, and the cats used to go in there and shoot up, and it was like blood on the walls and shit, just horrendous in there a lot of times. Back in the '80s he was back at that studio, but he had cleaned up. He had been a practicing Muslim for quite a while. And he went back in that same bathroom, and he said when he realized where he was and the journey that he traveled, he just stayed in that bathroom and wept.[24]

This story of Higgins's struggles with drugs is not shared with the reader to provide salacious content or fodder for judging Higgins as a human being. It is provided only to illustrate how far Higgins had evolved as a person and what motivated him to do good works during the second half of his life. Islam was a tool Higgins used to evolve as a human being. His conversion to Islam was an attraction not to dogma but to self-discipline. As Kamau Daáood explains, "He was a practicing Muslim but he did not believe in dogmatic Islam. You know those lines we used to have as kids to help us write straight? Islam provided that for him. When you pray five times a day, it's kind of hard to make that next prayer and have a lot of craziness in between. You are either going to pray or not pray."[25]

Saxophonist, composer, and close friend Jackie McLean introduced the teachings of Islam to Billy Higgins during a flight to Japan, and it was while on tour in Japan that Higgins visited his first mosque. Though he was eventually given the Muslim name Hassan Ahmed Abdul Karim, Higgins chose not to change his birth name; he believed his deeds had to be beyond approach for him to fully adopt his Muslim name. As he told interviewer Rasul Muhammed, "I studied the attributes of the names. Abdul means slave servant [*sic*] of Allah and Karim is, you know, also generous and deserving. So I have to live up to that name. If I can live up to that name, then I'll be eligible to take it. You understand? You have to watch what name you take because you have to live up to that attribute, you see."[26]

There is a correlation among Higgins's refusal to be known by his Muslim name, his unwillingness to be a "star," and his resistance to being pigeonholed into any one style of improvised music. Yet the social context around the culture of intellectual and aesthetic openness that Higgins championed banged up against strict religious mores that were used as a gatekeeping tool by certain followers of Islam in the community. Black musical place-making reflects the life strategies and choices Black people make in life to survive (and transcend) imposed constraints—including institutional structures that commodify their art yet negate their quotidian needs. Yet the space can never be utopian because of the racism, patriarchy, and homophobia that also exists in that space. How ironic that one of the most democratic and culturally open spaces of music, forged through the legacy of Black enslavement and dehumanization, can also be prescriptive, biased, and closed-minded.

According to anthropologist João H. Costa Vargas, who researched the cultural scene in Leimert Park Village and specifically the World Stage, the promotion of innovative music and humanity happened within a patriarchal context of toxic masculinity.[27] It is clear that Higgins's musical, spiritual, and community development missions were intertwined. After all, his adoption of Islam was deeply connected to his mission of communicating a deeper level of humanity through innovative musical practices.[28] However, because the Muslim sect Al-Islam and, to a lesser extent, the Nation of Islam were the predominant religious contexts of Leimert Park in Higgins's time, Muslim religious values were used to enforce a version of Black self-respect and decorum rooted in Black male patriarchy that also worked to police class distinctions among Blacks. Vargas explains that those who did not comport with the dominant patriarchal view of Blackness were considered outsiders:

> Intolerance toward race, gender, class, and age differences, as well as marked suspicion toward those who lived in areas considered degraded, were some of the most readily observable traits of Leimert's social life. Non-Blacks and poor Blacks, as well as women and non-heteronormative persons, were viewed as having personal essences that, in principle, placed them in different and distant worlds across which communication and understanding were, if not impossible, at least very difficult.[29]

Having grown up in the Los Angeles area and having performed at the World Stage sporadically in my youth, the permutations of intolerance claimed by Vargas to exist in the village was not immediately legible to me. However, it is possible for a jazz community to embrace universal openness on the surface while being invested in protecting its values, maintaining racial exclusivity in confrontational and subtle ways. Still, despite the overwhelming Black patriarchal structure, young women and male musicians, many of whom were from the poorest parts of the ghetto, were enthusiastically supported—which shows that Blackness is never static but is always being negotiated.[30] Vargas articulated these complex contradictions in the World Stage community when he wrote that "improvised black music can be seen as a privileged conduit for emancipatory practices and thoughts—even when unmistakably permeated by principles and attitudes that frontally contradict radical liberation and decolonization."[31] Black respectability politics and patriarchy was also seen in the promotion of jazz over other Black music art forms.

Higgins viewed African American improvised music as a higher form of music than codified forms of the twelve-bar blues and hip-hop music in general. Higgins believed Black youth were not being educated about Black music culture outside of hip-hop:

> Because the stuff that they feed kids now, they'll have a bunch of idiots in the next millennium as far as art and culture is concerned. I play at schools all the time, and I ask, "Do you know who Art Tatum was?" "Well, I guess not." Some of them don't know who John Coltrane was, or Charlie Parker. It's our fault. Those who know never told them. They know who Elvis Presley was, and Tupac, or Scooby-Dooby Scoop Dogg—whatever. Anybody can emulate them, because it's easy, it has nothing to do with individualism. There's so much beautiful music in the world, and the kids are getting robbed.[32]

It would be easy to write off Higgins's criticism of Black popular music as the conservative cantankerousness of an elder statesman pining for the good old days. Yet his criticism stemmed from a legitimate concern for the nature of musical education in the inner-city public schools of America, which systemically deprives children knowledge of the great Black music culture that has given this country its identity. This dearth of knowledge among the young African American generation extends throughout their adult lives unless a curricular intervention is made. Higgins knew and loved the history of Black improvised music because he *lived and made* the history of Black music. A master drummer, Higgins worked in the improvisational schools of composer-pianist Thelonious Monk and drummers Roy Haynes and Art

Blakey. From Monk, Higgins received observational lessons about space and time; from Haynes, about applying taste to sound. Working with Blakey, he learned the technique of building gradients of sonic texture, or "shading." On Blakey's playing, Higgins remarked: "As strong as he plays, he always starts down there with the shading. It's something that comes with age."[33]

Higgins wanted Black children to know the rich history of improvised music so that younger generations would have a cultural literacy to buttress their self-worth. As Daáood explains, "The music is really coded in the story and the history of our times and the lives and the things that we go through on our journey through this life, and a lot of these stories, because of the commercial nature of this world, do not get told, you know, and a lot of these voices are not heard."[34] Despite his anger over the lack of cultural education among Black youth, Higgins radiated positive values as a core member of the Leimert Park Village community through his street music pedagogy. The late community stalwart and musician Juno Se Mama Lewis noted that Higgins evolved into a model of generosity, peace, and inspiration in the community:

> He [Higgins] wasn't born like that, you know. Billy's worked a lot on all his stuff. You can feel him when he speaks, you feel him when he listens to you. Coltrane was kind of an angel—everybody who met him felt the same—and Billy's got that type of vibe. He's nice to everybody, works a lot with the kids; he even gave one of his drum sets—the one that was at the Stage, remember?—to a young kid, and man, his playing is so fresh, so meaningful.[35]

Lewis's comments connect Higgins's cultural work to his ability to shimmer with, joy, love, and spirituality as a musician. The African drum ensemble at The World Stage, which is still active in the wake of Higgins's death, remains an extension of Higgins's philosophy about serving the African American community where he lived. His vibrant practice of producing Black musical space through improvising cannot be separated from his mission to have a positive effect on the lives of Black people in the Leimert Park community as well as throughout the world.

Family Sound and the Negation of Ego in Higgins's Practice of Black Musical Space

Higgins's statements during interviews regarding his philosophy on teaching, orchestrating individual sound, and improvising with other musicians evinced a recurring theme, one that reflected his belief system of collective family sound. Higgins believed improvised sound needed to achieve a kind of familial balance, where every musician in the ensemble could be heard, so that every musician and audience member could receive a kind of spiritual food that exists at the core of "the music."[36] He also believed that having a big ego locked a musician into a style of improvising that played to audience expectations and blocked the Creator from working through him/her in the moment. Higgins enjoyed not being famous and was happy just to concentrate on evolving as a musician: "Now, everybody wants to be out front, but the drummer's supposed to give a little and take a little and give a little and so on. When you're not a star, there's a lot of pressure off you and you can just be yourself. Sometimes I've seen people who've become stars, and it's all over for them."[37] Consequently, Higgins generated Black musical space through forgetting himself and practicing deep listening as a kind of spiritual fellowship with other musicians, regardless of their race. Higgins believed in subtlety and not forcing musical ideas.

"Sonny Greer once told me something," recalled Higgins. "He said finesse is very important on the drums. Because you can always relate to music if you use finesse."[38] Such sophisticated subtlety was a part of Higgins's drumming philosophy, and he believed drummers acquired finesse as they became more experienced in the music. Musicians on this creative level signal ideas through subtle gestures, often leaving space where a more anxious improviser would play a musical idea in an obvious manner. Drummer Andrew Cyrille observed how Higgins orchestrated the musical spaces through mental imaging for improvisers by steering the tempo flow with a kind of pushing and pulling:

> It's what you see in your mind as you are listening and how you fill those spaces up. A lot of times, we as drummers fill in the spaces. Cats play a line, then they stop for a minute, and you give them something to keep moving, give them a little push. And those little pieces of music that he would put in, moving from one phrase to another, were also very magical and wonderful.[39]

Recalling his experiences of performing with Ornette Coleman, Higgins defined empathic improvisation this way: "That's what people are supposed to do. You make me do something and then I make you do something. It's give and take."[40]

Many cultural critics will often box Black musicians into an essentialized space, arguing that African American improvisers only articulate Black identity. But African American improvisers do not see themselves in such stark and simplistic terms. Rooted in Black musical space, they see their musical expression and cultural work within the larger context of the arts and the human condition. This is why all the musicians in this book reject being identified with prescriptive, nationalistic discourses that can mean being locked into an improvisation school or a musical style. These musicians, among many others, also prefer the alternative schools of music education rooted in the Black community and not the conservatory, a white space that privileges Western European art music modes of thinking. Kamau Daáood explained it to me this way: "Just because you have allegiance to where you come from, that does not have to stop you from embracing a larger humanity and family structure. That's the problem with a lot of us that become more educated and refined in our thinking. A lot of times we kinda forget about where we are at, and there is real work that needs to be done here."[41] The real work that Daáood is talking about is the fight for equality alongside anyone from anywhere who is committed to social justice. The practice of Black musical space-making is about feeding the entire community.

Higgins believed that a musician who listens closely to other musicians in performance feeds them by improvising in a way that sonically supports their creative efforts. Like a great conversation between sensitive, empathetic listeners, the heart of successful improvisation is strengthened by the ability to interact with other improvisers in a way that allows them to communicate their ideas. Commenting on the progress of his Monday night African drum ensemble, held at World Stage for children as young as toddlers, Higgins remarked, "Now it's sounding together. . . The sound is a family. Everybody got to get fed."[42]

Drumming helps people breathe together and has been used to create a connection of human expression in the midst of life-and-death conflict. Calling drumming "a powerful resource for reconciliation," Ghanaian master drummer Nicholas Djanie maintains drumming has a way of synchronizing the breathing process among people, often helping resolve conflicts between African tribes by creating a musical and spiritual path to reconciliation: "When we bring together people from communities that have been in conflict, people from groups that have been perpetrators or oppressors and people from communities that have been victims, they will all breathe in different ways. The drums will balance their breathing."[43] Higgins made a similar argument about drumming when he recalled playing with Ornette Coleman: "Once you start playing together, a whole lot, you start breathing together and then it becomes natural. It's like speaking to your wife, or whatever; it's something that becomes part of you, and it becomes so natural that it's no mystery."[44] Higgins believed that playing extensively, without sheet music, with musicians who were also open to the process led to similar breathing patterns during improvisation. Breathing during improvisation allows musicians to interpellate into each other's space-times.[45]

Magical Blowing: Landscape of Musical Possibilities

Higgins's conception of space and air involved creating a flow within his solos and within the various ensembles he worked with, and this connected to his space-making. The evidence of this methodology is in the testimonies of his colleagues, who watched and studied Higgins's performance strategies through the years. Drummer Andrew Cyrille observed the inhalation and exhalation cycle integral to Higgins's approach to drumming and musical risk taking. He saw how Higgins's breathing patterns enabled him to articulate his imagination through the topography of his drum set, continually astounding his drumming colleagues and international audiences:

> I'd go watch him play, and he'd start playing something on the rim of the drum, and breathe-in, breathe-out, etc. He'd go for it. Just do some stuff that you wouldn't expect. Just the element of surprise. That's really what was so great about him, and all the great drummers also. That's in a sense what the essence of jazz is all about—the element of surprise. What is this guy going to do next? And he was one of the great exponents of that.[46]

The risk improvisers take is already a success because victory is in the attempt to say something musically truthful, regardless of whether an arbitrary musical goal is achieved. The heart of the Black aesthetic belief system is found in the advice that Thelonious Monk whispered to Abbey Lincoln as she recorded "Blue Monk": "Don't be so perfect."[47] The African American music tradition is never about perfection in the conventional sense of the European aesthetic. It is about asymmetry, trial by fire, disavowal of the monochromatic, and joyfully coloring outside the lines. If an improviser has attained perfection, then there is no more story to tell and therefore nothing to live for. The late, legendary drummer Elvin Jones spoke of the importance of storytelling in improvisation:

> When I was a young man, my parents and their peers had ways of encouraging the young people, and there was an expression they would use: "Tell your story." What the people meant was, "Do it your way and make it for all of us." This is the way I believe a song is supposed to be rendered, whether it is a drum song

or a saxophone song or any other. The composition should be expressed in a form that can be recognized as a story.[48]

Telling one's musical story through improvisation is a continual journey and never an arrival point; the same holds true for the sound that a musician is trying to achieve. Yet, because serious listeners of improvisational music can identify recordings of a creative musician by his or her touch, attack, and phrasing, young improvisers are often taught that developing one's signature sound on one's instrument is among the most important accomplishments for a musician. It's a sign of reaching a certain level of creative maturity; once you have found your individual sound, you have arrived. Higgins disagreed with this idea. In 1990 a jazz journalist asked him if he felt that he had arrived at "his sound": "No, no, no," Higgins replied. "Because the sound keeps changing. Once you 'arrive,' it's all over. You've got to keep evolving from day one till the time you leave the planet. It's a process. It's a journey, not a destination."[49] It was the beauty of the never-ending search for one's sound in that Black sense of place that motivated him. Every new breath brought new possibilities for human expression.

Creating a sound on one's instrument is a regenerative process of renewing energy, similar to breathing. And it is the hearing of one's sound in relation to other vocalists or instrumentalists—the internalization of a spatialized community of sounds through the deep, genealogical study of sonic innovation in the history of Black improvised music—that is how one develops a personal sound as an improviser. The improviser does not create the community; the community creates the improviser.

Higgins, speaking about the process of creating one's own sound, invoked the concepts of air and space: "I don't like to fight the drums. If I've got to fight them, then it's a physical chore to play them. I try to get a little 'air' with the instrument. . . . Space and air. . . . The drums are a vehicle for all instruments to bounce off of."[50] Higgins believed the mastery of air flow promotes innovation within a collective, and that musicians need to allow music to breathe instead of forcing the articulation of unexpected musical ideas. He also taught that less could be more:

> Most of the drummers that are working are people who know how to make the other instruments get their sound. Kenny Clarke was a master at that. It sounds like he was doing very little, and he was, but what he implied made all the instruments get their sound. . . . You try to add your part, but the idea is to be part of the music and make it one. That's the whole concept for me.[51]

Parables of this lesson, that *implying* a musical idea is more powerful than *playing* one, have been passed from one improviser to another on band-stands and stages all over the world for generations. When Higgins talked about other instruments bouncing off his drums, he was not only making an acoustical observation but remarking about the way other instruments breathe colors and tonalities together. This can occur only if musicians leave musical space within their performance, giving music air by avoiding the playing of conventional notes in a chord or a scale.

The first time I heard drummer Billy Higgins's breathing during his impro-vised accompaniment for Brad Mehldau's piano solo on "Georgia," I heard how he used his breath to launch musical ideas, *insufflating* (blowing on or into) the moment. In this recording (which receives a fuller analysis below), Higgins's breathing for me is an audible cycle of his imaginative thinking, displayed through his split-second musical choices in the moment. The practice of improvised Black musical space in real time extends, as does the space itself, from lived experiences. Kamau Daáood believed that Higgins's breathing and vocal sounds represented a repository of living musical ideas learned from living and playing with other masters of improvised music. Here Daáood reflects on the sound of Higgins:

> When you listen to Billy, and you hear all of those little grunts and stuff like that, there are so many motifs, and patterns, and stories in the music, he got that library at his disposal. You have played with Monk, Lee Morgan, Jackie McLean and played with Trane; to have them cats be a part of his life, to spend days together and time together—laugh and tell jokes together—he is pulling from all that.[52]

Higgins's improvisations through his breath phrasing pointed to his ability to hear Mehldau's ideas; execute sympathetic, parallel ideas; and then create oblique but complementary rhythmic angles of divergence, along with other improvisers. Higgins was invested in his collaborators' musical expression on the macro, conceptual level of the compositional form—as evinced in his expansive pacing through the whole of the ensemble—as well as in the shape of musical ideas on the micro level with each individual performer.

Breathing is connected to how musicians listen to each other as they fearlessly communicate musical ideas with each other. This is "the space of breath," defined as the process of the outside communicating with the inside of the body.[53] Higgins's space of breath is imagined here as something shared among improvising musicians, who breathe not in synchronicity like a classical string quartet, but asymmetrically as they negotiate the creative energy between them. Breathing while improvising tells us how musicians think about musical and physical space and the way they intend to expand that musical space with unpredictable musical gestures.

Higgins's improvisation strategies reveal a continuum between breath and improvised creative expression in real time. When I asked Kamau Daáood if he ever observed breathing strategies in Higgins's performances of improvisation, he explained that all of the breathing sounds and grunts Higgins made when he performed were rooted in his experience in the Black Holiness church: "Billy's Mama was Holiness, Holiness church, so he came up around all that hummin' and all that groanin', and stuff like that. He knew about that, he carried that around with him."[54] Ashon Crawley writes in his study of the whooping sociality of the Black church, "Not only does spirit give life, but that life is evident in how one leans toward others, how one engages with others in the world. *We do not merely share in sociality; we share in the materiality of that which quickens flesh; we share air. Breath, breathing through the process of inhalation and exhalation*" [my emphasis].[55] African American improvisers do not own this practice of creating musical space and community through breathing practices. In some social worlds breathing strategies, in connection with body positions, are used as a portal into wondrous spiritual worlds.

Lowland South American shamanic breathing through wind instruments and its relationship to the spirit world have been studied by missionaries and ethnomusicologists for generations. Ethnomusicologist Jean-Michel Beaudet argues that "it is by this experience of blowing, by this mode of knowing through the senses, that men enter into the world of extraordinary beings."[56] Anthropologists Jonathan D. Hill and Jean-Pierre Chaumeil write that seventeenth-century Jesuit missionaries documented the connection between breathing and sacred flute rituals in indigenous Amazonian rituals of lowland South America. Amazonian shamans who practice these sacred rituals believe they can communicate with ancestors and cure an array of illnesses. The prevalence of aerophones (wind instruments) in their culture evinces how indigenous peoples of this region understand breath as a spiritual "life force."[57] Aerophones provide a way of channeling breath to "ensure the continued fertility of animal nature as well as the regeneration of human social worlds."[58] For the Wayapi people in French Guiana, breathing through the aerophones makes the invisible spirit world visible. Through these wind instruments the chosen shaman calls upon animal spirits and ancestors that other community members cannot see. Waiwai people think of flute rituals as "magical blowing" used to call the spirits into existence.[59] Flute rituals through shamanic breathing increases the sound volume of breath so that it travels distances. Sacred wind instruments have also been used as "auditory masking devices" to obfuscate the identity of individual players, in order to promote a group identity while expressing the mystic power of shamanic breathing cycles.[60] Whether or not the widely traveled and open-minded Higgins was aware of these cultural practices by the Amazonian peoples is not known. Though grounded in an Afrodiasporic worldview of improvised music, Higgins explored the space-making practices of various music cultures; this allowed him to cross bar lines of the institutional reification of codified jazz forms prevalent in our time. Higgins's openness and breadth of knowledge allowed him to operate above epistemological walls and cultural borders maintained by the policing of musical categories. "You should also check out all kinds of music from different countries and put it in with your own conception. Because it's all valid. If it wasn't valid it wouldn't be there," he once remarked.[61] Drummer Billy Hart, a colleague and keen observer of Higgins and the evolution of African American improvised drumming, has this to say about Higgins's knowledge of world music cultures:

> As we move more towards a world view of music and of drumming, as we are more and more interested in the South American rhythms as an evolution from Africa through South America to here, as we get more advanced or more progressive or whatever, we realize we are really going back and studying all those musics from before. And Higgins' contribution seems to be some kind of innate awareness of that in advance.[62]

Hart's insightful comments provide a valuable perspective on Higgins's approach to learning from drum community cultures around the world.

Saxophonist and composer Charles Lloyd worked with Higgins from the age of eighteen; some of their collaborations were eventually released as *Which Way Is East* (2004).[63] Four months before Higgins passed away, he spent a week at Lloyd's house in Big Sur in 2001. Sometime during the recording process, Lloyd played a digital recording of the two of them improvising for an African man who had come along with a family member to pick up Higgins. As Lloyd tells the story, "[W]hen they came to get him after the week was up, there was an African brother. And we played this stuff for him. So the guy said, 'You know, Billy, he's so incredible. If he came to my village, the people from my village will say that he's one of us because of the way he sings and plays. If he went to *another* village they'll claim him!'"[64] Lloyd's story attests to Higgins's ability to create an Afrodiasporic sense of musical place without attaching to any style, despite his commonly being associated with the 1940s–50s bebop and 1960s free jazz eras. Lloyd's telling of this story shows he appreciated Higgins's music being recognized as culturally, musically, and spiritually descended from Africa. However, the roots of Higgins's "ontological amplification,"[65] his improvised speaking in tongues, were in the Black Holiness church of his youth.

Higgins was not the only African American drummer who meditated on the relationship between his breath and his creative practice. Drummer Elvin Jones reflected on the relationship he observed between his own breathing, practicing, and the performance of improvisation:

> I think it started when I would go through my exercises late at night on the drum pad. Instead of hitting a cymbal or reading a rest, I would sometimes make a noise with my mouth. This would create a kind of continuity for me. It was a habit I got into way back then and it's never left. I sometimes make these sounds, but can't sit down and relate them to the piece.[66]

It would be too grand a statement to say that Jones's breath was the dynamic blueprint of his polyrhythmic sound and overall concept of rhythm. However, it is clear that he would breathe a sound, not *instead* of striking a drum, but as *part* of his drumming sound. Jones's breath was an invisible, inner drum that guided the central pulse of his humanity; it was the chief orchestrator of his sound, not a forced insertion. Though Jones understood manipulating his breath was integral to his creative process, he found it challenging to articulate how his creative breath related to the compositional forms he performed. Breathing transcends any compositional forms a musician would interpret. Breathing is how improvisers cross bar lines of compositional forms and engender musical space.

"It's All Spiritual Now": Facing Mortality in Black Musical Space

Billy Higgins was transparent about his weakened physical condition due to his nephrological challenges during the 1999 recording sessions for Lloyd's *The Water Is Wide*. Higgins's transplanted liver was failing and the hospital at UCLA denied Higgins another transplant.[67] Higgins told Lloyd that he wanted to record in Los Angeles where he lived, so he could use his own drums. Staying in L.A. also gave Higgins access to a mosque close to the recording studio, which facilitated his practice of praying. Lloyd explains Higgins's request to be near a mosque: "I knew what he meant. He needed comfort. Around that time, I was very sensitive to his situation. We would

take a break and he would go to the mosque in Hollywood."⁶⁸ Lloyd believed
Higgins was coming to terms with his imminent death on their *Water Is Wide*
recording sessions and the home recording sessions at Lloyd's house. The
signs that Higgins accepted his mortality showed in his drumming, singing,
and guitar playing on a homemade recording made in Lloyd's house. Lloyd
recalls how Higgins played the guitar and sang the blues on "Blues Tinge"
(2004) as a way of processing his failing health, saying goodbye to his close
friends, and making peace with a hostile but beautiful world:

> Did you notice that blues? Did you hear what he was saying? I can't remember
> the first part, but he sings, "It's a cold, cold, day when the world turns its back
> on you...." That's a man who was dealing with a big truth. And he was a man of
> a big truth. Why do you think a man with his realization would come here [Big
> Sur] and leave his stuff with us, make his last communion?⁶⁹

What Lloyd refers to is Higgins's actual lyric "It's a sad, sad feeling when the
world turn his back on you,"⁷⁰ but his point is well taken. Higgins's apparently
improvised lyrics could be understood as betraying a feeling of abandon-
ment by the world and also defiant fortitude while facing despair: "Well,
strange things happen but you gotta keep pushing on."⁷¹ In Lloyd's comments
about Higgins's embrace of his mortal truth, one hears the deep connection
between the two men documented in their duo recording of January 2001,
mere months before Higgins died in May 2001. This music was later published
as *Which Way Is East* (2004). However, Higgins had also embraced this same
truth a year earlier, in December 1999, as he produced space on "Georgia."

"The Cleansing Thought of Circles":
Billy Higgins's Sculpting of Black Musical Space

Billy Higgins's improvised accompaniment on "Georgia" reveals his use of
breath as an ontological launching pad of dynamic, timbral colors through
his brushwork.⁷² He spontaneously composes melodic-rhythmic ideas that
encircle the piano soloist, spreading air around the ensemble. Higgins's
sculpting of musical space reveals his values of inclusion and love. Breathing together with his colleagues, Higgins puts into play living musical phrases
that bounce off the interrelated human expression in the session for the common purpose of a joyful, spiritual, and thrilling musical exploration. He is a
man playing more on spirit than physical strength. Higgins is working both
on the broad structural level, coloring the group sound, and on the micro

level, improvising ideas in encircling dialogue with saxophonist Lloyd, pianist Mehldau, and bassist Larry Grenadier.

Revealing the topography of his intellect and soul, Higgins allows the listener to hear the air in his improvised breathing patterns, which would have been lost in the recording mix had he used wooden drumsticks instead of brushes. Using the skin of the drums, Higgins's brushes create a compositional backdrop of angular, rhythmic splashes of fluid textures for the other instruments. He articulates ghostly textures through his drum cymbal rivets that linger in the air, creating a cascade of spherical sound in the wake of his initial musical gestures. Higgins's vulnerability serves as the pathway to creating a unified sound with the other musicians.

The improvised interaction between Higgins and Mehldau is embedded in cultural cues and social codes that players understand from their respective worldviews as they endeavor to articulate something musically original and human in their manipulation of space and time. Yet there is much more going on here than achieving a balanced sound. They are playing in a Black space, in an ensemble platform that blends sonorities, supplanting the Western aesthetic ideas of tonal balance that inform orchestral or chamber groups. The production of Black musical space does not adhere to a hierarchical plane of soloist versus accompanying instrumentalists. Though the mark of a great soloist is the individual sound, the idea of the improvised solo has been theorized primarily as an individualistic action. Yet creative improvisation is never about individualism; it's about community.

Higgins's breathing strategies both inspire him and give air to pianist Brad Mehldau as he improvises on the AABA compositional form of the 1930 standard "Georgia (On My Mind)."[73] Though Higgins is in conversation with the genealogy of performances of this song that he'd heard in the past, he is not signifyin' on those past performances.[74]

Saxophonist Charles Lloyd states the first part of the theme in the two A sections of "Georgia" followed by the contrasting B section that begins at 1:34. After Lloyd plays the first phrase of the B section, Higgins breathes his ideas softly, translating his musical imagination into an execution of his idea. In the open space after Lloyd's phrase at 1:43, the bold subtleties of Higgins's musical gesture articulates the dissolution of quantized time. I hear in the alternation between Higgins's left and right hands the permutations of sixteenth notes as he skillfully puts space between smaller independent rhythmic units that add to the sound in its entirety.

Because Higgins's improvisation is as distinct as his breathing, I hear him breathe his ideas as he rolls his brushes in short bursts during the last bar of Lloyd's statement of the theme. Since Lloyd has already told his story through playing the melody, or head of the piece, Higgins begins to create a new rhythmic topography within the compositional form two bars before the new beginning of the compositional cycle in which Mehldau will be the featured improviser.

Higgins does not play sectional transitions in an obvious or predictable way, with clichés. Guitarist Kevin Eubanks remarked on Higgins's ability to cue transitions in the compositional form with simultaneous flair and subtlety, without interrupting a soloist's idea:

> He plays very melodically. He doesn't force the bass drum up your rear, and when he does a fill it's not, "Look at me, I'm the drummer playing a fill." When he plays a fill, he doesn't play it louder than when he's keeping time. Sometimes the fill is lighter, so he gets everything in without jumping in and interrupting your conversation. He's just adding to the discussion, so to speak. When a lot of drummers play a fill, it's louder in dynamics than everything else. Or they telegraph the bridge a mile away. After a while, the music becomes desensitized by all that because it's telegraphed too much. You don't get a sense of the suspense of the music, or having it resolve in a different way.[75]

Whereas some drummers would change from brushes to drumsticks when the next musician begins to improvise through the chord cycle, Higgins does the unexpected, remaining with brushes after Lloyd's statement of the melody.

The energy level now rises as Higgins provides a new coloristic backdrop, with a higher gradation of energy, for Mehldau's improvised piano solo. Higgins changes the sound color and texture of his rhythms by manipulating the brushes through his breath. In the measure before Mehldau's piano improvisation at 2:46, Higgins exhales a short breath on beat two, then rolls his brushes with a crescendo through beats three and four into the first measure of the improvisation. Higgins vocalizes the sound "eh, eh" during the beginning of Mehldau's first spooled-out melodic line through the E♭ major7 and the G7 chord at the beginning of his improvisation. Blowing short breaths into the new sonic landscape, Higgins works to uplift Mehldau through a musical and breath cue, to inspire with his exhalation.

Around 3:10 I hear Higgins breathe and sing rhythms that he does not play on the drums; instead, Higgins's breath becomes an additional drum. Before the repetition of the second A section, Higgins sings eighth-note triplet rhythms, absent the first eighth note, at 3:19. By leading Mehldau with a masterful flair of virtuosic subtlety, Higgins allows improvisational events to happen through love and the manipulation of air and space. He conducts Mehldau with his rhythmic breath, and Mehldau in turn takes those musical ideas and conducts Higgins.

"Conducting" is a signifier that brings to mind an individual standing on a podium in front of an orchestra. In the European concert music tradition, the conductor is in aesthetic control of his or her large ensemble. That, of course, does not apply to the interplay among improvising musicians. The late cornetist, composer, and conductor Butch Morris defined his conduction method in a way that better describes such improvisational interactions: "There is a process of construction, and this construction can move and turn in many ways at any given time, based on anyone in the ensemble."[76]

In response to Mehldau's left-hand rhythms and sparse chord voicings on the C minor chord going to E♭7 at 3:32–3:36, Higgins breathes the sound of quarter notes as a way of articulating a rhythm pocket, in which they are both in sync at that moment. What you hear in this exchange is an ontological conversation of intersecting musical spaces firmly embedded in Black musical place-making. Time is a wave that constantly expands as these musicians dance on the contours of their collective consciousness.

At the close of the second A section, from 3:44 to 3:56, Higgins crosses bar lines with a cross-rhythm pattern of three and four notes between his snare drum and ride cymbal. Higgins prepares the B or contrasting section, as they have played through the repeated A section. When the band enters the B section, Mehldau responds with a triplet rhythm and melodic pedal point in his right hand that inspires Higgins to respond with a simplified pattern on the ride cymbal.

In the last A section, at 4:30 of Mehldau's spontaneous composition on the form, the pianist begins a chordal solo on E♭ major7 through the chord cycle until he arrives at D♭7 at 4:47. At 4:34, Higgins grunts and catches on to Mehldau's triplet idea—a gradual accelerando offbeat pattern to which Higgins responds with offbeat patterns that complement Mehldau's idea, until they both resolve the idea on D♭7. Higgins is a master of making a crucial adjustment in real time by waiting, listening, breathing, and then flowing with the soloist.

Master Traveler in Black Musical Space

He called it the zone; it's a sacred space, man. He was a master traveler in a sacred space. He'd be sittin' there, and he wasn't there. He was there, but he wasn't. He had this smile on his face when he was playing, and he was looking at you but not looking at you.
—Kamau Daáood[77]

Listening to Higgins improvise on "Georgia," I hear a performance emanating from a zone of spiritual strength rather than physical prowess. As Higgins stressed, "Music don't *belong* to *nobody*. If they [other improvisers] could just realize that music doesn't come *from* you, it comes *through* you, and if you don't get the right vibrations, you might kill a little bit of it. You can't take music for granted."[78] With that, Higgins stated his philosophical views on being a conduit for music rather than a master of improvised sound.

Masters of improvisation, like Higgins, deny mastery: they are in service to Black music rather than believing that Black music serves them. By curbing his ego and embracing the limitations of his physical strength, Higgins entered into a Black musical space-time of increasing spiritual refinement. Had he the musical personality and playing habits of indiscriminate, percussive bluster on the drums, with the content of stock rhythm clichés, the weight of that ego-fortifying façade would have suffocated his deteriorating body as he improvised on "Georgia" in the twilight of his life.

Higgins was in dire physical shape in the last year of his life, stating, "I can't play anymore, from a physical standpoint—it's all spiritual now."[79] And so it is clear that Higgins's last performances were not heroic, mind-over-matter musical statements but the grace of breath over the limitations of matter. Higgins's commitment to truth in Black music was stronger than his physical ability. His breath was his portal to creativity, and he sculpted his trap set into variegated colors of his humanity.

I experienced Higgins's empathetic listening ability when I performed with Higgins in a late-afternoon World Stage jam session in the late 1990s. Higgins held up a mirror to my own playing. His sound was open yet inescapable. Higgins played with a big, open beat, and grinned at me while I struggled to find my way within his rhythmic frame on that small bandstand. Veteran drummer Louis Hayes told me over twenty years ago that "the best way to learn how to play is to play with drummers who have a big beat."[80] Higgins's big beat embraced me and pushed me out of my comfort zone. I realized he was challenging me with love to improvise my humanity in real time. Finding a way to articulate my ideas in the midst of Higgins's effortless groove, I felt no disdain or criticism from him—only the generosity of his years of experience. Higgins also kept guitarist Kevin Eubanks honest about his strengths and weaknesses, inviting him to embrace the musical moment instead of forcing an improvised musical idea to create moment: "Whenever I played with him it always felt like there was room to do things. But at the same time, if you did too much you'd know it right away. Somehow he just made me feel aware when I was overplaying."[81]

Elasticity, expansiveness, listening, and breath were the way Higgins produced and shared Black musical space with other musicians. His concept of
rhythm had little to do with keeping time but much to do with insufflating his
fellow improvisers with permutations of renewable time cycles. As Mehldau
remembers, Higgins had a "circular quality to his playing in relation to the soloist, constantly weaving around each player, perpetually interacting with them."[82]

It did not matter that Higgins's instrument was not a wind instrument.
He insufflated the space in and around his drums and blew magical breath
through his instrument onto the musicians with whom he played. As Eubanks
puts it, "There are particular individuals that paint the music and at the same
time keep the time moving ahead, not always driving the beat home. They
spread the responsibility of keeping the time. Billy was more like the other
instruments. It's a very delicate balance that he just seemed to have naturally."[83] Higgins's improvisations through breath allowed him to cross bar
lines into the tonal character of other instruments, infusing his sounds with
their character. He broke the taxonomy of instrumental groupings, musical
genres, and conventional drumming methods.

In his last years, months, weeks, and days, Higgins kept finding the breath
and energy to record music despite his physical decline. Brad Mehldau, in
a tribute statement, recalled: "Although he wasn't physically 100 percent by
the time I got to play with him, he still carried that energy with him. When
he died, I was aware that one of the real creators was gone now. There would
never be a replacement."[84] Thirteen years before recording "Georgia" with
the ailing Higgins, Mehldau had studied his approach to playing the drums
when he came to New York in 1986 and observed Higgins's performance
strategies with the Timeless All-Stars. "When I heard the shimmering of that
ride cymbal, and felt his beat up close like that, I got it."[85] Higgins used the
sizzle ride cymbal to create a sustained wall of timbral color while allowing
him to create other nuanced timbres on his family of drums.[86] "Because it
does a lot of work itself, without you having to do it," Higgins explained. "It
adds a certain picture. While you can do the rest of the stuff it sustains."[87] In
addition to being a sound that helped drummers achieve employment by
various bandleaders, Higgins believed the sizzle cymbal sonically sustained
the other band members by giving "everybody a cushion."[88]

My reading of Higgins's performance shows that he presented us with
examples of breathwork on two levels. Higgins used breath physically to
execute complex cycles of thematic and improvisatory musical ideas while
using his breath to produce musical space with the musicians around him.
Listening to Higgins's improvisation on the level of breathing reveals how

he demarcated time not by playing time but by breathing his ideas into the sound of the other musicians.

Higgins improvised beyond any historical or pedagogical epistemology that would exclude any group. He showed us that what makes Black musical space radical is not the notes, innovative compositional forms, or so-called avant-garde practices. I have witnessed, through the lens of Black sound, what makes the music radical: the love of humanity as a politics, even with full knowledge of the systemic perpetuation of historical crimes that continue to shape Black people's experience in the world. Though the ability to listen is crucial, being a masterful improviser is not the foundation of Black humanity but the product of being Black and human in the world. Higgins crossed bar lines through breath, breathing past hateful racial divisions and segregation. Kamau Daáood said the practice of improvised music is about

> the ability to internalize your life experiences into your being until you radiate it. You radiate it, but you radiate it for good use. You choose the things you wish to emit into the world (if you are a drug dealer or murderer, you don't radiate that). You internalize your life experience and it goes through a process inside you, and when you give it back, the best of yourself comes out—that's important.[89]

Higgins breathed past his failing body and survived on his spirit in the final days of his life. His life is an example of service to improvised music and his community as practiced within the contours of Black musical space.

praise him upon planets, cymbals swirling
flying saucers more than
mere keepers of time
space creators, rhythm liberators
a winged clock, birds clapping
a blind man tapping in time[90]

3

The Social Science Music of
Terri Lyne Carrington

I have been arguing that African American musicians articulate their human-ity through space-making practices. While I believe that improvised music is the most inclusive form of aural art, it has not embraced everyone equally in that musical space. The subject of inclusion relative to the degree in which all marginalized people feel welcome in that space needs to be examined. In this chapter I discuss how, through the cultural work of drummer, composer, arranger, and producer Terri Lyne Carrington (b. 1965), the gendering of improvisation, instruments, and innovation has suppressed women impro-visers. Carrington is at the vanguard of contemporary jazz improvisation. An analysis of her career, musical innovation, and activism highlights the gender disparities that women improvisers face in a patriarchal jazz culture and academic world.

Carrington has won several Grammys and was the first woman to receive one for Best Jazz Instrumental Album for *Money Jungle: Provocative in Blue* (2013). She also won Best Jazz Vocal Album for the first iteration of *The Mosaic Project* (2011), which will be discussed in detail below. However, the extent of her accomplishments and the artistry of Carrington's numer-ous recordings and performances with leading musicians in improvised and popular music over the last several decades, is not the focus of this chapter.[1] Instead, I focus on the important connection between her practice of improvisation and space-making activism for women musicians and other marginalized people.

Using the Black feminist epistemological lenses of Patricia Hill Collins, bell hooks, and Angela Davis, I discuss how Carrington links her improvised musical expression, compositions, and arrangements with social justice issues, creating a musical and intellectual space to examine the barriers obstructing the full participation of women improvisers in jazz culture. As artistic director of the Berklee Institute for Jazz and Gender Justice (founded in 2018), Carrington has taken on gender inequity in jazz culture. She utilizes her international reputation as a musician and experience in the music industry to create an African American woman–led musical space within a prominent musical institution, one rooted in gender equality and inclusivity for people who identify across the gender spectrum. This is the frame I use to understand her cultural work.

I analyze the arrangement by her *Mosaic Project* (2011) of Bernice Johnson Reagon's composition "Echo" (1989) performed and published by the African American women vocal ensemble Sweet Honey in the Rock (SHR). Finally, I analyze several selections in her recent project *Terri Lyne Carrington & Social Science* (2019) which takes on such subjects as police brutality, gay conversion therapy, missing Native American women, and the power of Black womanhood. None of Carrington's projects operate in thematic and aesthetic silos. Carrington's arrangement of "Echo," as well as her current effort to bring attention to intersectional issues with her collective *Social Science*, are not mere musical exercises but an intertextual weaving of Black radical music within the larger quilt of Black feminist thought.

Improvisation Studies and Gender

Writing about improvised music within Black musical space is incomplete without discussing how power is spatially distributed through violence, oppression, racism, and sexism in our society. After all, these systemic constraints shape the music industry and male-centered jazz discourse. To have a discussion about Black musical space without considering how Black feminist thought has helped define alternative spaces and repositories of street theory makes for an impoverished dialogue. Many books on improvisation written by male scholars fail to consider the contributions of African American women improvisers because most male scholars are more comfortable writing about male improvisers. While for more than a generation Black music scholars have argued that separating Black musical aesthetics from their social context within history and culture leads research and analysis down a formalist rabbit hole, they have not adequately addressed gender in their analysis. Many male jazz scholars do not consider gender in their analysis of the contributions of African American women improvisers—apart from mentioning who they consider to be the nonpareil women improvisers.[2] The contributions by women improvisers continue to be considered "feminine" and therefore less impactful than those of their male peers. As a consequence, the sexism faced by women improvisers translates into undocumented cultural contributions in the history of American improvised music. Julie Dawn Smith argues, "The particular challenges encountered by women improvisers due to gender and sex oppression, including the gendering of women's performances and audiences as feminine and/or lacking, are rarely acknowledged."[3] Smith explains that male musical critiques of social inequity through free improvisation have not addressed critiques of gender inequity in their quest for liberation. In Smith's view, this is because free improvisation has always struggled for recognition as an artform. In other words, women improvisers are marginalized in the scholarly discourse because male improvisers individually and collectively struggle for resources and recognition.[4] Freedom is defined in the Black intellectual tradition in broader terms that pivots "around the collective well-being of a people."[5] While Black male leaders in social movements and bandstands have historically relegated Black women to secondary status, Black women themselves have led the struggle against all forms of inequality. Yet Smith's justified focus on gender ignores the central role played by race in the economy of musical prestige and reward. What Smith does not say is that the struggle for resources by Black male musicians—some of whom have also been historically guilty of excluding women improvisers in their social critiques and as colleagues on the bandstand—have not had the same power and access as white male improvisers in the field. Smith's analysis omits the consideration of race as a factor in her critique of gender exclusion. Critiques of gender inequity in improvisation cannot exist apart from the discussion of race.

Sherrie Tucker's history of women big band jazz bands in the 1940s, in her book *Swing Shift: "All-Girl" Bands of the 1940s*, argues that women instrumentalists who improvised were historically treated as social aberrations or imposters because both male and female musicians are "gendered before anyone blows a note."[6] Women instrumental improvisers were considered singers or dancers who happened to play instruments. When they received any notoriety due to exceptional musicianship, they were considered the female versions of male icons.[7] The race of the women improvisers was also a factor in why all-girl orchestras were left out of the predominantly white narratives of swing music histories and jazz history in general.[8] Carrington has had to contend with race and gender in her music career in order to cross the bar lines to success. Yet she understood that success in the music business without freedom for all is not success. This caused her to evolve from a focus on her own exceptional career to a focus on creating a more inclusive space in jazz culture for women improvisers and marginalized communities.

My approach to Carrington's work analyzes the evolution of her political consciousness over the recent years of her career. I briefly discuss her childhood as an African American female child drum prodigy who developed musically in the nexus of patriarchal jazz culture. As common with familial structures of all patriarchies, jazz culture could be both nurturing and exclusionary, picking and then mentoring select female instrumentalist improvisers who master the invisible, male standard of excellence in improvisation. Carrington mastered those male-defined musical codes, evolved them into part of her own sound, and eventually developed a stance that exclusionary male-dominated jazz culture was unacceptable. Carrington's early childhood and subsequent career as a young female musician illustrates how mentorship intertwines with the patriarchal nature of jazz culture and racism in the music world.

A Female Musical Anti-Prodigy in a Predominantly Male Space

Carrington was nurtured by male musicians from the beginning. Born in Malden, Massachusetts, on August 4, 1965, Carrington revealed precocious talent at an early age while playing the drums of her deceased paternal grandfather. Her father Solomon Carrington, an accomplished musician in his own right, exposed Carrington to a panoply of his musical colleagues who came through Boston to play engagements. Solomon had hoped to have a son who would continue the family tradition of playing music, and despite having a daughter, he loved and cultivated his only child's talent. He was the one who had steered Carrington toward her deceased grandfather's drums. Like her father, the jazz musicians who entered their home circle and community were impressed with Carrington's musical abilities because she could play time almost immediately. Carrington describes how her father's promotion of her musical abilities had an impact on her career: "He had the relationships with the musicians and was able to walk me into these scenarios, talk to the musicians, and tell them I could play, and they would let me sit in because they knew and trusted my father.

He was not afraid to ask them to give me a shot. The whole thing would have been very different if I didn't have that support. I'm forever grateful for the circumstances I grew up in."[9] Yet Carrington never thought of herself as a child prodigy but rather as a student of mystical time. For her ears, a musical prodigy may have mastery of instrumental technique at a young age but may have not internalized the intangible musical codes of improvised expression: "I never embraced that term [musical prodigy] . . . to me, prodigy is about technical prowess. With me, it was always more about time feel, which is inexplicable."[10]

Carrington's mother, Judith Carrington, was as much a part of the community of musicians as was her father Solomon. Carrington explains, "It was a team effort . . . her support was just as important to me as my father's."[11] Judith, who trained in classical piano for many years and worked for the Polaroid Corporation in Cambridge, Massachusetts, was there for Terri Lyne at every stage of her career. Solomon, who sold insurance, took Terri Lyne to music lessons at Berklee College of Music on Wednesdays. He could schedule his own hours and had more flexibility.

Apart from her musician father, Carrington's earliest male mentors included the late trumpeter Clark Terry, who gave Carrington her first professional gig at the Wichita Jazz Festival when she was ten years old. Terry was a very important mentor to Carrington. For Carrington, Terry was the bridge to Duke Ellington; he often told the eighteen-year-old Carrington stories about his professional and personal involvement with the legendary bandleader. Carrington explains, "He would say that he was from the 'School of Ellingtonia.' He was my connection to Duke Ellington. That's how apprenticeship happens."[12] She demonstrated Terry's importance in her life by featuring his vocal improvisations on her arrangement of Duke Ellington's "Fleurette Africaine" on *Money Jungle: Provocative in Blue* (2013). Carrington's Money Jungle project revised the original *Money Jungle* (1963), an album that featured a trio of Duke Ellington, bassist Charles Mingus, and drummer Max Roach. In the twilight of Terry's life, when he was experiencing rapidly failing health, Carrington flew to Arkansas to record Terry for the project but Terry was too ill to play the trumpet. Terry suggested he sing or vocalize. His improvised cadenza on "Fleurette Africaine" from 5:27 to 5:44 is not only musically brilliant but is also a commentary on their close connection over a generation.

Carrington obtained her union card as a preteen and a full scholarship to Berklee College of Music, where she is now an endowed professor and recipient of their 2003 honorary doctorate for her impact on the music world. She has also been mentored by pianist Herbie Hancock and saxophonist

Wayne Shorter. Recalling their advice to not play music but to play life, she explains, "They taught me to look at life and to look philosophically at things in general, which affects your music."[13] While many male musicians have provided Carrington with mentorship and opportunities to grow as a musician, Hancock and Shorter stand out because they have also functioned as spiritual mentors to Carrington through their participation in the Soka Gakkai Buddhist movement.

In the 1980s Carrington was part of a community of musicians that later formed into the group called M-Base led by saxophonist Steve Coleman.[14] M-Base was a Brooklyn-based collective started by a group of young African American improvisers in the 1980s. M-Base, which stands for Macro-Basic Array of Structured Extemporization, is a term created by saxophonist Steve Coleman in 1985, with the influence of saxophonist Greg Osby and trombonist Robin Eubanks. The term itself was influenced by Coleman's interest in computer programming. M-Base was founded on self-determination and the practicality of offsetting the fierce competition in the jazz scene. They shared music concepts during rehearsals in their various apartments.[15] The collective was influenced by the Black musical space-making organizations Association for the Advancement of Creative Musicians (AACM) and the Black Artists Group (BAG). She describes her experience with the group as one that shaped her approach to composition: "I was on the outskirts but close enough to let it shape a little bit of me, especially the odd time signatures."[16] You can hear this odd-time-signature influence in her recording *Terri Lyne Carrington and Social Science* (2019), which features compositions "Purple Mountains" and "Trapped in the Amercian Dream," both composed in the uncommon rhythm cycles of ten beats. Carrington never played in the official M-Base band but had "one-offs" with M-Base members such as pianist Geri Allen, trombonist Robin Eubanks, and recordings with saxophonist Greg Osby. She left New York City in December 1988, which took her out of the community of musicians that later became the movement called M-Base.[17]

At age eighteen Carrington concluded that being an African American and a woman was a double liability. Yet she had some success ignoring the sexism of male improvisers in various working environments stating, "If those feelings are underneath, I don't pick up on it. It's a waste of time. I get along with all the men musicians and I always have. It becomes passé, that mentality. I am getting involved with other scenes."[18] She had to get along with men and ignore their sexism in order to survive. This tactic allowed a young African American woman to be supported by important male jazz musicians in the field. She explains her attitude at that juncture in her life and career: "'The hell with it [being Black and a woman]. That's my karma,' and

I haven't looked at it since." Though she coped with the sexism of the music industry, she realized more female representation was needed in jazz culture.

Carrington left New York City in December 1988 and moved to Los Angeles to explore the pop, rock, and fusion music scenes and to be among colleagues like pianist Patrice Rushen, who was also labeled a music prodigy. In these music circles Carrington felt more accepted because male-led bands ostensibly wanted women who were competent musicians who could help them appear egalitarian and diverse. Yet Carrington believed that her employment was about more than having a Black woman on the bandstand. Diversity of band members was linked to the crossover aesthetic of the popular music of that time. Blending different musical genres signified an aesthetic of tolerance for racial and gender diversity and open-mindedness. Carrington claimed in the 1990s: "there are a lot more women playing and coming into their own. It's no longer a matter of women being fashionable or a fad. It's really serious. When a woman says she plays, you have to listen and find out now."[19] This snapshot of Carrington's thinking in her early thirties indicates she believed she was able to rise above the sexism of male improvisers to pursue her career. But it also reflects an early interest in, and support for, representing the talent, tenacity, and topographic diversity of women improvisers.

While navigating the Los Angeles music scene, Carrington was hired as the first staff drummer by comedian Arsenio Hall for his late-night eponymous television show. Playing drums on *The Arsenio Hall Show* five nights a week gave her a visibility that surpassed her East Coast reputation as a jazz drummer. Despite the success and notoriety she attained working in various "non bebop" bands in Los Angeles, the lack of women in the jazz scene and other issues of gender representation continued to disturb her. This gender chasm planted the seeds for future music projects and her current institutional work.

Black Feminist Thought and Black Musical Space-Making

Black feminist thought is a productive intellectual space to redefine theory and intellectual work. The Black feminist thought of Patricia Hill Collins, Angela Davis, Barbara Ransby, Kimberlé Crenshaw, and bell hooks is particularly helpful in framing the work of Terri Lyne Carrington. The practice of improvisation is a social interpretation of lived experience. Black feminist thought—and African American women improvisers like Carrington who exhibit that thought through their performances—are articulating their lived experiences as Black women by producing Black musical space. The musical and institutional contributions of Carrington require us to think differently about what constitutes intellectual work.

Black feminists call for a reconsideration of how the words "intellectual" and "work" are defined. Collins has written:

> Producing intellectual work is generally not attributed to Black women artists and political activists. Especially in elite institutions of higher education, such women are typically viewed as objects of study, a classification that creates a false dichotomy between scholarship and activism, between thinking and doing. In contrast, examining the ideas and actions of these excluded groups in a way that views them as subjects reveals a world in which behavior is a statement of philosophy and in which a vibrant, both/and, scholar/activist tradition remains intact.[20]

The continuity of such academic prejudice and the irrepressible creativity of Black women leads to Black feminist thought flourishing in the work of Black artists who create Black musical spaces. When improvisers like Carrington are taken seriously as human subjects and their musical practices are analyzed according to who they are in the world, their performance practices reveal a philosophy and a connection to an intellectual tradition.

Jazz festival stages, small clubs, and recording studios can all be thought of as geographies where Black feminist thought is cultivated and practiced by Carrington. This cultivation will be discussed below in my musical analysis of Carrington's arrangement of "Echo" (2011) and her *Social Science* (2019) project. Carrington's musical cartography is in a dialectical relationship with Black feminist thought because she is a musician, intellectual, and cultural worker who implements her socially conscious music projects through her compositional practices, her musical and intertextual arrangements of political musical material, and her numerous performances with different band configurations.

Take, for instance, Carrington's mission statement regarding the latest iteration of her social justice and improvisation project, *Social Science*. Here she explains how she self-consciously uses her music and platform as an established artist to bring attention to important social issues, such as police brutality and homophobia. For Carrington, musical practices should reflect the current local and geopolitical situations. In her view, music is a way to express the humanity of those whose daily lives are impacted by the social inequity that continues to marginalize them: "I feel it is our job as artists to carry out the responsibility of reporting and commenting on

what is going on in the communities we are a part of—regarding humanity, politics and anything else that affects our life condition."[21] An organic
intellectual, Carrington's musical and social projects can be classified as
Black feminist thought because she is an African American woman creating a Black musical geography of inclusion to educate her audiences about
issues that affect Black women, Black people in general, and people from
other marginalized communities. Carrington's *The Mosaic Project* (2011),
a recording that features all women improvisers, emerges from the Black
feminist tradition. Her musical project exposes this false binary between
musical activism and scholarship. But how does Carrington define space-
making through improvisation?

Black Musical Space and Gender Justice

When I told Carrington during our personal interview that Black musical
space was inclusive, she immediately disagreed and challenged me to further explain what I meant by the word "inclusive." I explained, for example,
that Black music culture has been used as a template for other cultures to
express their own marginalized identities. She agreed, but further argued,
"It's culturally inclusive but when it comes to gender it has been very not
inclusive and that is what has to change." As I mention above, African
American improvisers fought for freedom and civil rights in the 1960s but
maintained patriarchal and sexist attitudes, treating most women improvisers as inferior collaborators in the movement. This patriarchal attitude
is inconsistent with inclusiveness and has historically been reflected in the
behavior of many male musicians who continue to connect improvisation with the struggle for Black freedom but remain threatened by strong
women improvisers. Yet Carrington is careful to create a balanced assessment of how that inclusion is defined. She does not dismiss all jazz forms
due to the hegemonic patriarchy in the culture. She argues that there are
types of improvisation that are more inclusive of women: "Just to clarify, I
do think that jazz is the most inclusive art form in music. There are areas
of jazz, such as contemporary improvisation, that are more inclusive to
women as opposed to mainstream jazz."[22] For Carrington, mainstream jazz
reflects more of a patriarchal mindset, as it reflects the gender codes of
the era it was created, whereas women can realize their humanity in the
space of contemporary improvisation. Carrington explained to me that
this space is likely more inclusive of women because the contemporary
improvisation field includes musicians who have studied the jazz tradition

and musicians who have not. While her experience has shown her that contemporary improvisation engenders a more inclusive musical space, she cares not for the futile and unproductive debate of what is, and what is not, legitimate jazz.

The Rule Should Be the Exception

Carrington spoke about how she internalized patriarchal thinking as a young musician. Early in her career she believed that, given the absence of women in jazz culture, rare was the female improviser who could improvise as well as a male improviser and also bring that masculine sound to her performance. She accepted her own status as a successful musician as proof that she was an exception to the rule and went on with the business of developing her career. Having become a professional musician at such a young age in a largely Black male space, she was more susceptible to the way the older male improvisers in her music community thought about women improvisers. After all, she came into jazz culture when she had little control over her career due to her age, and adapted to the musical models her father provided through his own musical associations. It should be noted, however, that Carrington was taken by her father to see African American women musicians like Mary Lou Williams, which means that he actively sought out women improviser role models for his daughter.[23]

Carrington devoured the vibrant African American composition and improvisational jazz curriculum that existed on the vinyl records and cassette tapes in her home. She also accepted uncritically, as children and younger musicians are apt to do, the Black masculinist improviser aesthetic regarding sound, energy, dynamics, phrasing, texture, and approach to drum cymbals. Even the unspoken definition of what it meant to be an innovative improviser was defined within Black male patriarchal terms, as any jazz record collection of that time will illustrate. Carrington recalls:

> When I was a kid, I had the protection of my dad. I was thinking like the male musicians: "Most women aren't trying to play this music. Most don't have that thing that we're looking for." And so you get into this thinking pattern about exceptionalism. When I played the drums behind Eddie "Lockjaw" Davis, my father would tell me that I had to "kick him in the ass." It wasn't about competition. It was about bringing that feeling of masculinity into the performance. I fell prey to that way of thinking because that was the

unspoken culture I was wanting to be in. For a long time, I was OK with that because I wasn't thinking about the big picture.[24]

The big picture, as Carrington defines it now, was the practice of selectively putting individual women instrumentalists who are brilliant improvisers on a pedestal. Considering a few women to be exceptional, however, renders the rest disposable. This parceling of woman improvisers creates a narrative that says brilliant women improvisers are rare exceptions in a sea of mostly mediocre women performers, whereas brilliant male improvisers are produced ad infinitum. Women improvisers, who should be viewed as integral to jazz culture, become less visible through exceptionalism. This leads to an imbalance in the literature on women improvisers in the jazz discourse because "the "exceptional woman" narrative functions as one more way of "invisibilizing" women as constituents of jazz culture.[25]

As she matured in the jazz life, Carrington adopted late pianist and composer Mary Lou Williams's approach to issues of gender discrimination by avoiding conversations and jazz journalism that would put her gender first and her musicianship second. Williams was focused on racial justice and saw herself as a serious musician.[26] Moreover, labels were anathema to Williams, as they are to most innovative musicians, because she did not want her life or her music to be categorized. Similarly, Carrington also wanted to be respected as an excellent jazz musician who happens to be a woman instead of being labeled as that rare woman improviser who could play as well as a man. Regardless of how gifted she was as a musician and her ability to navigate the music and education business, growing up in largely male music environments that included festivals all over the world and largely male-dominated student bodies in education institutions was frustrating and isolating. Her musical mind was developed through these social experiences and her courage is evidenced by how she struggled to get beyond them. It was only after she achieved a level of autonomy, career success, and exposure to Black feminist thought that she began to challenge the edifice of patriarchal music values that has depleted the female population in jazz culture, making jazz less diverse, less ebullient, and less democratic.

Improvisation has been gendered as male because the male improviser has been represented as the standard of excellence in jazz publications, jazz research, on the bandstand, and in the movies. According to Carrington, male and female improvisers have been inculcated with male-dominated standards of jazz culture over generations by listening and imitating male standards of improvisation and compositional excellence on landmark jazz recordings. Many of the jazz standards in the American songbook that young improvisers are expected to learn were mostly written by twentieth-century white male Tin Pan Alley tunesmiths who promoted what they imagined to be heterosexual, white women's point of view on love. Carrington explains:

> We [both men and women] have been conditioned to think how music is sup-posed to sound. Everything we have heard [in jazz] sounds a certain way. There is a masculinity built into the music, even in how the American songbook is written from the male point of view. None of the jazz standards we play come from a woman's perspective. Nobody has been trained to wonder what it would sound like if jazz has a different aesthetic.[27]

Carrington concedes, "I'm just as guilty as anyone. I'm listening for that sound that I've heard over the years as being great. So the measure of that album's [*The Mosaic Project* (2011)] greatness is according to whether it lives up to male standards of great improvisation."[28] Carrington's point, which echoes civil rights icon Angela Davis, is that African American improvised music culture has not expressed all of its musical possibilities because it has not supported contributions from women improvisers and composers.[29] Davis explains, "Because the music itself is gendered, the music has never been allowed to reach its own potential."[30] In books like *Blues Legacies and Black Feminism* (1998), Davis has tackled these issues through writing about autonomous Black women vocalists like Ma Rainey and Bessie Smith who were, independent and assertive women.[31]

Space-Making in the Berklee Institute for Jazz and Gender Justice

Over the last ten years, Carrington's political consciousness has grown to the point where gender justice has become the forefront of her activism and is embodied in her founding of the Berklee Institute for Jazz and Gender Justice in 2018. Describing the original idea for the institute, Carrington recalled: "I realized there was something really wrong with that thinking about excep-tional women improvisers–because if you say somebody is an exception, that means there is a rule they are not a part of. Being an exception is not good. That's like when you say this Black person is so articulate."[32] Being singled out for being Black and articulate might initially feel validating but, more often than not, a white person's assessment of codeswitching is in itself rac-ist and reflects a system of white supremacy. Carrington wants to eradicate patriarchy in jazz culture, even if she personally benefited by mastering its codes and improvisational language. She shared an analogy concerning the importance of caring about mass incarceration even if one has never been incarcerated because both mass incarceration and gender injustice are supported by systems of white supremacy and patriarchy, respectively, and "are effectively accomplishing what they set out to achieve."[33] Similarly, male improvisers should care about gender justice even if they have never experienced gender discimination.

In the American education system, girls and women are socialized to play "feminine" instruments, which often leads them away from pursuing the life of a jazz musician. And when they do pursue music in schools that have music programs, they are generally steered toward instruments gendered as feminine, like flute, whereas young male musicians will be encouraged to play the trumpet. According to a study by Kathleen M. McKeage, instruments like the trumpet, saxophone, and trombone continue to be gendered as male.[34] In her study, fifty-eight college students were asked to rate instruments from most masculine to most feminine. McKeage found that drums were viewed as the most masculine and flute was considered the most feminine. Carrington has noticed this trend in her own experience, remarking, "The trumpet is loud and strong and women have been socialized to be quiet."[35] She argues that this kind of socialization is similar to how boys are socialized toward pursuing mathematics and females are tracked toward English literature. And because instruments are gendered feminine, the women who play these instruments are kept out of jazz ensembles whose enrollments are capped, creating intense competition for those few "feminine" instrument chairs in the band.[36] As I stated before relative to Sherrie Tucker's study of all-girl bands in the 1940s, women who play "masculine" instruments have long been perceived as endangering the careers of men. They have been given less lucrative platforms and venues, and their musical skills were rated lower than their potential for novelty and "showwomanship." Tucker writes, "when musicians did cross these lines they were often perceived not just as making aesthetic choices but as disturbing social norms, either in threatening, ludicrous, or titillating ways. When women chose careers playing instruments associated with men, their 'novelty' potential often overshadowed the likelihood of their being heard as skilled players."[37] Moreover, young girls and women have been kept out of jazz culture because the training grounds of improvisation occur in mostly male spaces such as performances in night clubs' male-dominated jam sessions. This creates isolated music spaces where men play with other men.[38]

Curriculum of Inclusive Respatialization

Carrington's pedagogical approach to transgressive teaching, composition and performance is evidenced in the curriculum that undergirds the institutional mandate, including writings by Audre Lorde, Sherrie Tucker, Nichole Rustin-Paschal, Carol Ann Muller and Sathima Bea Benjamin, bell hooks, Eileen Hayes and Linda F. Williams, and Alan G. Johnson.[39] The Black feminist, poet, and lesbian Audre Lorde taught that different tools are required to disassemble structures that oppress and marginalize people defined outside the norms of humanity and white civil society. Oppressed people cannot thrive and live using the same tools that have been used to oppress them. Lorde understood that building coalitions across every type of social division was necessary for a more just world to blossom, writing, "It is learning how to stand alone, unpopular and sometimes reviled, and how to make common cause with those others identified as outside the structures in order to define and seek a world in which we can all flourish. It is learning how to take our differences and make them strengths. For the master's tools will never dismantle the master's house."[40] This coalition-based inclusiveness is what Carrington strives for in her institutional work. Carrington believes that the fight for true freedom cannot be parsed, it cannot be based on conditions of race or sex. Freedom cannot be argued and fought for in one area while supporting suppression in another. As I stated earlier in this chapter, the core issues of African American women improvisers who identify as feminists have been addressed by neither mainstream feminism led by white women nor the patriarchal jazz culture. Carrington continues to experience this isolation:

> My institute [Berklee Institute for Jazz and Gender Justice] deals with gender but I can't talk about gender without talking about race. Black women have to deal with both of these worlds because in the world of feminism, we are still outsiders—not Black feminism, but the overall movement of feminism. The music came out of that tradition *and it was a space where Black men could be free* [my emphasis]. Jazz was at the forefront of the justice movements but never gender equity. How are you awakened in one area and not another? I don't have that luxury.[41]

Carrington admits her Black political thought didn't always consider gender justice because she had to adapt to the male musicians' way of thinking about improvisation to survive and thrive as a female player and composer. Though she met Angela Davis thirty years ago while working as the first *Arsenio Hall Show* staff drummer in 1989, her musical expression was not explicitly aligned with Black feminist politics: "Honestly, I wasn't thinking like a feminist. The problem with the music I played and the times that I grew up in, including going to clubs with my dad and meeting all these great jazz artists—I had to fit in. Luckily, I had that thing where I could fit into this largely male-dominated culture. If you don't fit in, you're not going to make it."[42] That "thing" Carrington discusses was the achievement of an instrumental sound and social attitude that reflected the patriarchal belief systems about improvisation.

The practice of inclusive Black musical space at its best is the social habit of accepting outsiders: those who have been discouraged, dehumanized, and devalued for not adhering to patriarchal social habits. The practice of inclusive space-making happens with the understanding that being an excellent musician has never been enough to succeed in the jazz world. Thus the male-centered, gatekeeping sociality of jazz culture has to be eradicated for the music to truly thrive in all of its possible and unimagined permutations.

Carrington is fighting against the anti-social behaviors of gender injustice in Black musical space because the injustice remains rampant in the improvisational social scene. Injustice is often quid pro quo. It could mean a male bandleader asking for sexual favors from a young woman improviser searching for performance opportunities. Or if the woman is hired, she may have to deal with flirtations from the majority of male members in a band. Rejection of these advances could lead to summary termination. Bassist Esperanza Spaulding complained, for example, about male musicians who perceive her to be the girlfriend of a male musician in the band: "You know, maybe it doesn't bother everybody who walks into that room and has to say oh like no I'm not somebody's girlfriend or a singer but like I'm here to play." [43] Male music critics and fans defined women improvisers roles in the post–World War II era jazz culture as either a "woman" or "bitch."[44] As musicologist Tammy Kernodle explains, a "woman" improviser functioned in what was considered by men to be the supportive roles as patrons, wives, or fans of the male musicians whereas the "bitch" improviser displaced male musicians by occupying the bandstand, taking their work opportunities, and challenging the patriarchal structure in jazz.[45] Women improvisers are still dealing with the residue of that gender-biased thinking today because some male musicians still assume a woman musician is a singer and not an instrumentalist; some male improvisers and industry people still hold the view that women are incapable of the mastery of improvisation. Well-known woman improvisers today, like saxophonist Tia Fuller or pianist Kris Davis, arrive at their gigs with vocal mics set up and are still told "You play good for a girl" or "You play like a man."[46]

The same musical codes of Black masculinity in jazz improvisation that Carrington mastered and that helped propel her career to great heights are the same musical codes that she is challenging in her music projects and institutional work. She has endeavored to create gender equity and an inclusive space for women musicians and musicians across the gender and sexual identity spectrum at Berklee. It can perhaps be argued that it is hypocritical for Carrington to disavow the same internalized patriarchal musical codes at this stage of her life and career when she has used those same codes to achieve significant success in the music business. Yet her mastery of the patriarchal music codes she critiques is not evidence that she is ungrateful but, having met them, finds them insufficient and not inclusive. Consequently, she has built a reputation with her detractors while creating a template for gender inclusion that inspires her supporters. Moreover, it is not only her view that gender justice must be achieved for all the women improvisers in jazz culture and not just a few exceptional woman improvisers. She also believes gender justice in jazz culture would benefit male jazz musicians who are also striving to achieve professional success in a sexist culture.

Jazz without Patriarchy and the Politics of Building Coalitions

bell hooks has stated that visionary feminism is the pathway to a more just society because it emphasizes "mutuality" and "interdependency."[47] For hooks, a mutual and interdependent society is not a perfect society but one where colonization, dehumanization, and gender subordination are lessened.[48] Carrington's music projects and the creation and mission statement of the Berklee Institute for Jazz and Gender Justice are founded upon this philosophy. In an informational video about the institute, Carrington identifies the core mission of the Institute: "to create a safe and nurturing environment for people of all gender identifications to study jazz."[49] The informational video also features a constellation of prominent African American artists and scholars such as Carrie Mae Weems, Gina Dent, and Angela Davis, who also argue that jazz will never reach its full potential without the inclusion of women. Artist Weems cites the irony of jazz being the most democratic music while it continues to exclude women.[50] Dent, a professor of feminist studies, argues that scholarship will never tell us what jazz sounds like without patriarch because "it's precisely the work the music will do."[51] Having said that, the Institute has taken seriously the task of developing a critical consciousness in the students in the program.

Carrington's fight for gender equality and a productive and generative space for female improvisers and improvisers across the gender spectrum is an example of Black feminist coalition politics that extends from a Black sense of place. The aim of the institute is to make musical space as inclusive as possible. Black women such as Patricia Hill Collins and Bernice Johnson Reagon are activists and scholars who have worked to transform institutions from the inside through a coalition politics that connects issues that affect Black women with more wide-ranging political and social agendas.[52] Carrington appreciates the past goals of Black nationalist critiques on improvisation represented in the writings of *Blues People* (1963) by Amiri Baraka who took on the 1960s white male jazz critic establishment in order to write his truth about Black musical space. Yet Black nationalism is contrary to the goals of coalition building with allies and the most marginalized peoples, such as those that come from the LGBTQ communities. Bernice Johnson Reagon says it best:

> We've pretty much come to the end of a time when you can have a space that is "yours only" just for the people you want to be there. Even when we have our "women-only" festivals, there is no such thing . . . To a large extent it's because we have just finished with that kind of isolating. There is no hiding place. There is nowhere you can go and only be with people who are like you. It's over. Give it up.[53]

Carrington's intertwined musical and intellectual projects stands on the foundation laid out by revered elder Black women improviser colleagues and ancestors like trombonist Melba Liston and pianist Mary Lou Williams, who created a social model based not on competition but on collaboration. This does not mean that Black women musicians don't strive to be the best musicians they can be; history shows us that musicians like Williams and Liston surpassed the accomplishments of many of their male peers in performance, arranging, and composition while also offering collaborative models of mentorship to those same peers. Both women not only had the ability to improvise but had a deep knowledge of African American language of improvisation and compositional technique that allowed them to give shape to large-scale music productions through arrangements that frame how individual improvisations are perceived. Liston was praised by pianists such as Randy Weston for her arrangements on his *Uhuru Afrika* (1961). Mary Lou Williams was not only a brilliant arranger, pianist, and composer but a known theorist in the musician community and teacher to musicians like pianist Thelonious Monk and others, sharing cutting-edge improvisational theory with her male colleagues in the wee hours of the morning. These models of collaborations show that musicians like Melba Liston valued their lived experiences as Black women. They also value face-to-face, oral trans-mission of musical knowledge, and holding each other accountable on the levels of Black aesthetic, intellectual, and spiritual values.[54] This collaborative model constitutes an epistemology that is the philosophical cornerstone of the Berklee Institute for Jazz and Gender Justice.

A Polyrhythmic Philosophy of Inclusion

The drums aren't just an instrument
But a necessary tool
They live within us
So let them be heard, let them be used
For tolerance, respect, sharing
These too are a drum thing
Polyrhythmic behavior in action[55]

These words from Terri Lyne Carrington's poem "I Am the Drums" show that she thinks of her instrument not as a mere tool of music communication but a weapon against intolerance. Polyrhythm, for her, is a set of musical and space-making social codes where improvisation is a creative practice and an opportunity to teach ways of thinking and being. She explains how her mission connects with her creative practice in this excerpt from a speech she delivered at a TEDxYouth@BeaconStreet event:

The magic of improvisation happens when we allow ourselves to be vulnerable and completely in the moment, surrendering our preconceived idea of what might happen next. Improvisation is truly ideas in action. Sometimes I think it's a way that God talks to us and through us. And when presented with a divine ideal, it becomes sound. Because when we are creative we are at our very best, fully integrating our mind, body, and spirit. And actually, I'm convinced that creativity saves lives, so every time I play, I think of that as my mission.[56]

Her values of love and inclusion have been influenced both by the practice of improvisation, and enunciated through the Venn diagram of Black feminist thought and Black musical space. She continues to weaponize her philosophy of inclusion by creating and implementing ambitious music projects that are as provocative as they are activist.

Carrington's arrangement of Bernice Johnson Reagon's "Echo" on *The Mosaic Project* (2011) is an example of compositional and ontological intertextuality as connected to Black sense of place. Both Reagon's original version and Carrington's arrangement bring attention to issues that Black people and other marginalized groups face in a society that has historically categorized them as placeless. Both musical groups include all women and each group supports gender equity issues. I would also contend that the multiracial *Mosaic Project* is based on the collective model of Black sisterhood in Sweet Honey in the Rock (SHR).

The importance of *The Mosaic Project* is that it presents a diversity of women improvisers who face forms of oppression as multifarious as the musical elements they expertly deploy on the bandstand and on each individual track in the recording studio. The coalition of multiracial women improvisers is based on the model of Black sisterhood and Black civil society civil society which, at its best, cultivates a musical space of inclusivity for all oppressed and marginalized people. As Patricia Collins argues, "Black feminist thought's identity as a 'critical' social theory lies in its commitment to justice, both for U.S. Black women as a collectivity and for that of other similarly oppressed groups."[57]

Carrington's *Mosaic Project* demonstrates the point that I have made about Black musical space and inclusivity. She stands in the tradition of the International Sweethearts of Rhythm (ISR), a Black women–led musical and multiracial sisterhood and social organization that opened its doors to white women musicians (sometimes at their own peril). Because the Black women of ISR knew that improvised music was the articulation of humanity and not exclusion, the criteria for entering that Black musical space were demonstrating your ability to play and not being racist. The Black women improvisers of ISR risked their lives in order to stay true to their values of justice and peace by going on the road in the South with white women improvisers, constantly in danger of being arrested, or worse, by the police. The ISR was not an openly integrated orchestra because Black women and white women musicians, some who wore nut brown powder to hide their whiteness, were not exempted from Jim Crow laws.[58] Yet their history prefigured the kinds of affiliations and alliances that Carrington and other Black feminists envision and enact today.

The Mosaic Project

Carrington's concept behind the first *Mosaic Project* album was about creating a musical space for women improvisers. *The Mosaic Project* realizes her vision of women musicians coming together to create cutting-edge music in a space almost free from patriarchy. I say "almost" because patriarchy is not an embodied power relationship but an internalized mode of thinking that influences the musical choices women improvisers make. While patriarchy is not a sound but a social or government system headed by a male or males, it has sonic manifestations in the ways it works to exclude women musicians based on gender bias. Generations of male musicians have been socially programmed to judge the talent of women based on poor assumptions about what women improvisers can accomplish. As I stated earlier, this exclusion of women improvisers leads to improvised sounds in a musical space that is neither fully democratic nor inclusive. By that logic, it would be reasonable to argue that we have not yet heard truly liberated improvised music.

Though Carrington took a stance about gender inequities in jazz culture by hiring only women for *The Mosaic Project*, Carrington believes the quality of the music is more important than focusing on the gender of the band members. The gender of the band personnel should not distract from a serious appraisal of the musical contribution to America and world culture.

The collective performance of her arrangement of "Echo" is not only a site of how Carrington and her colleagues think about the subjects addressed in the piece. The performance reveals how the musicians think about what it means to improvise music together as women because, as Eileen Hayes argues, "'women's music' is less a type of music than it is a site of thinking about music."[59]

Carrington's first *Mosaic Project* (2011) is a weaving together of a coalition of women improvisers who come together from various racial, ethnic, religious, and geographic backgrounds to create a collective quilt for gender justice. Black musical place-making in this case is the cultivation of sonic quilting led by an African American woman, a kind of maroon space for gender justice created in real time by women improvisers who tell stories. These weaved connections form what Barbara Ransby has called "modern maroon spaces" where organizers can seek refuge "and forge new levels of consensus."[60] Though Ransby was discussing political quilting within the context of Black Lives Matter organizations, Carrington's Black women–led musical space is also formed by the stitching together of women improvisers to create an opening for nonhierarchical and nonpatriarchal spaces for advanced spontaneous composition called improvisation.

Carrington's promotional video for the first *Mosaic Project* features the percussionist Sheila E., who dares male musicians to accomplish what Carrington and her woman colleagues have achieved on *The Mosaic Project*. Facing the camera while flanked in triangle formation by pianist Patrice

Rushen and Carrington, who also face the camera and laugh along at inter-vals, Sheila E. speaks to the imagined male audience: "I dare any man to try to do this right here, what?! Any man. C'mon, c'mon, c'mon, c'mon. I dare you. This right here? Woah! Powerful. Y'all don't understand, but you do. It's all good; we love you anyway."[61] While Sheila E.'s comments appear to be said in jest, her claims are serious and meant to frame and draw attention to Carrington's accomplishment of bringing women improvisers together to achieve a space of aesthetic possibilities that critiques racial and sexual hierarchies. Despite Sheila E.'s verbal challenge, Carrington admits that, while her Grammy-winning project seeks to address the problematic aesthetic barometer of male-gendered musical excellence in improvised performance and jazz composition, it was still necessary on some level to produce work within the hegemonic sonic codes of male musical standards in order to be successful in a male-dominated industry.[62] Yet Carrington's cultivation of inclusive Black musical space and talent for organizing women improvisers should never be solely defined as a response to male patriarchy and white supremacy in jazz culture. Her music reflects the many facets of the Black experience, including Black sisterhood, gender fluidity acceptance, and Afri-can American understandings of "unconventional" love relationships.

Not a Legacy but a Reverberation

Carrington has had a close relationship with members of Sweet Honey in the Rock (SHR) for decades. Her father Solomon Matthew Carrington III attended Albany State University in southwest Georgia with founder and legendary civil rights song leader Bernice Johnson Reagon. In her twenties, Carrington became a dedicated fan of SHR repertoire. The original Reagon composition "Echo" was particularly appealing to her. Reagon is known for her decades-long participation in civil rights activism, her scholarship, and the founding of Sweet Honey in the Rock as well as other vocal groups. The original recording of "Echo" was released on SHR's *Breaths* (1989). A vocal-ized "Echo" is built on breath-produced sound vibrating through time. An Echo returns to you even as it fades away. "Echo" here is conceptualized as an intertextual idea where breath is a receptacle for history and connecting lived experiences across time and space.

Carrington liked the sound of the melody in "Echo" and was so moved by the social issues the lyrics address that she promised Reagon that she would arrange the piece. She fulfilled that promise with an arrangement of the com-position on the *The Mosaic Project*. Carrington has developed a compositional process that works for her demanding touring, teaching, and institutional leadership responsibilities. She has found a way to maintain productivity while on the road through the use of GarageBand software to record musical ideas: "When I arrange a song, I go on GarageBand. I sing the melody. Then I get a tempo that I like, then I add a little drumbeat, then I'll sing a melody and hear a foundation and the foundation is that baseline. I sing the melody and try to hear the harmonies." After Carrington records her musical ideas in GarageBand, she sends the files to a transcriber who creates her charts. This outsourcing of musical transcription is a testament to how busy Carrington is as a musician, cultural worker, professor, and leader of a demanding institute. She explains, "Because I travel so much, I use a two-octave controller to put sounds in the computer. People transcribe what I write, and those are the charts I send people." Despite what might appear to be an unorthodox methodology, her writing process yields complex scores that her colleagues have to internalize and then interpret on a high musical level. She has to remind her colleagues that her complex scores represent the basic sound of her ideas and that they are required to internalize her music to the point where they can then "open up" and self-realize the music from their unique points of view. She explains, "I have to spend time helping musicians get free with it."[63]

Carrington's arrangement of Reagon's composition "Echo" adds complexity on multiple levels with the orchestration of the melodic material across different harmonies and a new rhythmic framework. Original melodic material is added in a complex, angular instrumental passage that interlocks in syncopated layers.

Carrington's arrangement of "Echo" revises not only the rhythmic, harmonic and melodic concepts; she adds lyrics, found in the last stanza of the *Mosaic Project* version. The epistemology of Black musical place-making creates intertextuality across time and space. There may be over twenty-three years' difference between the recorded versions, but the spirit and the content of the song are the timeless issues Black people continue to struggle with over generations. The struggles and lived experience of Black people are connected to a single vocal blues line throughout history.

The SHR performance "Echo" tells the story of Black life and resistance through the performance of vocal echoing. This sonic overlap and intimate imbrication of SHR communicate interlocking historical stories that goes beyond gender and translates into a message for all marginalized communities that have been historically silenced. These echoes, these interlocking stories must continue and must be maintained in our current culture of individualized downloading and streaming music where contextual liner notes continue to be divorced from music files.

Carrington did not arrange "Echo" in relation to a historically specific event. Yet the themes of the composition as they relate to a critique of anti-Blackness are always relevant. Carrington explains, "Those themes I was listening to in my twenties addressed by Sweet Honey and the Rock, it's never not going to be relevant."[64] Carrington argues that the subject of "Echo" is even more relevant today because she is witnessing a rise in political consciousness about various social issues raised by the Black Lives Matter movement. Carrington remarks, "I'm amazed to see that white supremacy and privilege is so alive and well and shocked to see it coming back so strong with this current administration. People are either going to get woke or get left. It's a beautiful time to comment on all that's been happening because many people are willing to hear it."[65] In that sense, Carrington's arrangement of "Echo" and her Social Science project, which will be discussed below, is in conversation with trumpeters Terence Blanchard's and Ambrose Akinmusire's critiques of police brutality discussed in chapters 1 and 4.

Reagon's lyrics and vocal arrangement in her composition "Echo" provide ample material for Carrington's arrangement. Reagon's original version is largely a cappella and sung freely in a nonmetrical style with lightly played percussion instruments. The original composition and arrangement features SHR members using vocal strategies that simulate echoing through layering the word *echo* in an Afrological hocketing style. The original version of "Echo" is also in C minor, pentatonic scale, hovering over the minor third of C–E♭. Only when we get to the chorus do we hear the music move to the F minor chord, creating a largely plagal relationship between the tonic of C minor and the subdominant F minor chord. Neither version of "Echo" uses conventional harmony or is based in the traditional system of tonality. Carrington's arrangement is also in the sound of a C minor blues but moves to other harmonic areas, whereas Reagon's original composition is largely based on the two chords of C minor and F minor.

"Echo" begins with a recorded statement by Black feminist and civil rights icon Angela Davis, from 0:01 to 0:36. Carrington explains, "The use of recorded voices, for example parts of speeches, represent 'ways to tell a story,' especially if the song is mostly instrumental."[66] She asked Davis to write and record an introductory statement for her arrangement of Reagon's "Echo" because Davis has been a leading scholar on mass incarceration.[67] Carrington clarifies, "I asked Angela Davis to write something for 'Echo' as an introduction. She's very passionate about the conditions and problems in the prison system in the U.S., so what she wrote definitely speaks on that. It's very brief but it's very powerful."[68] Carrington has long used technology throughout her recent career to record important political voices that help contextualize the subject matter of a song. Davis's literature on music and Black feminism has been an important influence on Carrington.

In *Blues Legacies and Black Feminism* (1999), Davis presents blues women like Bessie Smith and Ma Rainey as exemplars of unapologetic Black female independence represented in post-emancipation itinerancy and performances of sexual expression that reflected newfound sexual "freedom." The blues woman proudly exhibited gender fluidity long before it was a term. Their performances told the stark truth in contradistinction to songs written by white men, who crafted representations of ideal heterosexual models of love. Those models, Davis argues, have always been incongruent with the reality of Black women's lives. *Blues Legacies* was published a few years before Carrington's *Jazz Is a Spirit* (2002) and Carrington was aware of Davis's book. Davis wrote the liner notes for Carrington's recording *Jazz Is a Spirit* (2002), arguing that Carrington was at the forefront of connecting the idea of democracy with her musical performances. Davis argues that Carrington refuses to operate within the strict confines of jazz as musical genre and declares that "Jazz is a spirit and thanks to Terri Lyne Carrington, that spirit is extricating itself from its exclusively male history."[69]

At the beginning of "Echo," Carrington simulates the connection between the past and the present by creating two separate but connected sonic spheres. She deliberately creates a darker, more distant sonic sphere for Davis's preamble through heavy reverb and compression. Whereas in the second, brighter sonic sphere that encompasses most of the tune, the instrumental and vocal arrangements from the larger ensemble are brighter and more clear. Davis's voice is presented on the recording in a grainy, constrained reverb designed to signify a past recording of Davis on a vinyl record. Before the first words are spoken, I hear what sounds like a skipping needle on vinyl or a hissing of a tape recording. This introduction was designed in post-production to signify Davis's statement traveling through time, literally echoing through time, by manipulating the sound of sonic space that encloses the words.

In this brief recorded statement, Davis discusses mass incarceration, poverty, and racism as the social legacy of slavery. She also criticizes the inhumanity of homophobia and hatred of immigrants in a statement uttered long before Trump's efforts toward creating a Muslim ban. For Davis, freedom is never static or finalized and the battles for freedom must be continually renewed:

> We inhabit our histories and our histories inhabit us. The prison system, with 2.4 million people behind bars, is a terrible specter of slavery. And if indeed we can say that slavery was abolished we cannot deny that it still haunts us.

The challenges of the past are challenges of the present and challenges of the future: poverty, racism, xenophobia, homophobia. Freedom itself is constantly transforming; echoes of the past and reverberations of the future.[70]

At 0:15 where Davis says the word "abolished," layered female voices transition in singing the word "echo" in improvised melismatic form, overlapping a pentatonic scale that focuses on the first and third degree, C–E♭, of the scale. Before the vamp begins, from 0:47 to 0:52, there is an accelerando that features a quick transformation from the compressed soundscape to a loud and bright soundscape, suggesting time travel between the time of Davis's recorded statement and the perceived contemporary time where the entire ensemble is introduced at 0:54. This juncture marks where the rhythm section enters with a bass ostinato–driven vamp.

Carrington deploys several time feels in "Echo." Carrington transforms Reagon's original "Echo" by putting the song in a clear meter, which is subdivided in complex ways among the bass ostinato and the congas improvisation by percussionist of Sheila E. The arrangement maintains a straight eighth-note feel but contrasts the time feel between the verse and chorus structure. Carrington emphasizes the feel on beat three, as a way of differentiating the sound during the chorus. The third feel is the one she demonstrates on the interlude of the horns, the unison interlude of the horns.

Melodic Material of "Echo"

Carrington told me that the melody of Reagon's "Echo" sounded to her like the melodic substance of African cultural memory. Carrington believes this melodic sound is rooted in African cosmology and is the foundation of Black popular music: "It's got elements of the blues, spirituals, and work songs. All that is in there, which is the essence of our music. That's the foundation of Black music, which is the foundation of contemporary music in the United States."[71] During the process of arranging the composition, she had challenges reharmonizing the melody with chords that spoke her musical truth. "When you have a melody based on a blues scale, its challenging to find harmonies to go with it."[72] Carrington developed a bassline groove over a vamp which led her to the more complex parts of her arrangements.

Carrington's composing and arrangement of the bassline also demonstrates intertextuality with singer and pianist Donny Hathaway's musical ideas. Carrington developed the bassline first when she was arranging "Echo." In that process of composing the ostinato, she was influenced by

Hathaway's "The Ghetto" bassline from *Everything Is Everything* (1970). Yet Hathaway's influence on the development of her bassline groove only became evident after she wrote it. Musicians develop a vocabulary from deep study and interactions with other musicians over a lifetime. How that study and sharing of knowledge manifests is often unpredictable, exciting, and revealing of the sonic archives that shape a musician. Carrington explains, "We are informed by all the music we listen to our whole life."[73] Her interpretation of Hathaway's bassline has thrown some of her bandmates off because the bassline phrase lands on beat four, anticipating beat one in the following measure whereas many musicians hear the ending of the phrase on beat one. Carrington describes what has often been a rhythmically off-kilter experience for fellow musicians: "What's interesting about 'Echo' is the bassline often turns the musicians around because I end on beat four. If you don't know that, you hear beat four as beat one."[74] The intertextual link between Reagon's "Echo" and Carrington's arrangement of "Echo" is brought to life in other ways.

When vocalist Diane Reeves sings Reagon's verses like: "The brother you lynched / a few years ago / the sister you raped / just the other day," the lyrics link past crimes against Black people to the crimes of the present. When Reeves sings "the sounds of the Wilmington Ten / are echoes of a massacre keeping Black freedom locked in," she reminds us that the failures of mass incarceration is not an issue of the past but a contemporary issue. The Wilmington Ten revolved around an early 1970s legal case that stemmed from a staged boycott by Black people who were protesting their maltreatment in Wilmington, North Carolina, by school officials from the segregated school system. During the uprising, some of the protesters burned down buildings of white business owners. Nine Black men and a white woman social worker were put on trial for arson and eventually sentenced collectively to more than 280 years in prison in 1972. Drawing international attention, the case was overturned by a federal appellate court in 1980 due to prosecutorial and judicial misconduct.[75] Though the time, geography, and circumstances of the cases are different, the lyrics regarding mass incarceration could easily be amended to reference the "The Exonerated Five" (E5), still widely known as the "Central Park Five" (CP5). A case about five juvenile Black and Latino men who were falsely accused of beating and raping a white woman jogger in 1989 and convicted in 1990 based on violent and forced confessions, their convictions were overturned in 2002. Director Ava DuVernay's Netflix film about the "The E5," *When They See Us* (2019), has put this case in my mind at the time of this writing because it is also a form of art that seeks to humanize Black and Latino men who were incarcerated. The truth of the matter, however, is that there are likely thousands of untold cases with similar circumstances that will never receive this kind of celebrity. Reeves's framing lyricism about the Wilmington Ten repaints these grotesque subjects on the canvas of our time, giving immediacy and recognition to the unvarnished truth of the Black lived experience of today.

Diane Reeves's performance of the lyrics stays close to the melodic character of the original version, which helps connect the subject matter notwithstanding the complexity of Carrington's arrangement. While lead singer Reeves sings the lyrics, background vocalists sing percussive vocal riffs that are tightly arranged melodic lines voiced an interval of a fourth apart. The singer(s) sing in vocables that use the sounds of La-La-La-Le-Le-La-Le-Le/Le-La-La. A new verse was added by Carrington to the composition to either extend the form of the arrangement or address a different topic in the lyrics. This extra stanza discusses income and educational inequality with the results of uneducated children who have less resources to cope with the world: "The blind eye you turn / To the poverty of our rich land / The unrelenting beat of ignorance in the streets / And children growing up with no tools to defeat."[76]

Carrington's arrangement of "Echo" is a study of harmonic and rhythmic displacement. Carrington's most daring display is the passage of the arrangement that is a complete departure from the original "Echo" but creates a contrasting dynamic melodic, rhythmic, and harmonic angularity during an instrumental passage that is designed to create a contrast to the verses and chorus. She revises the harmonic form of the original piece by adding additional chords, which gives the story in "Echo" more harmonic vibrancy. This occurs in the instrumental interlude from 3:35 to 4:08.

This interlude is followed by Ingrid Jensen's flugelhorn solo with effects from 4:08 to 5:09. During Jensen's solo, the Carrington-led rhythm section frames her abstract melodic lines by abandoning any obvious beat patterns, perhaps giving the lay listener a sense of temporal dissolution. While the temporal grid appears to dissolve, the musicians are always cognizant of the pulse because they have internalized the compositional form. These rhythm section explorations are common in Black time and have been happening for generations in African American improvised music. To cite three examples, this was a common musical strategy most famously used by trumpeter Miles Davis and his rhythm section in recordings of "Stella by Starlight" on the album *My Funny Valentine* (1964) or *Bitches Brew* (1970). This temporal dissolution is also demonstrated when pianist Mary Lou Williams plays abstract, solo piano free blues on recordings of her composition "A Fungus A Mungus" (1963).

"You Learn from Us Then Murder Us"

Carrington has continued her socially conscious music in projects like *Money Jungle: Provocative in Blue* (2013), in which she criticizes American financial institutions for greed in the self-titled track. *Money Jungle* was inspired by the original *Money Jungle* (1962) project that features pianist Duke Ellington, bassist Charles Mingus, and drummer Max Roach. Her most recent release, *Waiting Game* (2019) by Terri Lyne Carrington and Social Science, is a reflection of her bringing into clearer focus her intersectional vision of gender equity and social inclusion, and interrelates with her institutional work at Berklee. *Waiting Game* is a lyrical and musical broadside against zealotry of religious fanatics who would have those in the LGBT community give up their identity in order to conform to their notions of heterosexual normalcy. She also addresses class, political prisoners, and mass incarceration by referencing and including on the recording the names and, in some cases the voices, of Mumia Abu Jamal, Angela Davis, Leonard Peltier, and Laura Whitehorn. Carrington defines her idea of social science here:

> Social Science came about in response to an ever-changing social and political landscape. We seek to inspire conscious thought and elevate a deep regard for humanity, addressing critical issues which disproportionately and negatively impact the lives and freedoms of many due to their race, gender, class, sexuality and/or faith. Along with a message of wakefulness, inclusiveness, and noncompliance, we've summoned our musical influences in various genres—jazz, indie rock, R&B, hip-hop, free improvisation, contemporary classical music and world music—to offer an eclectic alternative to the mainstream. Music transcends, breaks barriers, strengthens us, and heals old wounds. Music is Social Science.[77]

Intersectionality, a term coined in a landmark article by American lawyer, civil rights activist and cofounder of critical race theory Kimberlé Crenshaw,[78] is a theoretical approach rooted in the quotidian experiences of multiple forms of discrimination that shape Black women's lives. Rising out of Black feminist legal theory, it seeks to disrupt the traditional view of discrimination by the American legal system, which separated issues of racism and discrimination. Since litigation models of sexism have been historically based on white women's lives and the models of racism have been based on "respectable" middle-class Black people's lives, Crenshaw has argued for a new paradigm that takes into account that Black women, especially the most socially isolated, face both issues of racism and sexism simultaneously. Carrington's approach to social commentary with Social Science reflects an understanding of the intersectionality discourse and its approach to social inequalities. After all, she is an intellectual who is close friends with some of the leading Black feminist scholars in the world. I am not arguing that Black feminist theory can be mapped onto a different domain such as Carrington's creative music. You cannot, for example, hear or see a hip chord voicing and say that that chord voicing is intersectionality. Unconventional compositional forms, creative improvisation, uses of multimedia, the bold mixture of instrumental mediums, and the embrace of other world music cultures cannot be called intersectionality because creative musicians and human beings are not compartmentalized like theoretical systems and are broader than social prescriptions. The humans produce the theory and the theory can never be universal. I am arguing that Carrington's counter-hegemonic, multilayered critical approach to artistically addressing multiple issues of race, gender, religion, homophobia, and mass incarceration in different compositions on the same album is an example of an intersectional approach that pronounces a thread of social justice through the work. Consequently, an intersectional approach to issues can be shown on the macro level in terms of the larger motivation for the compositional ideas but cannot be mapped onto a specific musical idea, such as a polyrhythm or specific lyric, for example.

Carrington's Social Science music relates to intersectionality because her music deals with many forms of inequality, such as racism, gender inequity, homophobia, love, and cultural theft. "Woke" improvisers, who are intersectionalist cultural workers in response to inequality, have historically created collectives that have cultivated radical imaginations in Black musical space-making. Intersectionality, as feminist theorist Vivian May argues, "has been forged in the context of struggles for social justice as a means to challenge dominance, foster critical imaginaries, and craft collective models for change."[79] At its most radical and conscious level, improvisation as respatialization has been intersectional on the level of musical fusion and activist critiques long before intersectionality became a term.

Carrington's Social Science music and cultural work is more intersectional than the work of the other African American male improvisers discussed in this book who focus on everyday police brutality in their critiques. Intersectionality is a framework for thinking about multiple interrelated sites of social inequality and how those sites effect daily life.[80] Like an improviser who must deal with compositional form, melodic architecture, scales, harmony, and rhythm while listening and responding in real time to fellow band members, intersectionality is a framework for handling multiple issues in play. Improvisation is a great model for intersectionality because to improvise is to theorize. Dealing with various types of social inequality is similar to a musician having to simultaneously hear the performance of multiple melodic lines in an improvisation. You have to hear all of those separate phrases, where they begin and where they end, if you hope to have any possibility of understanding the compositional form or scope of an issue in order to jump into the fray and make change.

Carrington's work is not so much an extension of the feminist philosophy of intersectionality but a musical illustration of conscientious music's natural character. I discuss here a few examples of social issues she addresses in her latest recording *Waiting Game* (2019). On this recording there is a critique of police brutality from the perspective of an African American mother who has lost her child to senseless violence, a lyrical broadside against gay conversion therapy, and a defiant anthem that celebrates women and Black sisterhood and invites cisgender men to join the fight against patriarchy.

Carrington's goal with Social Science is to address the social and political issues of our time in a multilevel attack on the ignorance of racism and the marginalization of gender-dysphoric people who have so-called alternative sexualities. The musical influences in Social Science are as vibrant, varied, and vital as the social issues she addresses on her latest recording. But more importantly, her goal is to elevate consciousness on the part of her listening and viewing audiences through her creative practice. It's not easy to address such stark issues with improvised music, and Carrington is aware of the complex audience reception to her work. She remarked at a NPR Tiny Desk concert on March 4, 2020, "I hope you are enjoying this music because it can be heavy and we've tried to figure out a way to make it feel good and still give these messages."[81] This is not a new goal on Carrington's part. Yet *Waiting Game* brings the strains of her Black political thought into pellucid focus. Social Science is not the culmination of her ideas but a harbinger of future, collectively composed cultural work that will continue to attack social complacency while seeking to create community. I will now briefly discuss a few compositions that address these complex issues.

"Purple Mountains" features the improvisational vocalist Kokayi, who rap-sings lyrics that address purported nineteenth-century Western military terrorism such as "small-pox blankets" used against First Nations people and the thousands of murdered and missing First Nations women in the true north (Canada): He sings, "Now what about my sisters missing in the north?" "Purple Mountains," a reference to the patriotic song "America the Beautiful" by Katherine Lee Bates, also critiques the commodification of Black cultural ideas in the entertainment industry forged from Black lived experiences and the simultaneous disregard of the humanity of Black people who produced the culture. For example, Kokayi sings over a ten-beat phrase, "You murder us you take from us / We give to you, you take from us / You learn from us then murder us."[82]

Carrington's composition "Bells (Ring Loudly)," co-written with Social Science pianist Aaron Parks, gives voice to countless Black women who have lost their sons, daughters, spouses to police violence. Carrington explains:

> He [Aaron Parks] had the music and the title, and the piano riff reminded me of church bells, which made me think of a funeral and the people that are left behind when someone is slain. I could not get the idea out of my head about Philando Castile and his girlfriend and her child that witnessed him being shot in the car by a police officer. These deaths leave more than one victim behind. So I wrote the lyric from the perspective of the spouse, mother or child of someone murdered. I think this set the tone for the rest of the recording.[83]

Bells are significant in American culture and are used metaphorically by Carrington and Parks. The bells in this composition are a metaphorical symbol of the absence of liberty for those unjustly killed by police. But bells also symbolize the sirens of police cars that ostensibly indicate that help is on the way and the bells that call mourners together to bury the victims of police violence. Observe these lyrics spoken by Malcolm-Jamal Warner: "Bells, siren swells, morphing into church bells, signaling another unjustifiable death." "Loudly / languishing ladies sing loudly / church bells ring loudly / bullets blurring, deferring dreams like it ain't no thing, proudly / Another brother slain in vain in the name of justice, no really, it feels more like just-them." Millions of tourists visit the cracked Liberty Bell in Philadelphia, taking selfies and perhaps unaware that the bell has yet to ring with the "harmonies of liberty" for all Americans.[84]

The compositional form of "Bells" is important for what it signifies. The critique of police violence is hitched to hope and this relationship between social life and social death is borne out in the semiotics of the music. The ringing tritone basis of the oscillating chordal riff communicates the occurrence and aftermath of violence in the Black community. The verse structure is built on the interval of a tritone, E♭–A, whereas the chorus is composed of brighter major seventh chords of F major 7th in first inversion over A, which eventually is inverted to root position, followed by D♭ major and E♭ major chords. This tritone relationship is important because it is an interval used widely in police and ambulance sirens for their perceived dissonance and ability to draw the public's attention to an emergency. The chords E♭ minor

7th and A7, a dominant seventh chord that has a tritone within itself, oscillates back and forth, simulating the ringing of bells while Parks pedals the melodic note D♭. I shared my semiotic analysis of this intervallic relationship with Social Science pianist and co-composer Aaron Parks after their September 13, 2019, concert at Cornell University. Parks had not realized the symbolism of using the tritone in the composition, but immediately saw the significance of his intervallic construction.[85] This so-called Diabolus in musical intervallic sound you hear under Warner's four-bar spoken word voiceovers and Debo Ray's sung verses constitute the sonic theme of the form.

Debo Ray sings from the perspective of Black womanhood with lyrics that discuss the loss of a loved one and the unavailing action of destroying another Black life: "You took my love away from me / I wanna know, how did it feel to watch him tremble and bleed / Tell me, what gives you the right to kill so senselessly / When you're alone, do you ever think of him, or pray for his peace." These verses occur over the chords connected through the tritone interval. However, in the chorus, the song presents that same Black woman—who is anguishing for her loved one—as someone who envisions a world where Black lives have equal value to white lives. Ray sings: "But when I dream / I see a world / Fearless and hopeful / Where my life matters." The contrasting vision in the chorus is signified with an F major chord in different inversions, which progresses to D♭ major and then E♭ major. These chords contrast the repetitive E♭–A relationship in the siren chords under the verses with bright harmonic colors.

"Pray the Gay Away" is a critique of gay conversion therapy practiced on members of the LGBTQ community. Conversion therapy is a religious and psychological intervention by zealots who try to change gay people to straight. This song excoriates any preacher or religious community that tries to erase an individual's gender identity. The song is not antireligious but suggests that it would be more humane and moral for the gay conversion therapy community to "pray the hate away" instead. Carrington suggests that praying should be used to work against hate and for supporting some of the most vulnerable members of our community who are often exposed to levels of ignorance and intolerance and, at the most extreme, murder. "Pray the Gay Away" dovetails with Carrington's institutional work at the Berklee Institute of Jazz and Gender Justice as she works to create a space for improvisers who identify as members of the LGBTQIA community. Messages of inclusion in jazz culture are wedded to messages of defiance regarding the woman's place in society and in jazz culture.

The track "Anthem" features the spoken word artist Rapsody and is a defiant treatise celebrating womanhood. Defiance is represented in Rapsody's anthemic spoken word and quest to eradicate patriarchy. In "Waiting Game," featuring the singer Debo Ray, the lyrics asks the listener when Black people will be truly free in every regard and how many more people need to sacrifice their lives for justice. The song provides a sense of urgency and an understanding that polite appeals to the listener's consciousness and sense of morality will no longer work. Ray sings, "How long can freedom wait before we can hear it ring" at 2:52–3:13, which is also part of the metaphorical bell trope that exists thematically throughout the recording. "Anthem," in comparison, is a more direct, unapologetic approach to social inequity, representing an in-your-face demand to end patriarchy through metaphorical lyrics. The "Negro National Anthem" is quoted and women and their male allies are encouraged to tear down the blockade of male domination: "The anthem / A new day for the woman / Break down the walls until patriarchy falls / Lift every voice, sing, spread your wings, cut the strings, take a swing. Fight to fight. . . ." "Anthem" tells the listener that woman should not be seen as a social aberration. The song invites men to stand with women in attacking gender inequality: "The woman is not an anomaly / Do you stand with your woman? / The woman my woman / I am she, she is me / Lift every voices is the promise to our queens, to their futures, to our dreams." From 4:46 to 5:03 the programmatic setting for these lyrics is a rising pitch with dynamically voiced horn chromaticism. The chromaticism of this section is emphasized by how the horn pitches rise in half notes as the sound crescendos passionately to the end of the phrase.

Carrington's projects are rooted in Black place-making and strive to make musical space inclusive for everyone. This entails making space for all types of musicians to thrive as improvisers. While her mission focuses mostly on gender inequity in jazz culture, she also welcomes the most marginalized improvisers so they can articulate their humanity and truth.

Carrington has studied the drum language of Roy Haynes and Jack DeJohnette, among others, yet their musical influences are not immediately discernable. This is not just because she has developed her own sound. Her drumming influences are less discernable because she has moved beyond prioritizing her individual sound to uplifting the group sound in the Mosaic Projects and Social Science. In this way she is an heir to empathetic drummers like Billy Higgins, who I discuss in chapter 2. Her empathetic geography travels beyond the stage.

Carrington does not only try to imagine what creative improvisation would sound like without patriarchy. Through the various percussive sonorities of her traps, she articulates her imagination of Black musical space. The conscious coloring of her symbols and the backbeat of her drums articulate her philosophy of racial and gender inclusion. She not only actively practices that imagination in the real time of improvisation, but she practices it in the preparation and choosing of political topics she addresses in her tracks, in the sophisticated use of technology to capture and record powerful voices of freedom fighters across generations, and in the musical partners she chooses to realize her visions. Though the African American musicians who have lived and embodied this musical and intellectual tradition have never had the pleasure of feeling safe and fully accepted in mainstream civil society, at their best they have never allowed their outsider status to keep them from welcoming others. Carrington's cultural work of crossing the bar lines should be included in that living, sonic archive.

4

Ambrose Akinmusire's
Satchel of Origami

People live before us leave a memory behind;
Actions done, actions written,
acts impressed upon our mind,
forming, moving in a circle,
ghosts appearing through the sound,
waving at us from the distance,
'cause the whole wide world is round
and round, and round and round
Yes the whole wide world is round
—Abbey Lincoln[1]

Through his improvised performance art and compositions on *Origami Harvest* (2018), *The Imagined Savior Is Far Easier to Paint* (2014), and *When the Heart Emerges Glistening* (2011), African American trumpeter and composer Ambrose Akinmusire's music reveals a complex understanding of Black humanity in his practice of musical space-making. This manifests in a spiritual relationship with ancestral masters of improvisation, a deep understanding of his complex positionality in the world from the nexus of Oakland culture, and a commitment to bringing attention to the murder of

Black men and women by members of police departments in communities across the United States. He exploits the sonic color line that Jennifer Stoever critiques, challenges the essentialized theoretical frameworks of Black music that Nina Sun Eidsheim deconstructs, and shamelessly expresses his sonic humanity in the performance and recordings of his music—a physicality of the kind that David Ake argues should be analyzed by musicologists.[2]

Akinmusire's poetic titles of his compositions point to his understanding of the multilayered liminality of Black musical space that comes from a Black sense of place, values he expresses in his musical work. A man of quiet intensity with a clear mission to deconstruct the binarial extremes that constitute the political field of American life, Akinmusire embraces these dualities by critiquing state violence and white supremacy with musical statements that reveal his concepts of Black spatiality.

His musical statements do not have innovation as a goal. Akinmusire's broad project is about realizing the unrealized ambitions of the ancestors that improvise music through him. Like the turf dancing of Oakland, Akinmusire's musical gestures are about freedom, generating a positive Black sense of space right where you are. Black codes be damned!

The cultural work of Ambrose Akinmusire (b. 1982) continues the African American tradition of using creative practices to expose injustice and critique racial violence. As I explain in the Introduction, I use the metaphorical phrase and theoretical hook "crossing bar lines" to describe the phenomenological relationship between African American improvisers' use of unconventional and experimental music strategies and their need to articulate Black humanity through improvisation. The artistic expression of Black humanity occurs on many different registers beyond resistance. Understanding how a Black artist like Ambrose Akinmusire practices space-making is to understand what is politically at stake for African American cultural workers in their fight for social justice.

Akinmusire's socially conscious music provides an opportunity for an exciting case study of why improvisation in the cause for human rights is always immediate and yet must be historically contextualized. I analyze four of his compositions—"My Name Is Oscar" (2011), "Confessions to My Unborn Daughter" (2011), "Rollcall for Those Absent" (2014), and "Free, White and 21" (2018)—to explain how Akinmusire crosses bar lines through the expression of his political views and lived geography.

Ambrose Akinmusire's compositions are connected to the African American tradition of performing critical consciousness through creative improvisation. It is important to understand Akinmusire's work within the context of the national grassroots movement to end police brutality. In recent times, the multiracial social protest to end police violence has congealed and resonated internationally under the Black Lives Matter movement.[3] Historical accounts teach us that the killing of African Americans is linked to the perception of Blacks; a perpetual criminalization of Blacks that motivates daily violent acts in America and abroad. As historian Robin D. G. Kelley argues, the American legal and political systems date from the history of settler colonialism and are predicated on the belief systems of white privilege and supremacy. The containment of Black, brown, and red populations was, and continues to be rooted in, seeing those populations as a threat to white property. While post-emancipation Blacks thrived in the Reconstruction period by holding public office, armed white citizens stripped Black people of those democratic gains. Not surprisingly, the techniques of demonizing Blacks by characterizing them as predators laid the groundwork for restricting Black progress through legal, political, and violent strategies.[4] Understanding this historical framework helps us understand the societal environment where African American citizens like Trayvon Martin, Oscar Grant, Yvette Smith, Rekia Boyd, and so many others are continually killed. I now turn to the particular story of Oscar Grant, a fellow Oaklander, whose death personally affected Akinmusire and motivated him to create his first recorded critique of systemic state violence against Black people.

My Name Is Oscar

Twenty-two-year-old African American butcher's apprentice Oscar Grant III was killed while handcuffed and with his face pressed against the ground by Bay Area Rapid Transit (BART) police officer Johannes Mehserle in the early hours of January 1, 2009. Judging from the cacophonous sound of shock and horror of many witnesses who viewed the incident through BART subway doors and windows, Grant was perceived to be executed by Mehserle. Evidence of the shooting is documented in the plethora of amateur videos taken by subway riders that continue to circulate on YouTube. The running commentaries below these videos are a narrative of immediate calls for justice and anger at the police.

One day after Grant's murder, the multiracial community outcry was swift, angry, and fierce. Major demonstrations in the Bay Area resulted in approximately 120 arrests. Widespread protests were not just a response to what was viewed by many to be another execution of a Black man by the police. The older protesters in the community remembered the "Riders Case" of the early 2000s, which involved a group of Oakland police officers accused of abusing and planting drugs on subjects. The case remains in the public memory, and the Grant murder stirred up angst and anger emanating from decades of distrust between Oakland's Black community and the Oakland police.[5]

Twenty-eight-year-old police officer Mehserle, initially charged by a Los Angeles jury with the more serious crime of second-degree murder, was found guilty in July 2010 of a lesser charge of involuntary manslaughter, plus a gun enhancement charge that could have added up to ten years to his sentence. Judge Robert Perry in November sentenced Mehserle to two years in state prison, overturning the jury's gun enhancement decision. Mehserle's prison sentence was widely perceived as insignificant and insufficient for the murder of Grant. This judicial asymmetry spurred some Oakland community members from peaceful protest to violent acts.

Under the theme My Name Is Oscar, various artists formed a collective stance against the Oscar Grant shooting and police violence through diverse artistic mediums. The songs, music videos, posters, poems, paintings, and graffiti that erupted in response to Grant's death are examples of artistic expression at "a critical moment in the movement to end police violence."[6] African American film director Ryan Coogler chronicled the last hours of Grant's life in *Fruitvale Station* (2013).[7]

Trumpeter and composer Ambrose Akinmusire's composition "My Name Is Oscar" (2011), from his first Blue Note album, is connected to the tradition of critical improvisation and the international movement to end police brutality.[8] Because Akinmusire is a Black Oaklander, it is no surprise that police brutality issues resonate with him. Akinmusire believes that music must ask the questions that challenge belief systems about race, systems that perpetuate ignorance about people who are different from those considered acceptable—in ethnicity, in power, in socioeconomic status. He notes: "these are real concerns I have. I read a great interview with Maya Angelou conducted by bell hooks, and in it she says, 'Art is not a luxury. . . . The artist explains to us, or at least asks the questions which must be asked. . . . that's what the artist is supposed to do, to liberate us from our ignorance.'"[9] Finding the space in his music to ask these questions did not come immediately or naturally. When Akinmusire was first signed to Blue Note records, he was ambivalent about creating work that critiqued police brutality in his community. Raised in North Oakland, he had "survivor's guilt" from not being one of the many Black people killed by the police. After releasing the album, he explained to me that his composition about Oscar Grant gave him opportunities to educate his national and international audiences about American police brutality while on tour:

I'm from a very poor community in Oakland. I didn't grow up poor. I grew up with my mom, and she had a great job. When I signed to Blue Note Records, I felt I needed to remind myself that I was still not only from there [Oakland] but, in a lot of people's eyes, I was equal to Oscar Grant. I was still just a Black man. I wanted to find a way to connect myself to my community on my albums. In America, when you're a Black person heading to success, the first thing they try to do is separate you from your community. They say, "He's different; he's a good one." I wanted them to know that I am the same; I am the same as the dude you just killed. I really am! These people are from my community, we have mutual friends.

   And later on, I began to have these conversations around the world. I would go to Kiev and other random places in the world. People would ask me about Oscar Grant, and I realized that it was an opportunity to tell people about my experiences as a young Black man, around the world. I've had a conversation about Oscar Grant in Johannesburg and realized many South Africans hadn't even heard about the murder of Grant. That's super deep. My critique of police brutality has become a leitmotif throughout my albums.[10]

For any serious listener of Akinmusire's music, this leitmotif is readily appar-ent—and what this chapter is dedicated to exploring.

   Recalling his musical and social training, Akinmusire tells the story of how he "almost grew up in a Black Conscious museum"; older African American male musicians, many of them former Black Panthers, guided his musician-ship and influenced his worldview.[11] The men of this Black activist generation were the postwar children of Southern migrants drawn to the Bay Area in the 1940s and 1950s to find work in the shipbuilding defense industry. As historian Donna Murch describes, the defense economy was strong, and the living conditions purportedly better than in the South. However, with "a disappearing industrial base" and segregation—fomented by white flight to the suburbs and growing populations of Southern Black migrants—job opportunities decreased.[12]

   In 1980, two years before Akinmusire was born, Oakland was majority Black, and had 131,127 more Blacks than whites. The state and city gov-ernments responded to the changing demographics by creating profiling programs to identify Black juvenile delinquents. These programs led to police harassment, which led to arrests and high Black incarceration numbers.

   Black Studies programs were the catalysts for the creation of the Black Panther Party (BPP) and not the product of the movement. The intellec-tual base of organizations like the BPP grew out of protests for curriculum changes, as colleges had no Black history courses that reflected Black people's contributions to the world. The "Black Conscious[ness] museum" that Akinmusire references was not a museum but a living, spatial repository of historical and cultural knowledge from community members who directly shaped his aesthetic choices. His understanding of his Blackness and music developed first in the Black church, then further through the street elders who taught him about improvisation and Black musical space from an alternative, pedagogy, one developed in those marginalized spaces outside of institutional jazz education. Akinmusire explains:

> That's the way I came to this music. I grew up in a Baptist church and I played piano in church from the age of three. Then I went to jazz camp when I was thirteen or fourteen, where I met all these old-school musicians. And they eventually took a liking to me. They would come and pick me up from my house, and instead of giving me a lesson with a horn, we would go to the record shop.[13]

Some of Akinmusire's mentors would take him to flea markets at six in the morning, and they would search the record bins for jazz records that would provide the curriculum that shapes his approach to improvisation today. The key lesson his mentors sought to impart was that improvisation is a reflection of life and not abstract notation or theory. In fact, he did not have traditional music lessons until much later: "I didn't start dealing with notes until college. Like Kenny Dorham is playing these notes over this chord. That's not the way I was taught. I was taught, 'He plays this way because he lives this way.' I was so lucky to come into it [jazz education] that way."[14]

As I argue throughout this text, the production of Black musical space comes directly from lived experience and reveals what is at politically at stake for the artist. Akinmusire's creative process confronts the extremes that constitute Black life. He creates compositions and performance art that addresses issues that have traumatized Black people in his community and throughout urban America. In comments about his album *Origami Harvest* (2018), Akinmusire describes his motivation to compose "My Name Is Oscar" as well as other compositions that seek to enunciate Black social life while drawing attention to systemic forces and ideologies that promote social inequality and Black mortality. His surreal visions reimagine Black life as harvesting beauty and freedom instead of pain:

> That is what Origami Harvest is about. It's about these extremes and putting them really close together and trying to experience them both at the same time in the way I experience life. Origami is about the different ways we have to fit into society. Harvest is the cycle of it. I put these words together based on my vision

of a sharecropper. It's a sepia-colored image of this guy at the end of the day with a satchel full of origami that he had been in the field folding. And instead of this painful thing, he was in the field creating beauty. At the end of the day, the sharecropper did not have a satchel full of cotton but a satchel full of origami.[15]

The extremes that Akinmusire feels and expresses in his music result, on the one hand, from his deep cognizance of the institutional and structural racism that shapes Black people's quality of life while, and on the other, having white friends for whom he cares deeply. "What is it like to feel and know all of these things, to have white friends that you really love but with a heightened awareness of how you are being perceived? With this album, I was trying to find an outlet for all of these things. Sometimes, it can be stifling, you know."[16] The experiences Akinmusire discusses here connect to what motivated Terence Blanchard to write the composition "See Me As I Am" (2015) which I discuss in Chapter 1. As sociologist Avery Gordon argues, the complexity of a marginalized people's collective personhood demands the ability to simultaneously face systemic inequality and violence while imagining a better future without those social ills. Embracing quotidian despair, while disciplining one's mind to imagine a better future, is a necessary critical praxis for surviving in the world.[17]

Akinmusire distinguishes his work from antipolice songs, such as those of the late 1980s Compton, California–based rap group N.W.A (Niggas With Attitude).[18] Though clearly saddened by the killing of Grant and the Mehserle verdict, Akinmusire decided to tell the story of Oscar Grant in a creative and provocative way that reminds the world of Grant's humanity:

> I just want people to know the story. I don't want it to become this "f*ck the police anthem." . . . Every time I go back home [Oakland] I'm reminded of it, people still talk about it, it's still such a big thing because he [Mehserle] got off with just two years, he didn't get charged with murder. It just really resonates with me because I feel like it could have been me or anyone. The piece begins with me observing what happens, then me talking in the voice of Oscar Grant himself.[19]

Crossing bar lines by letting the deceased Oscar Grant speak through his voice, the performance of "My Name Is Oscar" reveals how fully Akinmusire identifies with being a possible recipient of police brutality. The analytical portion of this chapter begins with a study of Akinmusire's first offering in his compositional critique of police violence, racism, and white supremacy.

The initial impression one may get from listening to "My Name Is Oscar" is of a spoken-word recitation by Akinmusire with improvised drum accompaniment responding in real time to his fragmentary poetic statements about the events surrounding the killing of Oscar Grant. Yet "My Name Is Oscar" is a presentation that manipulates listener perception. Akinmusire's spoken word is performed and choreographed in response to the arc of drummer Justin Brown's prerecorded improvisation. This drum improvisation was removed from a different recording session (specifically, from a composition by saxophonist Walter Smith III). Both Brown and Smith III are longtime members of the Ambrose Akinmusire Quintet. "My Name Is Oscar" features a stark contrast between Brown's asymmetrically vibrant drumming and the calm voice of Akinmusire. In this way, Akinmusire's spoken-word performance breaks with conventional jazz performances; audiences often imagine improvising musicians responding to live poetry readings, exemplified by New York City's East Village Nuyorican Café poetry slams. Akinmusire devised a musical strategy for recording the poem dedicated to Oscar Grant: he practiced reading the poem with the prerecorded drum improvisation several times and then choreographed the reading to Brown's prerecorded, improvised drum solo.

Treated with vocal effects throughout the composition, Akinmusire's voice sonically represents Oscar Grant, a man physically dead but whose spirit here is reanimated. Eschewing the linear narrative common in traditional storytelling, Akinmusire has orchestrated his words into a nonlinear list of signifiers related to the events surrounding the killing (see table 4.1). Embodying Grant's spirit, Akinmusire constructs him as a lone voice who humanizes himself in fragmentary declarations.

The first phrase, "My name is Oscar," begins at fifteen seconds. Akinmusire states this introductory line in monotone fashion. The rhythm of the phrase comprises a staccato sixteenth note beamed to an eighth note for "my name," then musical space followed by an eighth note and two sixteenth notes for "is Oscar." The words "Fruitvale," "human," "apology," and the remaining phrases are deliberately stated, with space in between for dramatic effect.

Complex hand drumming continues, with the drummer's left foot keeping a steady quarter-note beat on hi-hat. Akinmusire uses his voice in a series of rhythmic divisions that include quarter notes, sixteenth notes, eighth notes, and eighth-note triplets. While Brown's hand drumming becomes more complex through increased rhythmic interplay between the snare drum and tom-toms, Akinmusire's voice remains contrastingly subtle.

Akinmusire also emphasizes the rhythm and meaning of the text by separating syllables and drawing out phrases. For example, at 1:46, Officer Mehserle's last name is divided defiantly and mockingly into three rhythmic syllables. The arc of Akinmusire's phrase is in stark contrast to the previous

Time of Verse Launching	Spoken Word(s)	Drumming Evolution	Vocal Dynamics & Rhythm
0:15	my name is Oscar	hand drumming	quarter-note cymbal
0:38	Fruitvale	hand drumming, ride cymbal crash	staccato (sixteenth note beamed to an eight)
0:50	human	hand drumming with quarter-note cymbal	monotone eighth notes/piano
1:07	apology	hand drumming, with quarter-note cymbal and tom drum	monotone/ eighth note and one grouping of eighth-note triplets/ piano
1:22	nineteen days	hand drumming with quarter-note cymbal	monotone/ two quarters and a half note/ piano
1:27	Inauguration [Obama 2009]	hand drumming begins to intensify	monotone/ four sixteenth notes and a quarter note/ piano
1:36–1:37	my name is Oscar	hand drumming continues to intensify	Sentence drawn out for dramatic effect. There is a space between "name" and "Oscar"
1:46	Meh-ser-le	asymmetrical interplay between drums is increased	calls out police officer's name defiantly and mockingly/ slightly higher pitch range
2:00	I Am You!	after some space, switches to drumsticks/ two cymbal crashes after spoken word	vocal intensity and speed increases; stated in a declarative fashion/ higher pitch range
2:09	Don't Shoot!	barrage of cymbal crashes in higher pitch range	more vocal drama and intensity/ pointillistic enunciation with drama
2:27	Oakland	fury of cymbal crashes continues	stated with defiance and pride in the city
2:39	Live . . .	Increased velocity of cymbal crashes mixed with snare drums	elongated, dramatic phrasing
2:52	my name . . . is Oscar	speed, volume and intensity of drumming climax	stated louder and more defiantly, but legato this time
3:17	we are the same	drumming still intense but begins to dissipate	even sixteenth notes in declarative style
3:23	my name . . . is Oscar . . . I am . . . Grant . . . I grant	drums fade out quickly with cymbal reverberation	Akinmusire's voice trails off with, layered echo effect

Table 4.1. "My Name Is Oscar" Performance Graphic
This table is a graphic representation of Akinmusire's performance of "My Name Is Oscar" (2011), which constructs a fragmentary narrative about key events surrounding the killing of Oscar Grant. Akinmusire uses strategies of timing, fragmentary spoken text, and various prerecorded textures of rhythmic drumming that articulates the narrative arc of the performance.

monotone statements. At 2:39 the word "live" is elongated for dramatic effect in response to the increased velocity and cymbal crashes of the drummer.

Akinmusire's use of space between his spoken phrases, combined with the subtle drama of his monotone voice, is the result of knowing in advance where drummer Justin Brown was going to switch to drumsticks from hand drumming, radically changing the texture, speed, and pitch of his improvisation. Knowing where Brown's solo would climax, Akinmusire chose that time frame to state the most dramatic, humanizing words of the poem, awaiting a barrage of cymbal crashes and rapid succession of sixteenth notes to declare, at 2:00, "I am you!" and at 2:09, "Don't shoot!" Such pointillistic speech is another strategy of Akinmusire's creation of musical space.

The last effect of Akinmusire's duo performance is the layered echo of Akinmusire's initial statement, "My name is Oscar." To emphasize this statement, Akinmusire's voice is treated with an echo effect just as the drums fade out with decrescendo cymbal reverberation. The reverb, applied to both the voice and the drums, connotes the doubleness and ephemerality that Black people feel when their lives are truncated by violent means.

"My Name Is Oscar" was not a singular event of music protest by Akinmusire. He continued the project of bringing attention to police brutality in his second album release.

"Rollcall for Those Absent": The List Grows

"Rollcall for Those Absent," a three-minute-and-thirty-eight-second composition from Akinmusire's recording *The Imagined Savior Is Far Easier to Paint* (2014),[20] represents the continuation of Akinmusire's project of drawing attention to Black males who have been killed by various police officers in the United States.

Foregrounded in the composition is the voice of a young girl, Muna Blake, who lists the names of Black males killed by police in recent decades. Blake's recitation of the names is designed to remind the listener that the slain Black men were somebody's children as well. Akinmusire explains, "Having a young voice read the names, it's like the beginning of life talking about the end of life."[21] Using children to sing jazz on protest albums is not without precedent. Archie Shepp's "Quiet Dawn" on *Attica Blues* (1972) features the singing of the seven-year-old daughter of its composer and flugelhornist Cal Massey.[22] Pianist and composer Robert Glasper, on the same Blue Note label as is Akinmusire, conspicuously uses the same compositional strategy of having a child read the names of slain Black people in his "I'm Dying of

Thirst" (2015); but Glasper's band vamps underneath the reading, whereas Akinmusire's music that features keyboardist Sam Harris on "Rollcall" is through-composed.

The youthfulness of Blake's voice is emphasized by the way she sometimes struggles with pronouncing this list of the deceased. Many of the names are recognizable because grassroots protests led to news coverage of their deaths. These names include Sean Bell, Amadou Diallo, Ousmane Zongo, and Trayvon Martin—he being the thematic anchor of the list. Killed two years before the release of this recording, Martin's death sparked the Black Lives Matter movement. Martin's name is recited strategically in the composition to emphasize his story and his youth relative to the slain adult Black males. Martin's name is made more prominent, not more important, by being repeated more than the others. Akinmusire understands all of these killings as equally tragic; yet he accentuates the pronouncement of the name Trayvon Martin, as his death was the most famous case of violence against an unarmed Black child at that time.

It is understandable that Akinmusire identifies with Black males killed by the police because he too is a Black male and sees himself as a potential victim of police violence. Still, his "Rollcall" is incomplete without listing the names of African American women. Critical race theory scholar Kimberlé Crenshaw argues that the dominant, analytical framework for understanding racial violence has been largely male-oriented, since racial violence, typically understood through the brutal and theatrically symbolic technology of lynching, has historically been designed to emasculate individual Black males and Black manhood.[23] The glaring absence of African American women's names in "Rollcall for Those Absent" is later addressed in "Free, White and 21," in which Akinmusire recites the names of Yvette Smith, Shereese Francis, and Miriam Carey, unarmed African American women killed by the police.

Akinmusire, who plays a Juno synthesizer, joins Sam Harris on the Mellotron to create the homophonic accompaniment that is the sonic backdrop to "Rollcall." Their combined sounds convey a funeral service, improvised music moving like a procession, flowing in nonmetric time and creating an aura of ecclesiastical reverence, gravitas, and solemnity. This composition is designed to suggest a public mourning for Black men. The layer of improvised drumming adds timbral dynamics to the organ sound and contextualizes the spoken text with splashes of rhythmic colors.

Akinmusire's Juno synth in "Rollcall" begins with a low-pitched rumble immediately followed by a slow, chromatic glissando into a brief major 7th chord. The opening chord is followed by increasingly complex polychords led by a higher-pitched melody. This sonic musical strategy is also used by

Akinmusire in his composition "Americana/The Garden Waits for You to Match Her Wilderness" (2018). There he plays a Casio SK-1 sampling keyboard manufactured in 1985 to juxtapose a snakelike, bending, high-pitched melody to contrast the texture of the strings. In both pieces, Akinmusire uses extreme pitch registers to represent the spatialized extremes that Black people face while living in the world. He endeavors to make those sounds sonically legible stating, "sounds that are really high and really low are like the beginning and the end."[24]

The nonfunctionality of the haunting chord progressions of "Rollcall" keeps me off kilter for its three and a half plus minutes. For those familiar with the standard repertoire of Black church music, there is no familiar hymn or refrain to orient the listener as we hear the names of the dead repeated by the young Muna Blake over the glissando melody. By using unconventional and haunting chord patterns, Akinmusire's music suggests that no social cadence or resolution is possible as long as these systemic patterns of anti-Blackness and violence continue.

At the very end of "Rollcall," Trayvon Martin's name is linked thematically and compositionally to Oscar Grant's, whom Blake names with echoing finality. The thematic link to "My Name Is Oscar" is clear: both compositions address the tragic deaths of Black males while humanizing them through the Black tradition of saying their names. A compositional link is also revealed in the production techniques: each name is enhanced with reverb effect and repeated several times in fragmentary permutations at the end of the composition.

In his composition "Free, White and 21"—a title borrowed from Howardena Pindell's video installation *Free, White and 21* (1980), which explores her tribulations with white racism as she appears as a white woman and her African American self—the list of those killed by the police now includes Black women as well as men. The expression "free, white and 21," no longer commonly heard today, was also a popular mantra in white character movie dialogues from the 1920s through the 1950s and cinematically reflected the unapologetic structural and systemic white supremacy of its time.[25] The core of Akinmusire's composition, however, is in how he points to another lyrical irony in a church hymn often sung in the Black church.

Akinmusire highlights the irony of how for generations Black people have been singing the Christian anthem "We Are Soldiers," which includes a lyric about "the blood-stained banner." Long considered a symbol of the fight for civil rights but also a term for a symbol of white supremacy, the Blood Stained Banner is the name of the third national flag used by Southern proslavery actors in the last month of the American Civil War. As part of the performance, Akinmusire whistles part of "We Are Soldiers," about which he remarks: "I wanted to sneak it in there. The only part that I vocalize is the 'blood-stained banner.' I wanted it to sound like it emerged and also do it in a way that was soulful enough to still be respectful to people that have passed away, trying to really extract the blues out of all that stuff."[26] The screams that Akinmusire orchestrates signify the insanity of the violence perpetrated on Black bodies throughout American history. The sounds of the snare drum connote the militaristic element of the song expressed in these words: "We have to hold up the blood-stained banner / We have to hold it up until we die!" Akinmusire wants to draw our attention to the lack of historical understanding among Black people who sing the song without understanding what the words truly signify: "I can remember that was a song we used to sing during the collection of offering. We would be marching around giving money to the church. That's dark."[27] When Akinmusire states that "we are not protest songs" at 2:35, as the string ensemble lays a harmonic bed,[28] he is telling the listener not to conflate Black people with the issues they perpetually fight to bring to the fore of society's consciousness for social change. He told me, "I have a problem with artists, both Black and other, using the deaths of Black people for commercial reasons."[29] Black people struggle against structural racism, but they would prefer for structural racism not to exist; they would prefer to be completely free, understood as fully human. Black suffering shouldn't be a fetishized soundtrack for the white imaginary and insatiable voyeurism. Akinmusire addresses the darkness in these historical racial codes in American culture because his mission is to be a musical truth teller, which is reflected in his production of spatially raw and glistening aesthetic that reflects his understanding of the Black aesthetic.

Grotesque Pulchritude: The Black Musical Space of the Glistening Heart

Akinmusire wanted his album *When the Heart Emerges Glistening* (2011) to be a statement against the production values of today's music. Whether it is the ubiquitous use of Auto-Tune to correct out-of-tune pitches or the use of Pro Tools music software to make a specific part of a musical arrangement or improvisation perfect, Akinmusire rebels against such aesthetic values by creating a less technologically mediated sound that viscerally brings listeners into his creative process. For Akinmusire, the practice of musical space-making must reveal the beauty and the imperfection of Black humanity, and humanity in general:

It's about encouraging people to reveal all sides of themselves. With modern technology, we have the opportunity to present what we believe to be perfect, and I think that has had an effect on music. With Pro Tools you can cut everything up, and you can play this passage over and over until you get it right. Nothing is really raw, and ugly things aren't valued any more, and I really believe that until people are comfortable with revealing the ugly parts of themselves as well as the beautiful parts, we can't really have an honest dialogue. So when you think of a heart and it's glistening, you think of it as bloody and raw, but it's also beautiful because it's a heart. So that album, there's some mistakes and sloppiness, and it's not overly mixed, and I think that's why it really resonated with a lot of people.[30]

The performance of the Black aesthetic is not polished, perfect, or refined in the way defined by what theorist George E. Lewis calls Eurological aesthetics.[31] Yet Akinmusire, like African American improvisers in general, does not believe in substandard instrumental performances. On the contrary, he has practiced countless hours over several years to achieve the opportunity to document his musical vision on a major label. Rather, Akinmusire believes and celebrates risk and intangibility.

Akinmusire uses the visual symbol of the exposed heart that is within him, yet displaced, as an abstract symbol of humanity. There is a direct link between his philosophy about open dialogue and his musical strategies of applying space between the notes, exploring the full range of his trumpet, the play of double consciousness between two extreme registers, and tirelessly searching for new ideas as he improvises.

"Confessions to My Unborn Daughter"

In "Confessions to My Unborn Daughter" (2011), the first track on *When the Heart Emerges Glistening*, Akinmusire's deployment of respatialization and a Black sense of time in his compositional and improvisational strategies merit careful analysis. "Confessions" has two sections. The A section of the composition is in E minor, where the ensemble of improvisers explore the mode with a blues sensibility. The recording begins with a solo trumpet improvisation by Akinmusire, who plays a meditative rumination over several scales. Moments later he signals the rest of the band to come in with a perfect-fourth figure from B to E. These notes are also played as a thematic interlude between solo sections as a way of tying together the musical narrative and compositional form:

Musical example 4.1. Perfect fourth figure from B to E.

When Akinmusire calls the rest of the ensemble with that perfect-fourth figure, the rhythm section responds. Pianist Gerald Clayton initially responds with chords in high and low registers of the piano, then eventually picks up and performs the B–E figure of the call. The rest of the rhythm section responds to the pianist's call on the first beat. The pianist responds in turn by playing on downbeats of the measures in response to the trumpet, as a way of grounding the rhythm section. Clayton then leads the rhythm section by taking up the perfect-fourth figure while the rest of the rhythm section responds in kind. The A section's focus on E minor during the solo is expanded through rhythm, and the form of the composition seemingly disappears. Musical illusions are created when the 3/4 time signature appears but then quickly dissolves into a sea of metric modulations. On hearing this performance listeners may believe the musicians have left the compositional form altogether. However, it is clear that they expand the sense of time as they cue each other through the form.

Akinmusire's concept of ensemble technique is revealed in the way the stated melody develops quickly into collective improvisation that features no particular musician. Akinmusire resists playing his composition's melody in a clear way, countering the approach typically taken to teach the listener the melodic and harmonic form of a piece. Akinmusire wants to envelop himself in Black sense of musical space because, for him, the performance is not about the individual soloist but about the lived geography of the collective group. Moreover, recent Black music, such as chopped and screwed music—recorded music slowed and treated with digital effects and choppiness—blurs clear distinctions.[32] Akinmusire explained his musical philosophy to me this way:

That's the way I grew up, man. You ride or die with your community and your homies. That's number one. I've been playing with drummer Justin Brown for twenty-two years. Walter Smith, the tenor player, I've been playing with him for eighteen years. Most of the people in my band, there was a time when they weren't the popular ones. We just stuck it out because it felt like a family. And as far as hierarchy is concerned, that's just the way I hear music, man. Sometimes I feel like a conductor as opposed to a leader. *And also the whole idea of taking a solo, that just seems so dated. I think in music in general, that has stopped. Even if you listen to things like trap and hip-hop, just music isn't like that anymore. Everything is melded into this collective thing in all styles of modern music* [my emphasis]: classical, hip-hop, jazz, R&B. You're like, "Is this a hook? Are they rapping or are they singing?" And also, I don't need the attention. If this music was just about me, if I was just doing this for Ambrose, I would have stopped touring a long time ago. I don't need the attention of the stage, lights, and glamour.[33]

There is no conventional hierarchy between bandleader and sidemen, no division of labor in terms of how the music is arranged or performed. Resisting small-group bebop convention, Akinmusire shares the melody equally with saxophonist Walter Smith III, who provides a timbral contrast and intellectual foil to Akinmusire's improvised lines. They are not communicating the space-making cartography of hierarchical domination but the opposite. There is no competition for musical space in the interplay between saxophone and trumpet.

The melody dissolves rapidly into collective improvisation between these two lead instruments and the rhythm section of piano, bass, and drums. The melody of the piece, which varies quite rapidly without any concern for establishing a clear centralized melody, occurs over a chord progression largely based in E minor. Akinmusire leads the band in blurring the lines between playing the theme and collective spontaneous composition, which traditionally are separate sections of a performance.[34] The band never repeats the melody in the same way, demonstrating Akinmusire's willingness to challenge traditional jazz performance hierarchies in terms of who states the melody and who improvises first. The improvisations among Smith, Akinmusire, and the rhythm section represent a balance between free improvisation and improvising within a clear structure. As Akinmusire explains:

Why do I have to wait until after the head to solo? . . . Why can't I begin with a solo? Why do I have to solo at all? For a long time, I've been trying to break through the forms. That's why I surround myself with musicians who are also willing to break down forms. When we play these tunes live this year, they won't sound like they do on the album. Anything I create is something to be manipulated and explored, and I trust the musicians to do whatever they feel. Even if I go, "Damn, why did they do that?" I still trust them. Sometimes you might be in the middle of the solo and someone else will come in, and that will be OK. Anything goes. And I mean anything.[35]

Harmonic Dissolution

Akinmusire's configurations suggest that he works within his own system of tonality while also working outside of that system in an E minor blues tonality. His harmonic scheme for "Confessions" avoids conventional harmonic resolution, and his melodic scheme reflects highly chromatic concepts. The harmonies of "Confessions" do not form a harmonic progression in the Western sense of the term but a repeated, acoustic bass–driven diatonic chord cycle that does not stray from the E minor modal sound.

The chord progression that Akinmusire creates in 3/4 is based on E minor, C♯ minor7(♭5), C major7, with a passing slash chord of G major/B. These cycles of chords are followed by the A minor chord, which precedes a whole step down to a G major chord, which "resolves" to E minor. The harmonic rate has each following chord shift on the third beat of the measure. For example, C♯ minor7 in the first bar, the E minor chord in the second bar, and G major on the third beat of bar 3 all demonstrate this pattern of shifting on each measure's third beat.

The contrasting B section is an exercise in harmonic oscillation between two major chords, C major and E major, a major third apart. After the rugged, blues quality of the extended E minor riff in the first section, these chords in the B section function as a release from the minor blues sound, bringing different harmonic colors to the composition.

How does Akinmusire musically address ideas of race, spatial marginalization, and time as he negotiates his personhood on the outskirts of civil society? The way he represents Black musical space and rhythm in his improvisation, the way he plays inside and outside harmony, relates to his being at both the center and the periphery of society at the same time. His performance simultaneously represents strategies of resistance and the exploration of Black ontological space through sound.

Akinmusire's unconventional melodic phrases are important because they demonstrate his conception toward shaping musical space. He plays several unconventional, asymmetrical phrases of large intervals in his improvisation; these are played motivically, with a repertoire of different timbres, and out of time.

Akinmusire represents his own timeline of Blackness by playing non-chord tones over E minor.[36] While he plays freely with a high degree of chromaticism, he is always mindful of his harmonic scheme or changes. Avoiding musical clichés, Akinmusire departs from the bebop tradition of trumpet performance that relies on scalar linearity to make musical statements. Although trumpeters

Clifford Brown, Henry Red Allen, Don Cherry, and other trumpet players have influenced Akinmusire's style, he is a conduit for their spirits while working beyond the musical vocabulary they expressed in own their time.

Many musicians and fans have asked Akinmusire about what they perceive as his innovative extended instrumental techniques he performs during his trumpet improvisations. Yet he does not want to be seen as an innovative iconoclast. His trumpet sound is not about his ability to innovate but reveals his deep investigation into the repository of improvised language that reflects lives formed in the interiority of a Black musical space.

His composition "The Lingering Velocity of the Dead's Ambitions," which closes *Origami Harvest*, is as much about his channeling the spirits of the improvisation masters as it is about honoring the Black men and women murdered through the legalized implements of structural racism. The term "lingering velocity" seems like an oxymoron on its face: "lingering" implies staying in place; "velocity" is about speed of motion in a particular direction. Consistent with his not feeling any duty to reconcile seemingly unrelated themes, Akinmusire juxtaposes these two signifiers to define spirits of past masters suspended with him in space, yet moving in a circulatory direction that inspires what Henry Threadgill called "spontaneous and extemporaneous" improvisation.[37]

Akinmusire also believes the ambitions of the dead are not buried with the ancestors but remain alive, waiting to be fulfilled by those still living. The "Lingering Velocity" section of the *Origami Harvest* trailer shows cinematographic evidence of Akinmusire's Black thought: blurred images of the ancestors of improvisation hanging on the wall of the Village Vanguard (4:41, 5:09), photos and posters of Thelonious Monk, John Coltrane, Pharoah Sanders, and others that most viewers would be unable to decipher in the blurriness of that liminal space.[38]

Those hanging images constitute a shrine toward which Akinmusire points his bell in reverence. The bell of his trumpet represents his hands clasped in humility, praise, and gratitude. Akinmusire does not worship the masters, but his music is a perpetual prayer in dialogue with their legacy and living artistic ambitions—ambitions suspended in that Black sense of placelessness, awaiting those open enough to feel them and technically prepared enough to articulate them through musical instruments. Akinmusire focuses not on being an innovator but on his commitment to connecting his work to his improvisation ancestors:

> If there is anything I pride myself in, it is my knowledge of the history of this music. And so it is very easy for me to imagine, in a very tangible way, what Booker Little would have sounded like at thirty, at forty, at fifty, at sixty; same

thing with Clifford Brown, same thing with Lee Morgan, same thing with someone like Henry Red Allen—who to me, was a master of extended techniques. It's
easy for me to imagine what Don Cherry would sound like if he sat down and
had a classical teacher for five years, and all this stuff was executed poorly. I'm
trying to be a conduit for all of those spirits to live through me; to play through
me in a straight-up, real way. I'm trying to get rid of myself enough for them to
come inside me and express the things they are not able to express in this physical world. A lot of people ask me about innovation or doing things that may be
new. Maybe I am, but it's really through them. Because, if we're being straight up,
I don't sit down and practice that stuff. I'm listening to my peers, and I'll get their
music to see what is going on today. But I'm listening to the masters and how
they expressed their time. That's the beautiful thing about the masters: they will
meet you where you are at. You can always return to it and hear completely other
shit. These recordings are alive, and I know that they knew the music was alive.[39]

Notably, in the list of trumpet players whom Akinmusire cites, Allen and
Cherry are the only ones who lived past the age of forty (each approached
sixty); Little died at twenty-three, Brown twenty-five, and Morgan thirty-three.

Melodic Conception and Akinmusire's Internal Ear

Akinmusire's melodic conception is related to his exploration of what he
calls his "internal ear":

To exercise the internal ear is to play exactly what the music wants. The better you
can do that, the more in line you will be with terms like "innovation." I also think
the music is living but not in some type of hokey or hippie way. The only thing is,
we can't see it. We can feel it and it changes you; sometimes you can even smell it.[40]

In this intervallic analysis, I study Akinmusire's melodic conception in his
improvisation on "Confessions," seeking to understand how he crosses bar lines
and produces space in musical performance during his melodic experimentation.

In the first four phrases of his trumpet solo at 4:41 in "Confessions," Akinmusire plays unconventional wide intervals that signify his conception of musical
space and intervallic exploration. While his exploration is facilitated by a limited
harmonic framework that mostly centers on E minor, there is no harmonic
stasis represented in his ideas. Through the performance of complex intervals,
Akinmusire superimposes harmonies that expand the ways E minor can be
heard through different sonic prisms. Yet he does not play modally. For example,
the first notes he plays are B–G–D, comprising intervals of a minor sixth and a
perfect fifth. The second phrase he performs, A–F#–D, is major sixth to minor

sixth, and the third intervallic configuration he performs is G–F#–B, which is a major seventh to minor sixth. The fourth phrase is A–G–F#:

Musical example 4.2. Akinmusire's unconventional wide-interval phrases 1–4 at 4:41.

Akinmusire's permutations of spacious intervals suggest risk and the celebration of the intangibility of Black musical space. More importantly, these intervallic configurations convey a departure from conventional forms of melodic improvising. The significance of this very untraditional way of improvising is found in the ascending intervallic permutations.[41] In phrase 6, Akinmusire departs from the three-note, wide-interval motif. This first such departure is in the ascending interval from A below to D above high C at 4:58—a span of nineteen notes:

Musical example 4.3. Akinmusire's performed interval in phrase 6 of A–D at 4:58. This interval of a nineteenth is a departure from the three-note motif.

His played D ascends more than two octaves. At this juncture, this is the shortest phrase and the longest interval in his improvisation. However, beginning with phrase 7 at 5:01, a pattern begins with phrases that pivot off of two notes. The next several phrases show how Akinmusire's melodic ideas are well thought out and consistent.

In phrases 7–13, Akinmusire plays motivic and varied ideas that pivot off notes D and E. Interval-wise, these phrases are more compact. Whereas the earlier improvised phrases only ascended, his melodic phrases now have both ascending and descending patterns:

Musical example 4.4. Phrases 7–13: examples of Akinmusire's motivic ideas beginning at 5:00.

Phrase 7 begins at 5:00 with D–E, a major second that rises a perfect fifth from E–B and descends a major second to A. These are more "vocal" phrases with clear melodic patterns. Phrase 8 repeats the permutation in phrase 7, to establish the melodic and rhythmic motif. In phrase 9, Akinmusire begins the first variation on phrase 7's permutation by playing D–E–A–B♭–A, then descending to A–G. The B♭–A are grace notes or decorative flourishes. The difference here is that B♭ is flattened and a G is added to the phrase. In phrase 10, Akinmusire ends his phrase in a different direction: he plays D–E–B♭–C and approaches D chromatically through D♭. This is the first time since phrase 6 that his phrase ends in ascending motion.

Akinmusire's phrase 12 is a reverse permutation of notes through octave displacement. The phrase begins on the pivot notes D and E, which ascend an octave but are performed in reverse order. Akinmusire's gesture of octave displacement foreshadows what he will perform later in the solo.

For the majority of his solo, Akinmusire exploits two registers of his trumpet. At phrase 13, when he pivots thematically on D and E, Akinmusire suggests bitonality by performing notes that are not traditionally within the scale of E minor. For example, he plays B♭–C–B♭–A, all note colors that indicate a different harmonic area. This thematic variation on what he played six phrases earlier prefigures his movement into the contrasting B section, which oscillates through the harmonic pendulum of C major and E major chords.

Analyzing Contrasting B Section

The contrasting B section, which enters at phrase 14, moves from C major to E major by way of a D major chord. Akinmusire's improvisation, characterized mostly by highly chromatic "out notes" so far, harmonically adjusts to phrase 14 when Akinmusire plays A–B♭–A–G. Akinmusire's melodic phrase begins in the lower range and then lingers in the midrange of his trumpet. Phrase 14 also appears to be a variation on phrase 9.

Whereas phrase 9 pivots on D and E, phrase 14 begins on G and A; however, the latter half of the phrase echoes phrase 9 in the melodic contour of A♭–A–G. Phrase 15, at twenty-one notes, is the longest in Akinmusire's improvisation at this juncture: it threads through the two major chords of C major and E major, which oscillate like a pendulum of bright colors compared to the dirge quality of the E minor performance in the A section, where it was the illusion of harmonic stasis that created an opportunity for Akinmusire and saxophonist Walter Smith III to play modal *harmonicpoint* while implying other modes. I avoid the Western signifier *counterpoint* because Akinmusire and Smith create spatial harmony through their interweaving melodic lines instead of countering each other. Except for perfect octave leaps and intervals of perfect fifth, Akinmusire's phrase is mostly composed of major second and minor second intervals, emphasizing chromaticism in the melodic line over the course of this long phrase. Moreover, phrase 15 is not fragmented, unlike most phrases in the beginning of his improvisation in the A section.

While it illuminates C major and E major chords, phrase 16, composed of ten notes, occurs only over the C major chord. Akinmusire reintroduces phrases split between two distinct registers after the B section. As noted above, his oscillation between two registers adds a unique character to the shape and sound of his improvised lines. He suggests bitonality in the A section and improvises more within the chord changes on the B section.

In phrase 17 Akinmusire plays "unconventional" notes in the mid to high and low range of his trumpet over E major and C major chords. Akinmusire's musical phrase sounds momentarily discontinuous but connects in one breath that crosses the literal bar lines. I contend that Akinmusire's performance of two registers of his trumpet represents a two-voice-out-of-one double consciousness.[42]

Musical example 4.5. Phrase 17 at 5:23 shows how Akinmusire plays an idea that is a double-voiced, timbral exploration of the high and low of registers of his trumpet over E major and C major chords.

Akinmusire exploits the full range of the instrument with melodic invention in two registers successively while maintaining a vocal timbre. His improvisational approach disavows codified styles of improvisation, and his melodic ideas may be displaced by one or more octaves. In this improvisation, Akinmusire never relies on diatonic melodies performed within an octave.

Further evidence of this representation by Akinmusire of double consciousness is that his registral gestures are repeated again in phrase 18. Whereas the seven-note phrase of G–F–E–F–G–A♭–A is performed in the high register of the trumpet, followed by a leap down an octave to A in phrase 19, the majority of the phrase, including the notes of A♭–G–B♭–G–A♭–D, is in the lower register.

Most of Akinmusire's registral leaps are separated into phrases. Continuing the strategy of performing in two registers, Akinmusire performs phrase 20, which shoots into the upper register again. The shorter phrase 21 is a continuation of the idea in phrase 20 but performed in the lower register. Akinmusire not only jumps between the low and high registers of his trumpet but also varies his musical statements between longer and shorter phrases. Again, most of his fragmented harmonic exploration occurs within the E minor non-progression of the A section, whereas longer, poetic melodic lines are performed over major chords in the contrasting B section.

Phrase 22 demonstrates a shorter four-note melodic idea in the upper register. Akinmusire performs a constellation of notes that are highly chromatic pitch sets. Here, for example, he plays the four-note series A–A♭–G–A:

Musical example 4.6. Chromatic cell idea in this entire phrase 22. This is a continuation of the four-note permutation idea.

Phrase 22 is a four-note permutation as in phrases 8,12, and 17. While there is much chromaticism in the varied melodic lines, these four-note permutations are connected in that no wide intervallic leaps are used. The first chorus, sixteen-note phrase 23, which includes several ghost notes, is the next-longest phrase after phrase 15. This phrase itself indicates that Akinmusire often thinks in smaller pitch sets as he improvises in this performance, but those smaller pitch sets often spin out into longer phrases. The series of improvised permutations in lower register phrase 23 is the first line with two intervals of tritones, B♭–E and A♭–D, lending them a momentary emphasis. The nine-note phrase 24, in contrast, occurs in the upper range of the trumpet. Phrase 25 is highly chromatic, with a large number of major seconds and minor seconds, and is performed in the lower range.

Phrase 26 marks a departure from Akinmusire's earlier melodic constructions; here Akinmusire begins to signal the end of one cycle of improvisation by playing a partial flatted fifth, a B♭ over the E minor blues figure in the beginning of the phrase. The actual ending of Akinmusire's solo is demarcated by phrase 27, a one-note phrase of F♯ played on a half-valved pitch. This half-valved F♯ signals a new improvisation cycle because, in addition to the previous altered blues figure and the musical space that follows the note F♯, Akinmusire then returns to the earlier idea of the wide-interval motif. This musical gesture of return shows that he is closing the narrative.

In this thirty-one-phrase improvisation, what distinguishes this new performance of wide-interval motifs in phrase 28 is that Akinmusire plays them within this one phrase, not in distinct, separate phrases as they were in the beginning of the solo. Phrase 28 contains two sets of ascending intervals. The first five-note pitch set in this phrase comprises C–E followed by the three-note E–F#–G. This is followed by a four-note passage: D moving a half step to E♭, followed by a perfect fifth to B♭, and then ascending, in slight vibrato, to A, a major seventh, to end phrase 28:

Musical example 4.7. Akinmusire returns to improvising wide intervals in this partial example of phrase 28.

The musical data from Akinmusire's solo reveals high-pitched growls and the splitting of melodic lines into two registers as strategies of musical resistance to codified constructs of improvisation. Akinmusire's improvisation represents spatial musical values on the outskirts of universal notions of musical beauty, agency, and humanity. His music is Black expression but not burdened with the rules and norms of what critics say Black expression should be. Akinmusire's unconventional musical gestures represent his immersion in Black musical space and time beyond any organizing epistemology of Blackness that seeks to confine Black expression to a limiting, discursive formation.

Akinmusire argues that the codification of improvised music language is a ruse designed to make students think Black musical culture can be *apprehended*—a verb that conveys not only "grasped with the understanding" but also "arrested, seized": "I live jazz; you can't take that away from me. If we have a whole community who understands that it's here [points to his heart], you can't take that away from us. That's the way it was with the beboppers, before jazz education came and made it this tangible thing and a lot of people started believing it."[43] Akinmusire believes, then, that the institutionalization of Black jazz culture has created a pedagogical jazz education culture based on the illusion of tangible Blackness. In his view, this tangible product of "jazz education" is dispersed so well among idealistic jazz students that some African American improvisers outside the conservatory begin to perceive that white cultural appropriation of their Black musical codes is tantamount to having their music being completely co-opted.

Akinmusire believes that if Black musicians understood that Black music culture is not a product to be bought, sold, or downloaded but is in the heart, and in the consistent, disciplined performance of that Black culture, then the argument of white cultural appropriation falls by the wayside. This understanding would uphold Black music culture as fluid, vast, unpredictable, and unable to be apprehended. Akinmusire's fight against the codification and concretization of Black music culture is seen in his rejection both of traditional methods of improvisation and of traditional hierarchy in his ensemble. Akinmusire plays music from that Black sense of space, music that may seem iconoclastic to conservative ears but is rooted in a kind of Black musical geography.

The space he puts between his notes represents the rejection of such tangibility as the musical figures in the tropology of clichés that fill jazz methodology books. The solution, in Akinmusire's view, is not to be distracted by the jazz product but to understand that culture is somehow internal to the glistening heart. This is the story that Akinmusire tells through his words and improvisation. It's a story of human complexity that articulates the day-to-day experience of Blackness as well as the Blackness that we may never know. The complex personhood embodied in Akinmusire's improvisation resides in his intention to resist ideas of music held up as tradition.

Akinmusire's narrativity is focused on a place beyond tradition. His music reminds us that African American musicians create stories that reveal how they view themselves in relation to a larger society that does not view them as equal. His compositional and improvisational practices are important for what they say about Black life operating in a sphere outside civil society. Akinmusire's techniques connect with the "traditional mission in blues history," described as "reasserting the blues idiom by critically boxing with it and evading attempts at formal standardization, as the old blues people and their jazz descendants and contemporaries had done."[44] Akinmusire's music clearly engages with that mission of evading standardization, crossing bar lines as he explores the contours of his imagination and while musically mapping radical Black musical space.

5

Unified Fragmentation: Andrew Hill's Street Theory of Black Musical Space

The man who merely at rare moments has this creative impulse and expresses that creativeness through perfection of technique, surely you would not call him an artist. To me, the true artist is one who lives completely, harmoniously, who does not divide his art from living, whose very life is that expression, whether it be a picture, music, or his behaviour; who has not divorced his expression on a canvas or in music or in stone from his daily conduct, daily living.[1]
—Jiddu Krishnamurti

Conceiving of diaspora as anaform, we are encouraged, then, to put (all) space into play.
—Richard Iton[2]

A philosopher as fluid as his composed and improvised music, pianist Andrew Hill was both direct and indirect as he expressed his opinions on politics and music over the course of his career. As I have been arguing throughout this text, the practice of Black musical space is both conceptual and from lived experience; its expression and theory are not monochromatic because the way African American improvisers view life and politics is not monolithic. This chapter grapples with the Hill that we do not know. A critical intervention into the largely formalist discourse surrounding his work is needed. We cannot ignore his understanding of his positionality relative to what he has said about music and race. Hill's approach to improvisation was forged in the jazz community of the segregated South Side of Chicago, and this experience informed his mission to bring the Black community aesthetic into the predominantly white musical institution. He wanted to close the gap between the listening community and improvisers. This is why he promoted creative community over the individual improviser's ego.

This chapter focuses on the complicated subject position beneath Hill's storied nebulousness. Hill stated in a 2006 interview, given almost exactly a year before he died, that Black jazz was dead whereas white jazz was alive.[3] Because Hill had a lifelong pattern of shrouding his past history and his life story in general, the manufactured mystery around his life has perhaps discouraged some scholars from theorizing his work through race and politics. In light of musicologist Nina Sun Eidsheim's warning against constructing facile frameworks built on assumptions that claim to know the interior logic of a musician, it is not enough to call Hill enigmatic, elusive, and mysterious.[4] This is why I have focused on finding out how Hill expressed his subjecthood, in part through his compositional and improvisational methodologies.

I begin with a brief biography and a discussion of how Hill's early life experiences in the segregated South Side of Chicago formed his musical philosophy and conception of Black musical space. I then discuss his complex political stance on nationalism and improvisation, as revealed in his discussion of his composition "Nicodemus" on *Marian McPartland's Piano Jazz*, as well as in statements he made at other points in his career. I also explore Hill's "street approach to jazz improvisation,"[5] an alternative pedagogy, based on his early training in the segregated clubs of Bronzeville, that he sought to bring to his teaching at Portland State University. Finally, I discuss Hill's conception of Black musical space through analyzing his melodic, harmonic, and improvisation techniques on "Malachi" from his final album, *Time Lines* (2006).[6]

Andrew Hill embodied Black musical space through his nonconformist philosophy and conception of improvisation, both at the micro level of improvised interval construction and the macro level of unconventional compositional form. He demonstrated his philosophy of Black musical space by attending to creativity and rejecting style, crossing bar lines by expressing his lived experience through improvisation and composition.

Born in Chicago on June 30, 1931, pianist, composer, and bandleader Andrew W. Hill was raised on its South Side. He later moved to the New York City area, and passed away in Jersey City, New Jersey, on April 20, 2007, after an extended battle with cancer. Despite the facts of his birth, he falsely claimed early in his career that he had been born in 1937 and was from Port-au-Prince, Haiti.[7] These tactics Hill used to survive in the music business were found in his liner notes and press releases, and his fabrications were repeated by unwitting critics in music reviews and various press stories long before search engines could help reveal historical inaccuracies. His archive also shows evidence of falsifying his curricula vitae and making several claims of college degrees never received in order to get academic positions in colleges and universities. As a fellow improviser, composer, and student of his work, I have no interest in judging Hill for his actions or hurting his legacy; I am interested in how his strategies reveal a man concerned not only with economic survival but also with knowledge production. Given his commitment to a musical vision built on unrelenting artistic integrity, it is important to understand how he accessed the university, which connects to his approach to learning and teaching improvisation in an institution of higher education.

In the liner notes of Hill's Blue Note album *Black Fire* (1964),[8] Hill created a myth around his birthplace to distinguish himself from other African American improvisers who were competing for concert bookings in the college campus market. A March 6, 1968, "Andrew Hill: Blue Note Records" press release written by jazz critic Leonard Feather describes Hill as "a native of Port-au-Prince" and states that "his name was originally Hille but the *e* was eventually dropped from his last name for convenience."[9] Later in life, Hill explained the motivation for his ruse:

> I lied.... I used to blame it on other people, but it was me, and AB Spellman was the one who helped me plot the crime. I was born in Chicago and had no interest in Haiti or patois, but that lie enabled me to get gigs on the college circuit, the Dave Brubeck thing, you know. People looked at jazz music as exotic and pretending you came from Haiti helped.... I'm not as pure as driven snow. It's just I've got more morally correct as I've grown older.[10]

Hill watched as critics latched on to his Haitian story, even linking Hill to the Négritude movement.[11] Yet he was motivated to correct the record later in his life.

Andrew Hill's Complex Stance on the Relationship between Activism and Improvisation

Hill's music philosophy, what he later called his "street approach to jazz improvisation," developed in learning environments and physical Black musical spaces shaped by the systematically enforced housing segregation of Blacks on Chicago's South Side. It was this segregation that facilitated the intense musical training for younger Black musicians like Hill. Historian Amy Absher has shown how segregation affected Black musicians and why they struggled for cultural space in Chicago between 1900 and 1967: "Black musicians needed diverse and complicated strategies for dealing with segregation because racism in Chicago was an outgrowth of the city's politics, which manifested itself at every level of life."[12] It was not unusual to see the same Black audiences at classical, jazz, and blues concerts, because "[t]he blending of genres and audiences was another manifestation of the influence of so many different types of people and musicians all migrating to and sharing a small piece of urban space."[13] Frankly, African American improvisers in this period didn't care about genre; their personal and aesthetic aspirations were broader than music market segregation and they had to contend with the economic realities of segregation. White local Chicago politicians and urban planners directed institutions of vice to the South Side because, for many of them, Blackness was equated with criminality and so African American musical improvisation was linked with crime. Black musicians responded by creating their own organizations, such as the Black musicians' cooperative known as the Association for the Advancement of Creative Musicians (AACM), to combat these stereotypes and to operate beyond the jazz clubs, unions, and booking agencies.[14]

The late poet, writer, and music critic Amiri Baraka (formerly LeRoi Jones) described Hill as a free, original, iconoclastic musician who was punished for his involvement with the Black Arts Repertory Theatre/School (BARTS). Baraka founded BARTS in Harlem in 1965 to expose the African American community to the wealth of Black art. According to Baraka, Hill in his capacity as music coordinator of BARTS actively recruited the leading African American improvisers and composers. Musicians like saxophonist John Coltrane, saxophonist Albert Ayler, and trumpeter Charles Tolliver brought creative music to the Black community in such "unconventional" spaces as public parks, government-funded housing, and empty parking lots. This was a space-making tactic that challenged the elitism of venues through the radical repurposing of public spaces. Baraka believed Hill's music career suffered as a result, and argued, without any clear evidence, that Blue Note Records delayed the release of several of Hill's albums for decades as retribution for the pianist's participation in such insurgent community projects: "The tragedy of Blue Note sitting on Andrew Hill's great works, e.g., *Time Lines*, *Passing Ships*, for nearly thirty years! Demonstrates once again how reactionary institutions can penalize artists if they think what the artists are doing in their private lives is not in tune with the corporation's ideological vision."[15] *Passing Ships* had in fact been recorded in 1969 but was not released until 2003; likewise, tracks released by Blue Note in 1975, such as Hill's *One for One*, had been recorded five to ten years earlier. But *Time Lines* was recorded in 2005 and published by Blue Note within a year, and most of Hill's other Blue Note albums had also been released within a year of recording. Perhaps assuming delays of Hill's work were consistent throughout his career, Baraka likely criticized the label for not releasing what he thought was a much older recording, until Hill's popularity had increased later in life—and while Hill was dying of cancer.

No Black improvising musician in America can be apolitical. Hill's attitude from this period, however, demonstrates a politics different from that of Baraka and of the Black Arts movement in general. In fact, the leading avant-garde African American musicians, such as John Coltrane, Sun Ra, Archie Shepp, Ornette Coleman, and Albert Ayler, had diverse, complex music theories and perspectives that could not be contained by the prescriptive belief systems of that movement.[16] Yet African American experimental improvisers do have some shared cultural codes, built upon shared experiences and cultural roots.

Innovative, free-thinking African American improvisers, such as Hill, view themselves as global citizens and resist being associated with Black nationalist ideologies that unify their musical expression and cultural work in reductionist ways. Ingrid Monson has argued that creative improvisers have aesthetic agency and do not let racial and gender categories determine who they are in the world: "Although the social categories one occupies may be given—Black, white, man, women, rich, poor—through the creative deployment of various kinds of practices, an individual just might succeed in doing a whole host of things that are not predicted by the social categories to which they belong."[17] Indeed, a core part of that creative practice is, either intentionally or unintentionally, an open rebuke and defiance of those categorical boxes musicians are often placed in. When Duke Ellington refused to categorize Black music, he was also refusing to categorize Blackness because he understood that Blackness is beyond category. The geographical placelessness that Black people and Black musicians experience continues to deprive them of the umbrella social category of human, and so it is reasonable to argue that the defiance of these musical boxes, what Monson calls "aesthetic agency,"[18] is a core part of ontological Black musical place-making as it relates to the practice of improvising a Black civil society, improvising humanity.

Though early in his career he was outspoken to the American jazz press about the economics of being a jazz musician, Hill's most stark comments on race were revealed to the foreign press only in his later years. Perhaps

Hill feigned an apolitical stance in the 1960s to get work and avoid being lumped in with activist African American musicians. Yet, according to Blue Note Records producer and discographer Michael Cuscuna, taking an apolitical stance as an African American improviser in the 1960s was to be an outlier in the political field of that time.[19] Cuscuna argues that African American improvisers who created politically themed albums in the 1960s were not punished for their politics but were rewarded with more press, more recording opportunities, and more gigs. He explains that Blue Note would have supported Black activism because it was a way to sell records by getting press or other types of attention. Yet Hill believed that overtly political improvised music was promoted over less overtly political music, and that this led to the alienation of the audience and narrowing of the fan base. Although Hill argued that jazz audiences were complex, came from all walks of life, and were not swayed by fashionable, political music trends in jazz, he believed that his audiences did not appreciate political improvisation and that they could not do the critical analysis required to understand his art. But though Blue Note itself may have seen protest music as a marketing strategy in the 1960s, African American improvisers like saxophonist Yusef Lateef (formerly Bill Evans) and drummers Art Blakey and Max Roach faced real consequences for being seen as associated with Black nationalism and Islam. Historically, record companies and journalists did not embrace what they understood as black radicalism. During the bebop era, the critical establishment was concerned that trumpeter Dizzy Gillespie would become a Muslim. Gillespie never became a Muslim but he did study the Qur'an. According to scholar Eddie Meadows, "A semi-boycott of jazz musicians with Muslim names took place . . . Yet in spite of these attempts to control their religious and social views, Muslim jazz artists were able to combat this racism through networking and sharing insider knowledge that, according to Gillespie, enabled them to prosper."[20] Those who made protest music did so out of real conviction, not to sell records.

In August 2002 Hill performed for the first time at the Beirut Blue Note Café. The performance was covered by Lebanon's *Daily Star* journalist Barnaby Skinner, who asked if Hill's improvised music connected to the legacy of African American musicians who rooted their creative labor in radical political consciousness. Hill responded, "Jazz isn't and has never been a political vessel. It's only about music; music has a right of its own."[21] This comment is representative of Hill's refusal to limit improvised music to political discursive formations relative to Black nationalism. He claimed to be more focused on art. French jazz critics Philippe Carles and Jean-Louis Comolli argue that African American free jazz improvisers who deny that their improvisations and compositions are political statements are incorrect about their creative practice not being shaped by politics. As the writers explain, "free jazz musicians produce work that is inevitably politically inscribed, not only because these musicians live at the heart of the same economic and racial contradictions as the Black masses . . . , but because their musical work targets the musical effects of these contradictions on jazz."[22] According to their reasoning, Black improvisers, and African Americans in general, cannot escape the effect of structural racism brought on by America's overwhelming participation in the transatlantic slave trade and the country's no less violent background in settler colonialism.[23] Hill is not a free jazz artist, yet Carles and Comoli would likely argue that Hill is subject to the same systemic forces that marginalize Black people. Therefore, Hill is a political musician whether he self-identifies as one or not.

In his study of Black artists and cultural politics, art historian Darby English argues that rigid ideas of Blackness are an unsustainable foundation for creating historical discourses on art, due to the multivalent complexity of Black modernist artistic production.[24] The Black artists whom English cites for his analysis believe that art has its own formulations, internal structure, and language, and that these are disconnected from ideological platforms rooted in "compensatory" cultural politics that focus on racial injustice:

What makes blackness an untenable groundwork for historical knowledge about art is the work of art's inseparable connection to concepts of art that bear no relation to the emplacements of culturalist ideology. I am talking about the part of art that is of the realm of things, that resists racing, gendering, et cetera, no matter how much these categories may mean to its maker or interpreter. When it comes to art by black Americans, though, advocates for the object's share have been few. *Black art and African American art history secure their conceptual coherency through a denial of the art in black art—this precedes a corresponding compensation on the side of the black* [my emphasis].[25]

Similarly, cultural historians often write about the politics of African American improvisers while ignoring the creative practice of improvising. The creative labor of African American musicians does not conform to any single political framework because its creators do not typically make allegiances to any single political cause. The prescriptive politics of the Black Arts movement was anathema to many African American improvisers, despite their strong belief in racial equality and other social justice issues. This is why Hill believed the work of African American musicians in the 1960s and early 1970s was being incorrectly framed by journalists as race music or hate music. This framing was incongruent with his philosophy and musical goals. Hill believed that Black musicians who performed overtly politically based improvised music alienated audiences and blocked possibilities of emotional connection.

Around the time Hill released *Compulsion* (1967), African American writer Ishmael Reed published an article called "The Black Artist: Calling a Spade a Spade."[26] Reed argued that even if a Black artist denied the influence of Black culture as the key framework for his or her art, Black culture still played a role in how one practiced art. Reed pejoratively compared Black artists who claimed their art transcended Blackness to a "buck-toothed and refined humanist," stating Black artists who foreground their Blackness in their work "will liberate those museums" and make America "swing once more."[27]

African American artist Raymond Saunders took issues with Reed's essay on Black authenticity and, in a partial retort, wrote the self-published pamphlet *Black Is a Color*.[28] This dialogue between Reed and Saunders illustrates the tension surrounding the question of Black authenticity in relation to art and music. Saunders believed that such frameworks reduced Black artists to political agents first and artists second. Two sentences of Saunders's essay are worth quoting at length here:

> certainly the american black artist is in a unique position to express certain aspects of the current american scene, both negative and positive, but if he restricts himself to these alone, he may risk becoming a mere cypher, a walking protest, a politically prescribed stereotype, negating his own mystery, and allowing himself to be shuffled off into an arid overall mystique. the indiscriminate association of race with art, on any level—social or imaginative—is destructive.[29]

Saunders believed the first priority of the Black artist was to make art that spoke to the whole human condition and not just the Black point of view. Trumpeter and composer Ambrose Akinmusire echoes Saunders's argument a generation later when he says, "We are not a protest song" (see chapter 4). Saunders also believed that imbuing art with messages of protest brought cynicism to the creative process: "pessimism is fatal to artistic development. perpetual anger deprives it of movement. an artist who is always harping on resistance, discrimination, opposition, besides being a drag, eventually plays right into the hands of the politicians he claims to despise—and is held there, unwittingly (and witlessly) reviving slavery in another form. For the artist this is aesthetic atrophy."[30] Saunders explains the irony of the protest artist fighting for freedom but being locked into an identity of protest, thereby being reduced to a political caricature. In many ways, Hill echoed

Saunders's stance when he stated that jazz has never been primarily a political art form. It is not my goal to label Hill as political or apolitical. Whether or not Hill defined his music as political or apolitical is not the core point. I only reiterate that Hill's music is contingent on understanding how the music is perceived within institutional power structures and social hierarchies. As Ingrid Monson explains, " . . . existing social structures empower individuals differently, according to their place in a configuration of social hierarchies and institutional organizations. Hence it is important to consider the social categories to which an individual belongs, as well as a person's position within institutional organizations. . . . Black and white musicians occupied different positions within this racially defined institutional and economic structure that musical communion alone could not alter."[31]

In contradistinction to Carles and Comolli's formulation and Ishmael Reed's general critique of Black artists who try to transcend race, Hill's positioning of his music as above politics and nationalism was never about transcending race. His goal was to produce Black musical space in ways that did not openly signify protest. Hill did not state jazz was apolitical because he was being ingenuous; rather, he showed political astuteness by positioning his improvised respatialization and musical space-making as oppositional knowledge to the hegemonic institutions of nationalism and white music criticism that circumscribes the creative potentiality of Black improvised musical expression in order to codify, crown, and commercialize.

Andrew Hill talked about race and Black humanity as it related to his composition "Nicodemus" in a rare radio interview on *Piano Jazz* with Marian McPartland on February 24, 2005.[32] His return to New York City sparked renewed interest in his work and he was now being seen as an artist who made an important contribution to American music. At the beginning of the radio interview, Hill performed his 5/4 composition "Nicodemus," then mentioned that he had named the piece "after a town that used to exist in Ohio." Hill explained: "So I heard the story, and you know, sometimes you write these compositions and don't have titles for it so I said well, that's a good title for it, 'Nicodemus.'"[33] It's not unusual for composers to write music first and then give the composition a title, imposing a meaning on sound. But Hill's explanation of the idea behind his composition "Nicodemus" was scant. Given the lack of evidence and Hill's habit of being mysterious and often coy with sharing information, I cannot say definitively that the socially conscious Hill was alluding to the profound history behind the biblically inspired moniker. And while the following narrative must be qualified as theoretical, its it is still worth exploring what imaginary connection Hill may have had to the historical town called Nicodemus.

First, there was no town called Nicodemus in Ohio, as Hill claims. Nicodemus was a town in Kansas, founded in 1877 and settled by formerly enslaved Black people between Reconstruction and the beginning of Jim Crow—"one of the first all-black settlements in Kansas, and the sole remaining western town founded by and for African Americans" in that era.[34]

For the newly freed former slaves of Nicodemus, its naming by that community signified a Black reinterpretation of the biblical character Nicodemus.[35] The biblical story in which he appears was symbolically powerful to African Americans because of his secret encounter at night with Jesus, who commanded Nicodemus to be "born again."[36] Nighttime was a crucial period when enslaved Blacks practiced Black Christianity in Invisible Churches. Night was also the time when enslaved African Americans ran away from plantations, sometimes only temporarily escaping the horror of slavery. For enslaved Black people, the rebirth of Nicodemus went beyond the white Christian's notion of salvation. Rebirth for them symbolized the constant renewal of spirit in order to thrive under the surveillance of the plantocracy.

For free Blacks, according to historian Rosamond Rodman, Nicodemus signified their refusal to be identified as slaves after they had moved out of the Confederacy to a free state. Rather than assimilate to white culture, the free Black residents of Nicodemus created a new spatialized epistemology of Blackness, one rooted in rebirth and a disavowal of slave identity. Hill may have been aware of the history concerning this Black settlement—he proved to be politically astute in several interviews over the course of his life. If he did know this backstory, he chose not to share the entire story on the air. As I have already noted, Hill showed a pattern of averting controversial positions.

Following his performance of "Nicodemus," he performed his composition "Blue Black." In the discussion after the performance, Hill revealed more of his philosophy about race and music to his radio host. McPartland commented that Hill's highly chromatic composition was appropriately titled, due to its unique range of musical colors.[37] Her theoretical appraisal focused on understanding Hill's creative process relative to harmony. But Hill pivoted to make a statement about how the idea of racial diversity was signified in his harmonic movement and chord voicings: "It's called 'Blue Black' based upon original Black men et cetera, but it's inclusive of all the races, 'cause like you said, it's something from every various [harmonic] color thrown into it and projected, and that's why I call it 'Blue Black'—not that it's just representative of one culture, but it's representative of all the cultures."[38] Hill's definition of blue Blackness, related to the production of musical space, was rooted in his belief in racial harmony reflected in his broader perspective on the human condition.

"Street Approach to Jazz Improvisation"

Though Hill was often not forthcoming about his musical philosophy to the press or to his bandmates, he did write an incomplete 1994 document titled "Project Acculturation" that offers some insight on his philosophy toward music. Written when he was a part-time artist in residence and jazz ensemble coach at Portland State University (PSU) during the 1990s, "Project Acculturation" reads like a preamble to a larger theoretical work on improvised music and Black musical space—a type of mission statement about reinvigorating institutional jazz programs through bringing a "street approach to jazz improvisation." This, Hill's central thesis, states that real progress in learning improvisation comes from interaction with more experienced improvisers and a reliance on one's musical intuition.

Hill wanted to expand the Black community's model of jazz apprenticeships, in which older Black musicians taught younger Black improvisers how to improvise in jam sessions outside of formal, institutional spaces. Musicians like Hill had been taught not traditional music theory but how to generate a sound on their instrument. As I note in chapter 4, Ambrose Akinmusire learned improvisation in a similar way, from direct relationships with older Black musicians who took him shopping for jazz records at flea markets. Elder statesmen of jazz who are hired to teach in jazz programs such as School of Jazz at the New School in New York City often complain that the improvisation they hear today has lost its sonic individuality. In his study of the institutionalization of improvisation, Anthropologist Eitan Wilf quotes a seasoned improviser who illuminates this binary between music learned in "the street" compared to music learned in the conservatory:

> . . . there's no *street* in it. And there are no characters! Everybody is so leveled down! . . . In those days your first goal was to get your own sound no matter what instrument you played to establish your individuality so people would know who you are. I have a hard time telling anybody from anybody else these days because there are very few distinctive, really distinctive sounds, because that's not part of the thing anymore.[39]

Jazz musician and musicologist Ken Prouty asserts that the majority of jazz programs align themselves with codified pedagogies of jazz because they must create manageable and "respectable" curriculums on which those jazz programs stand. This allegiance to codified methodologies reflect Eurological approaches to teaching music rooted in Western European art music and by default dismisses alternative approaches to teaching improvised music knowledge that extends from the archives of street knowledge:

> The institutional narrative excludes many of the important processes by which the techniques of jazz were transformed and formalized into a viable academic practice. Intentional or not, this can be seen as an attempt to more closely identify with the *institutional* community rather than the *jazz* community . . . by placing itself squarely within the institutional community, jazz education sought to pacify its institutional critics by emphasizing its relationship to *their* methods and histories, rather than its ties to a larger jazz community.[40]

Because we live in a capitalist society built on the rubric of white spatiality, improvised music continues to be practiced within a larger struggle for resources and racial ownership. Attempts at owning an art form in the political economy of jazz often translates into codification of musical expression. Sociologist Herman Gray argues that jazz generates its vitality outside of institutions that attempt to codify the art form through attempting to canonize its musical gestures and repertoire and painting this sidewinder musical expression in the lifeless colors derived from the politics of respectability: "the locations and conditions of production where jazz maintains its motion and movement, innovation and expansion, continue in those cultural spaces outside canonical discourses and institutional practices of legitimation."[41] Gray's comments dovetail with the spirit of Hill's theory about how one should approach the pedagogy of improvised music. Hill's definition of his "street approach to jazz improvisation" is worth quoting here at length (with misspellings and grammatical errors conserved, to stay true to the original archival document):

> When jazz was part of the black community, aspiring musicians could serve their apprenticeship in the streets by participating in the many jam sessions held on Blue Monday or sit in with local and guest musicians. Musicians twelve (12) to ninty [*sic*] (90) years of age would assemble on the same stage to play together. The younger musicians were given the fundamentals of sound during the intermission which enables the younger musicians to correct any error they made on the bandstand and improve their sound at each session. Most of the young musicians became working musicians within eight months.[42]

The "fundamentals of sound" part of Hill's treatise points to Hill's sense of Black musical space-making in the alternative music schools of the Bronzeville Black community in South Side Chicago. Hill later spoke of a certain intangible feeling in Black spaces, one linked to how generations of Black people had listened to music: "You go in there and it was a certain feeling . . . people weren't just lying with their heads back. The audience was very much into the music. They've been listening to it since slavery."[43] Hill valued the alternative musical education he had received from the Black community on the streets of Chicago, where learning from his musician elders provided a direct way to submerge himself in rich cultural information. In the year before his death he claimed he no longer heard the practice of Black musical spatio-temporality in present-day improvisation because, as he explained, "The musicians became more literate and more into self, so they started playing for the literate crowd and forgot the people who pay at the door."[44] Hill felt the community sound he loved was absent and that, as his interviewer remarked, "it had a different feel to the jazz of white players. 'But now,' [Hill] says, 'there's no difference. It's like white jazz survived and black jazz died.'"[45] Hill was critical of the elitism of Western musical theory pedagogy for its traditional emphasis on labeling music through the use of memorized theoretical terms instead of learning music in a more lived, less abstract way: "The aim of street approach to jazz improvisation is to take the emphasis off non-functional labels; example, atonal music. Jazz musicians negate tonality through free use of all tonality. In the blues non-diatonic notes seek a balance among all twelve notes of the chromatic scale."[46]

Hill viewed the Western, *diatonic* music system of tonality, which is based on the hierarchical theory of how chord progressions should move in various keys, as limiting, and wrote that there were alternative systems of tonality in the world. Criticizing such Western labels as *atonality*, which indicates the absence of a tonic base or key, he understood that African American improvisers worked beyond this basic system of tonality develop their own theories of harmony. It is clear that he connected his most important training and growth with cultural values rooted in his experience with the communal Black musical spaces within his community.

Hill likely had an uphill battle bringing his street approach into music institutions grounded in Western European art music training practices. In fact, he believed that most young jazz musicians he encountered had an abundance of technique and book knowledge but no feeling for the music: "Before, people were saying 'such and such is playing by ear and they're a natural musician.' And the natural musician seems to have some type of synergy with the audience. But now they are not natural musicians. They are academic musicians who come out wanting to do their own thing, not recognising that jazz was communal, it was shared and participated in by audiences."[47] Monson argues that such statements by African American improvisers—that Black improvised music was more "natural"—buttressed stereotypes about Black musicians as adverse to exploring theoretical frameworks and "had an effect of 'deauthenticating' a long history of Black intellectual engagement with music by associating the abstract and intellectual with whiteness."[48] Yet it is important to understand that Hill was not indicting intellectual engagement or prodigious technique. He was criticizing institutionalization; what he understood as the application of rigorous value systems of musical institutions that focus on performance practices that devalue or ignore the most important aspect of music performance: creating human connection through sound. In the process of musical training, mastering technique and learning repertoire, many musicians have forgotten—and in some cases can no longer express with clarity—the fundamental reasons why they became musicians in the first place. But they have technique. In contrast, the "natural" musician has never let go of or forgotten that initial, most intrinsic, attraction to the sonic art. Hill understood it as the feeling of the street in the "natural" musician. The "natural" is only the regeneration of that basic impulse that motivates improvisers to do their work in a society where many music listeners prefer recognizable forms of sonic art as they would prefer the predictability of a chain restaurant.

Hill's 1966 comments about the political economy of jazz and the need to subsidize jazz musicians who were trying to learn improvisation dovetail with his writings about the street approach: "Why not give an award to musicians coming up and trying to make a living so they can subsidize themselves? Sure, give scholarships to work on computers, work on plastics, or something that will pay for itself, but give grants to those who are already suffering in self-imposed poverty."[49] Hill's passionate argument for such subsidies was connected to his imagining a place where musicians composed without the pressures of conforming to the demands of the marketplace. He stated his occupational objective as follows: "To compose and perform without the constriction of the market-place, so I can continue to make quality performances available to all people, creating a situation where neophytes both young and old can participate in a positive environment that would enhance their lives."[50] Though he may not have achieved this "hilltopian" goal, Hill's vision of an ideal, inclusive musical space, rooted in the values of Black place-making, reveals a musician missing his community sound and lamenting how the jazz music business had evolved to cater primarily to the elites. I now turn to an exploration of Hill's approach to improvisation and composition.

Unified Fragmentation

I have coined the neologism "unified fragmentation" to describe Hill's practice of improvised respatialization. This term takes into account Hill's pointillist sound of musical fragmentation through melodic interval formation, ghost chords, and floating rhythm within his larger wave of sound. Just as seashells wash up on shore within a wave, those individual melodic fragments performed by Hill create a radiant array of colors within his sonic surge. Hill often ignored the notated map of music that he himself created, improvising in a way that defied Western time constructions, creating pianistic wave crests that functioned within their own logic and musical space. Hill's piano technique was often described by music critics as staccato, but his fragmented playing was integrated in the sonic sphere of the legato of his piano pedaling.

In Hill's performance (analyzed below) of "Malachi," for example, the haunting specter of uneven, cascading notes and chords he plays is soaked in the foggy gloss of his pedal work, telling a story of harmonic maps that ebb and flow, with intermittent, sharp finger attacks on the black-and-white topography of the keyboard.

Hill's fragmented playing reflected the way that he spoke: in subtle, asymmetrical utterances that require study to ascertain his deeper, more hidden layer of knowledge. His former colleague and founder of the Portland State University (PSU) Jazz Studies program, Charley Gray, remembers the way Hill spoke to his and Hill's students: "Andrew always communicated in short, deliberate sentences. He seemed to take time to express his thoughts just right and in the fewest words. I think this was partially a way of working around a slight speech impediment and an attempt to express thoughts in an original way."[51] Though Gray approached Hill about conducting an oral history, "Hill said, respectfully, no," because he focused on the future and not on the past.[52] Gray's oral history project would have put Hill in a position of looking back on his career when he was determined to look forward. His reticence toward retrospection has been the central challenge of this chapter: how to write about a musician concerned much more about what lay ahead than about his legacy, who cared about his compositions but was often not careful with how he documented and stored them. Hill's forward thinking was manifested in his approach to spontaneous composition or improvised space-making.

Analysis of Hill's "Malachi" (2006)

Bassist Malachi Favors (1927–2004), known for his timekeeping, ability to improvise melodic counterpoint, and Pan-African worldview, was a long-time friend of Andrew Hill and the bassist in his first prominent piano trio during 1955–59.[53] Favors played on Hill's first album, *So in Love* (1960; recorded 1955). He later joined composer and pianist Muhal Richard Abrams's

Experimental Band in 1961, which later evolved into the Association for the Advancement of Creative Musicians (AACM). Favors was also a member of the Art Ensemble of Chicago for thirty-five years. "Malachi," the tribute Hill composed to honor his friend and fellow creator of Black musical space, demonstrates Hill's concepts of such space through his musical strategies of melodic, rhythm, and harmonic invention. His solo piano performance in this piece reveals Hill as a master of orchestrating, sonic texture with his hands and creating a sonic wall of pedaled imbrication with his feet.

A Timeline Method

The time signature notated for Hill's melodic line in "Malachi" is 3/2, suggesting the half note as a rhythmic unit. Yet this time signature, indicated in musical example 5.1, is only a suggestion, and is typically ignored in both the ensemble and solo piano performances of "Malachi" on the *Time Lines* (2005) album. Consequently, the musical score of "Malachi" functions only as a reference point and not as literal notation. These half notes, quarter notes, and rests are a proportional representation, a guide to the actual music Hill performed as a solo pianist or with members of his band onstage.

Hill has a unique way of composing haunting melodies. The contour of his melodic writing rises and falls in unpredictable ways yet reveals a clear pattern. "Malachi" is held together by six separate melodic phrases in a twelve-measure form that contain valuable information regarding how Hill thought about melodic invention.

In the first phrase, Hill opens m. 1 of the melody by writing an ascending and descending perfect fifth pattern of notes A–E, followed in the second measure with a whole step to B. The note B in m. 2 ascends to a stepwise melody from D–E–F. In the third measure and second phrase, Hill varies the first melodic gesture with a leap of a major seventh F ascending to E, followed by a step down to D in m. 4. F–E is the widest interval in musical example 5.1 so far, but is surpassed at the end of the third phrase (B–A–B–A–D–E–F) in mm. 5–6 when F crosses the bar line and drops an octave from F–F in mm. 6–7. The descending three-note pattern of C–B–A in m. 4 answers the rising three-note pattern in m. 2, although the two phrases contrast in rhythmic phrasing: the first follows a half note in m. 2, whereas the second, in m. 4, descends immediately at the measure's start.

Measure 5 with repeated notes B and A creates a variation of the first phrase in mm. 1–2 by repeating the first note of m. 1 (A) and the first note of m. 2 (B), which creates a cell of intervallic tension released in m. 6. This musical gesture in m. 6, the last three notes of the third phrase (B–A–B–A–D–E–F), is a repetition of notes D–E–F, first written in m. 2. Measures 7–8, which features notes F–E–A–E–F–G–F (tied to F of the following quarter-note triplets), is the fourth phrase and in a lower register, is harmonized with Hill's oscillating B minor 7 (♭5) and F major7 chords during his solo performance.

Musical example 5.1. My transcription of "Malachi" into concert key as Hill performs it on *Time Lines* (2006). This was transposed one whole step down from the original B♭ score for tenor saxophone found in the Hill archive so the transcription would reflect the harmonic sound of Hill's solo piano version.

Since the notes repeat, m. 8 is a short extension of the melodic idea in the third phrase of m. 7 (B–A). The last two notes of the quarter-note triplet, B–C, begin a melodic ascent to a descending three-note pattern of half notes in m. 9, a rhythmic augmentation of the other stepwise three-note ascending and descending patterns throughout this twelve-bar form.

These three half notes—G, F, followed by a minor third descent to D— prepare a pathway to the climax of A, the highest note of the piece, above the staff. Measure 11 repeats m. 3 in both notes and durations. The most interesting melodic sound in "Malachi" is how Hill crafts the ending of the sixth phrase that begins in m. 11, landing on D, the eleventh of an A minor11 chord (the chord is not shown here but can be heard on the recording). Hill accomplishes this sound through the melodic route that begins in m. 12 from the G that is the seventh of A minor followed through by F to the final D. This is Hill's own idiosyncratic way of creating a cadence in the melodic space.

Hill's melodic writing reveals patterns that occur in unpredictable and asymmetrical places in his score. This reflects his understanding of musical space, which is revealed in how he avoids melodic clichés and codified standard compositional forms—an understanding also conveyed by what I call his "ghost chords."

Ghost Chords in the Solo Piano Performance of "Malachi"

Andrew Hill's use of *ghost chords* in "Malachi"—those implicitly created, though not necessarily played, through remnants of tones shared by other chords—shows his conception of harmonic fluency between the chords

F major 7th (or *F–A–C–E*), B minor 7th (♭5) (or *B–D–F–A*), and A minor (11) (or *A–C–E–G–B–D*). Like many of the notated compositions I viewed in the Hill archive, however, "Malachi" has no chord changes or harmonies written below the melody. I transcribed the three chord scheme by listening to the recording.

Hill appears not to have thought of harmonic rate, the movement of chords in a composition, as connected to a strict number of chords per bar. Instead, he considered harmony in a way that allowed him to cross bar lines, which helped him avoid harmonic stasis. In other words, his chordal patterns unfolded asymmetrically. Hill created the compositional form but then deliberately left the form behind in his performances.

The chords that Hill played are loosely connected to the phrases in "Malachi." Hill discussed this harmonic strategy of common-note relationships, that is, connecting several chords through shared notes, a few months before the recording sessions: "F7 really remind[s] me of an opportunity to play in two keys at once, because you have a A♭ and you have a F." Hill went on to imply that you can superimpose either the A♭ major scale or the B♭ dominant seventh scale over the F7 chord.[54] While it is unclear to me which scale Hill is referring to, his way of thinking about common tones in chord relationships is not peculiar to Hill. Many advanced improvisers use common tones to improvise through chord changes. Yet Hill combined chords in his own idiosyncratic way, creating a unique sense of spatiality.

Hill's melodic and harmonic improvisations on "Malachi" avoid musical clichés by employing short, single melodic lines mixed with percussive groups of semitones. His strategy of playing permutations of two-, three-, and four-note clusters creates *harmonic ambiguity*. The result of not spelling out with clear chord voicings what the chord is strategically denies the listener a clear idea of the harmonic sequence of the composition. Whereas other pianists, such as Bill Evans, often voiced 7th-chord voicings absent the root, the educated listener still had a general idea of the chord quality. Hill, though, used this improvisational strategy, creating tone clusters in his left and right hands, over the course of his career. Biochemist and musicologist Roger T. Dean explains, "Hill uses clusters systematically, sometimes only two adjacent semitones, much more often several notes in a range of four tones. This again helps from time to time to dispel any sense of tonal centre, and it depends partly for that effect on its regular intermittent juxtaposition with clear tonal implications."[55] I disagree with Dean that Hill was trying to imply tonality in any form: Hill understood Western tonality on a deep level, and that was his platform for leaving the system altogether.

Hill's signature tone cluster voicings relate to his unconventional construction of melodies. Hill did not perform set harmonies for "Malachi" because he did not want to be held to one particular harmonic color linked with any melodic phrase of the piece. Beyond that, Hill's performance of Black musical space extended beyond his use of common tones across various chords. His overall conception of sound and his approach to the performance of "Malachi" were evidence of a deep framework of Black musical space that represented adherence to form while always expanding that form in real time.

Ride the Rhythm

Andrew Hill had an open approach to rhythm that was connected to his melodic writing. Hill credited the alto saxophonist Charlie Parker for teaching him the concept of "melody as rhythm."[56] Hill's former PSU colleague Charley Gray stated that he observed Hill's approach to teaching rhythm in improvisation: "He was very much into rhythm, I remember a phrase he used a lot, 'ride the rhythm.' He didn't explain it much. He left it up to you to figure out what it meant."[57] Hill's approach to teaching "ride the rhythm" reflects a sink-or-swim street theory pedagogy historically practiced by Black male bandleaders who believed experiencing an idea musically was more important than a lengthy verbal explanation of a musical concept. Hill was communicating his idea of rhythm to PSU students within the context of Black musical space at a predominantly white institution of higher learning. I believe Hill saw rhythm as an open form, and that trying to dominate the rhythm would lead to predictable, linear, repetitive grooves. Such grooves, being both memorable and easily understood, are used to market music as a *product*, but they do not foster inspiration for improvisation. Being free of repetitive grooves allows more space for playing complex melodic and harmonic rhythms, especially when advanced improvisers always know where they are in the compositional form.

The rhythmic complexity that Hill achieved through his collective and solo performances challenged his audiences throughout his career. Yet Hill did not conceive of his music and improvising as "free" or "avant-garde." As a composer, he believed in the structure and clarity of compositional forms, and he was always aware of the compositional form while improvising within the form. Bassist Calvin Jones, who played with Hill as a sideman in the 1990s, told me about Hill's deep awareness of his own compositional forms:

The one thing that took me to many places each night, besides Andrew's great sense of melody, was his freedom to play whatever he heard yet always knowing where he was in the form. He would play something incredible and out of nowhere hit a note from the melody of the song form. It was the most extraordinary thing I ever heard. Hill had complete awareness of his complex song form at all times, no matter the freedom or context of the improvisation.[58]

From Hill, Jones learned how to be open and allow creativity to thrive within himself. Here he articulates what he learned from performing with Hill in the 1990s: "I would say, let the music drive itself (don't try to micromanage) and to always be present during the journey (know where you are in midst of the growth and dynamics of what's going on at all times)."[59] This is truly an apt definition of riding the rhythm, and from a sideman who learned lessons about musical space-making from Hill. Roger Dean argues that Hill's performance of polyphonic rhythm was most obvious when he played with his ensemble, "who could play in strongly pulsed music almost as if without regard for the pulse, while yet remaining acutely aware of its status and position."[60] Although I agree with Dean, it is important to assess Hill's polyphonic rhythmic strategy within the context of his lived experiences, which motivated him to avoid creative complacency. Hill desired to foster a musical experience that kept him, his ensemble, and his audience on edge. Jumping into the abyss of musical space that Cornel West describes in my quote of him in the introduction, Hill rode rhythm believing he was going to fall on something. Knowing that he had no control over the music, Hill surrendered to the creative process to access the unknown. This is why I believe that terms like syncopation, polyrhythm, and hemiola (three beats against two, or vice versa) fail in the description of Hill's sound and overall music strategies, and quite honestly, Black music in general. These common musical terms suggest that Hill tried to impose order on the music or tried to control the outcome.

In conclusion, much of the academic scholarship on pianist and composer Andrew W. Hill avoids discussion of the man behind the complex music. Scholars have been much more comfortable analyzing his compositional and improvisational strategies while ignoring the political and social context that formed his musical practices. I suppose on some level this is understandable. Hill rejected labels, obscured his biography, and disavowed his placement in the teleological discursive formations called jazz history. He positioned the story of his life and his music on his own terms. Yet it is clear to this writer that Hill's statements throughout his life about race, space, and music reveal a multivalent understanding of his racial positionality.

Hill's "street approach to jazz improvisation" theory represents "a self-actuated quest for knowledge and understanding."[61] He would not be confined by the traditional rhetoric of jazz theory though his archive reveals clear respect for mastering the formal elements of Western music theory. While he did not write a complete treatise on his theory of composition and improvisation, Hill's commitment to musical nonconformity was reflected in how he avoided conventional articulations of musical Blackness in codified jazz forms. His "self-actuated quest for knowledge and understanding" was focused not on himself but on bringing street music theory relative to improvisation into music institutions by exposing students and colleagues to the alternative improvisation school born out of the segregated Black community.

Hill respected his own timeline. His understanding of his own Black sense of musical place was demonstrated in not conforming to codified Black musi-cal styles. He did not work in the socially accepted sonic codes of Blackness dictated by the capitalist music business and blessed by the mainstream jazz gatekeepers. I would hope that other music scholars explore how his complex, non-monochromatic politics shaped his musical practices based on an approach to music that questioned all conventional improvised and compositional forms.

EPILOGUE

The Sonic Archive of Black Spatiality

I don't think it speaks to getting older. I think it speaks more so to understanding space, and our relationship to space, and how much of it exists.[1]
—Saul Williams

Empowerment? You can't empower me. People have all the atoms they need. We impose meaning on structures.[2]
—Douglas Ewart

While writing this book I discovered that I was writing not about African American improvisers and their music as much as about the luminescence of Blackness manifested in the improvised expression of humanity. This required working outside the confines of what constitutes musical knowledge while remaining in conversation with the vocabularies of the accepted musicological orthodoxy. Traditional musicology is rooted in the philosophy of positivism, where statements about music must be backed up by evidence and a perceived critical distance from the research subject. This is why music analysis has been linked to formalism.[3] Joseph Kerman explained: "Musicology is perceived as dealing essentially with the factual, the documentary, the verifiable, the analysable, the positivistic. Musicologists are respected for the facts they know about music. They are not admired for their insight into music as an aesthetic experience."[4]

This book does not abandon positivism. After all, I have done my due diligence of verifying my claims with citations and, in some case chapters, detailed musical transcriptions of improvised music. As an African American improviser, composer, and theorist, I have approached this book by never privileging traditional research musicological methods over my lived experience, as well as the lived experiences of the improvisers I discuss in this book. This book will hopefully provide further insight into the relationship between African American improvised music and cultural notions of spatiality in relation to improvisation. The lived experiences of musicians is an equally valid base of knowledge, even more so over the application of objective musicology. Poet Aimé Césaire said: "scientific knowledge enumerates, measures, classifies and kills."[5] I have the same aims as other critical musicologists but I have tried to present my truth about African American improvisation and politics in the most honest way possible. Call me a practitioner and theorist of Black musical space.

Black musical place-making operates on the outside of the dominant Western house of music aesthetics because Black people have been placed on the outside of that house.[6] Practitioners of Black musical space resist the dominant notion of Western aesthetics because Black musical space is not concerned with defining beauty in that way. Freeing ourselves from the aesthetic straitjacket of beauty defined by whiteness has meant that African American improvisers find liberation in what is often considered grotesque cacophony. The distorted, bending pitch of Akinmusire's trumpet and keyboard performances is one example of how his rubric of the raw, glistening heart is about the search for the realness of human expression. In this sense the phrase Black musical space has disavowed the common associations with the word Blackness in relation to space: emptiness, void, or negativity. Blackness here is understood as a productive, fluid space that features the wealth of Black value and imagination, an ontological portal to endless possibilities in musical practices.

Black musical space is not defined by a defiance of whiteness or white supremacy. It is defined by joy, struggle ad infinitum, and reliance on community. The well-known performance artist Marina Abramović has written, "I constantly create systems that allow me to be free again."[7] In contrast, African American improvisers create musical space not to free themselves or their community again, but to affirm their humanity—in the first place—through vibrant musical practices. For African American improvisers, musical systems are only useful insomuch as they become platforms for expressing the immense radiance of Black humanity through the various instrumental mediums that become cornucopias of brilliance and risk taking.

I have not endeavored to reduce the improvised music that African American improvisers make to "socially and culturally categorized and evaluated" improvised sounds.[8] The theory of Black musical space is not about reducing improvised music to "essential markers" because Black musical space has no such markers.[9] Black musical space expressed through humanity ultimately escapes attempts to codify it. It can never be in vogue because it is not a style. Trumpeter Don Cherry remarked: "Style is the death of creativity."[10] Black musical space is both the blues riffs in the capable hands of Mary Lou Williams and the pointillistic, improvised cells in Henry Threadgill's music.

I have focused on how the improvisations and compositions of Blanchard, Higgins, Carrington, Akinmusire, and Hill articulate Black musical space, or what Nina Sun Eidsheim calls a "vibrational field."[11] In writing this book I have had no interest in canonizing or classifying Black musical space as a tangible category or school of music. When I asked pianist Andrew Hill for advice in 2006 in between sets at his Birdland show, he said, "Don't conform."[12] Similar to Fumi Okiji, who argues that the crack in vocalist Billie Holiday's voice should be made our own and used as an opportunity to take risks and fail in scholarship,[13] I believe that Black musical space is a theory of place-making through risking everything in musical practice, giving oneself to the possibility of failure in order to discover something new and truthful.

I have analyzed Black musical space through the theme of improvised breath in the activist work of trumpeter Terence Blanchard and drummer Billy Higgins's philosophy of creating community through sound. Whereas Blanchard meditates on Eric Garner's death and the struggle for Black people's collective ability to breathe freely in American society through orchestrating the continued sonic exhalation of breath textures, Higgins has shown the joy of Black life through improvising Black musical space by conducting himself and the band through his breath-inspired rhythmic phrases and melodies. Higgins promoted love through his music time and time again, showing us that Black musical space is about inclusion and not separatism.

Terri Lyne Carrington's socially scientific work of making musical space more inclusive provided an opportunity to explore Black feminist thought more closely as I endeavored to understand the arc of her political thought and growth as a socially conscious musician. At the end of the multivocal track "Bells," you hear the faint, almost subliminal, voice of spoken word artist Kasso Overall from 5:18 to 5:26, who states, "I am one of the people—who built this country / I am one of the people." This subtle recitation interchanges in a cross rhythm with Malcolm-Jamal Warner's saying of the word "Bells" that represent the morphing of police sirens church bells at a funeral. At that moment, the track at this juncture demonstrates the tragic juxtaposition of the often perceived fungibility of Blackness banging up against the evidence of African American cultural contributions to America. Indeed, I am one of the people who are building this country. The intersectionality of the social issues that Carrington brings to the fore in her revision of "Echo" has only grown more powerful in her musical commentary on *Waiting Game* (2019), which is both painful to hear and necessary to say.

Trumpeter Ambrose Akinmusire's work on drawing attention to the murder of African Americans by members of police departments in works like "My Name Is Oscar" (2011) and "Free, White and 21" (2018) articulate the immediacy of these life and death issues through his sonic strategies and performance art.[14] Akinmusire's goal is never to be musically innovative or to be identified as an innovator. His goal is to disappear in the music so the "lingering velocity" of his trumpet-playing forebears can live through him on the stage. While Akinmusire understands he can only communicate the events of his time, the spirits of trumpeter Lee Morgan and Booker Little, and other musicians, live through him.

Up to this point, there has been no scholarship on Andrew Hill that focuses on his understanding of the relationship between race and sound. While Hill's political stance appeared inconsistent throughout his career, he had clear opinions on Black sound and space. Akinmusire's and Hill's work are connected because they both talk about Black musical space as a feeling, an intangible phenomenon that extends from lived experiences. For Hill, it was a feeling missing in jazz, a feeling he first felt in his community on the segregated South Side of Chicago in the 1940s. Akinmusire prefers his art to remain intangible since making Black sonic art tangible is akin to institutionalizing and commodifying the music.

This book has not been about clever note placements or melodic, harmonic, or rhythmic phrases that cross a notational, organizing symbol called a bar line. This book has been about African American improvisers who express their positionality by articulating their life experience through sound. While Blanchard, Higgins, Carrington, Akinmusire, and Hill express their ideas differently in the language of Black musical space, they are all connected by how they cross bar lines to emphasize the social context connection between their lived experiences and their improvisational and compositional practices.

Black musical space-making is characterized by liminality and aims to be culturally inclusive of all expressions of humanity and all genders. Black musical space is open because it comes from the lived experiences of people who were treated like machines for capitalistic production for centuries and lynched due to anti-Blackness. Improvised music has been a welcoming space because Black people know what it means to have their humanity repeatedly questioned, challenged, disregarded. There is joy that that extends in improvising Black humanity. This joy does not come from overcoming the evil of white supremacy. Improvisation cannot solve racism. This joy comes from a recognition of one's humanity through creating space for affirming humanity through improvised music in the face of ongoing failed attempts at dehumanizing Black people. As Douglas Ewart states, we impose meaning on structures.

ACKNOWLEDGMENTS

Over the years I had to learn that successful scholarship is never done in isolation. As musicians, we learn to thrive in collaborative environments in order to achieve the highest gradations of musical expression. Sometimes a hostile climate encourages us to contract into ourselves, but that is exactly when we should reach out for help, because no one can do this work alone. I stand on the shoulders of scholars like Robin D. G. Kelley, who told me to trust my own ideas as I wrote this book. I thank him for the wonderful Foreword. Over twenty years ago, Kelley introduced me to the work of Cedric Robinson and the Black Radical Tradition. Kelley, Ingrid Monson, Fred Moten, Leonard Brown, George Lipsitz, Travis Jackson, Robert Walser, David Ake, George E. Lewis, Greg Tate, Sherrie Tucker and many others have set a high standard for scholarship on critical improvisation studies, and I thank them for their exemplary work. The Black Geographies scholarship of Katherine McKittrick helped me form the theoretical core of Black musical space. Artistic collaborator and mentor Fred Moten, who recommended McKittrick's work, has been an unselfish source of intellectual and artistic inspiration at my most difficult junctures in academia. The Black feminist thought of Patricia Hill Collins and Kimberlé Crenshaw, Audre Lorde, among other Black feminists have provided invaluable frames for much of this book. I am indebted to all of my fellow improvisers who allowed me to interview them for this text. They helped make this book the vibrant project it is. I have been fortunate to learn from Terence Blanchard, Billy Higgins, Terri

Lyne Carrington, Ambrose Akinmusire, and Andrew Hill. I am also grateful for Henry Threadgill, James Newton, Wadada Leo Smith, Nicole Mitchell, and community activist and poet Kamau Daáood. Sharing my writing with others gave me needed perspective.

I am immensely grateful to scholars who have read various drafts and individual chapters of this book. They include Robin D. G. Kelley, Fred Moten, Amy Kallander, Guthrie Ramsey, Theo Cateforis, Gayle Wald, and George Lipsitz. Lipsitz has especially lifted me up at a crucial time while growing as a scholar. I am equally thankful for the several anonymous readers, dedicated colleagues who helped shape this book with their constructive and helpful suggestions. Over the years, I received moral support and advice from Anthony Davis, Anthony Burr, Carrie Mae Weems, David Borgo, Norman Bryson, Kwame Dixon, Linda Carty, Ken Frieden, Amanda Eubanks Winkler, Gerald R. Greenburg, Karin Ruhlandt, Vivian May, Kimberly Blockett, Roshanak Kheshti, Wadada Leo Smith, Leonard Brown, John S. Burdick and Carla Ponti. Kamau Kenyatta introduced me to Terri Lyne Carrington's *Mosaic Project* and allowed me to use his UCSD music department office for several years so I could have a quiet space to write and think. Cecil Lytle has been a great life mentor, teacher, confidant, and model of human elegance. My colleague Maiya J. Murphy's support and friendship during our multi-year writing accountability fellowship in different time zones helped me through the writing process.

During the process of writing *Crossing Bar Lines*, I received research support from the Syracuse University Center and the SU Associate Provost for Faculty Affairs, LaVonda Reed. The librarians and staff at the Institute of Jazz at Rutgers University supported me with navigating the Andrew W. Hill archive. I am grateful to Robert G. O'Meally and the Jazz Study Group at the Center for Jazz Studies at Columbia University for allowing me to participate in the meetings. The Jazz Study Group experience, the fellowshipping with artists and scholars who treat improvisation as a serious research subject, partially laid the fertile soil for this book many years ago. Thanks to University Press of Mississippi Director Craig W. Gill, his wonderful and gracious team, and the university press board for helping me bring this multi-year book project to fruition. This book is dedicated to my parents Eulah Y. Williams and the late Robert Gordon Jemmott-Williams whose sacrifice, vision, and love provided opportunity of life, which allowed me to thrive and eventually write this book. Finally, I thank my very supportive partner Consuelo and my two sons Sebastian and Julian, all of whom sacrificed time with me over many years in order for me to complete this book. You continue to be a source of encouragement, strength, and love. I celebrate this musical space with you!

NOTES

Foreword

1. Ashon T. Crawley, *Black Pentecostal Breath: The Aesthetics of Possibility* (New York: Fordham University Press, 2017), p. 33.

Introduction: Entering a Theory of Black Musical Space

1. American painter Amy Sherald, who famously created a portrait of Michelle Obama, remarks how ironic it is that Black children are treated badly in the Museum of Fine Arts, Boston by staff and visitors when that work was meant to build up these very Black kids by disrupting a cultural space dominated by Euro-American art with her paintings. Her art is welcome but the Black children are not. See https://www.nytimes.com/interactive/2019/10/08/magazine/black-women-artists-conversation.html?searchResultPosition=2, accessed October 28, 2019.

2. bell hooks, "Choosing the Margin as a Space of Radical Openness," *Framework: The Journal of Cinema and Media* 36, no. 36 (1989): 23.

3. Nathaniel Mackey, "Breath and Precarity," in Myung Mi Kim and Cristanne Miller, ed., *Poetics and Precarity* (Albany: State University of New York Press, 2018), 13.

4. Robert Farris Thompson wrote about the philosophy of the people of Senegambia and how they created their textiles: randomizing the patterns, avoiding the congruency of straight lines in their functional art. Robert Farris Thompson, *Flash of the Spirit: African and Afro-American Art and Philosophy* (New York: Random House, 1983), 207–22.

5. During a sight-reading lesson with the drummer Dion Parsons in the late 1990s or early 2000s, he pointed to his electric piano and asked me to tell him what it was. It seemed like a silly question with an obvious answer until he told me what I should have known: that the instrument I played was a reflection of my mind, the way I thought about the world. In

my many years of conservatory and college training, no one had ever mentioned that. It was almost as if we were supposed to forget about our own minds, our own ideas, and kneel at the altar of jazz greats.

6. See Patricia Hill Collins, *Black Feminist Thought: Knowledge, Consciousness, and the Politics of Empowerment*, rev. 10th anniversary ed. (New York: Routledge, 2000).

7. Katherine McKittrick, "On Plantations, Prisons, and a Black Sense of Place," *Social & Cultural Geography* 12, no. 8 (2011): 947–63, 949.

8. Katherine McKittrick, "Rebellion/Invention/Groove," *Small Axe: A Caribbean Journal of Criticism* 20, no. 1(49) (2016): 87.

9. Katherine McKittrick, *Demonic Grounds: Black Women and the Cartographies of Struggle* (Minneapolis: University of Minnesota Press, 2006), 141.

10. hooks, "Choosing the Margin as a Space of Radical Openness," 23.

11. hooks, "Choosing the Margin as a Space of Radical Openness," 19.

12. hooks, "Choosing the Margin as a Space of Radical Openness," 19.

13. Transcription of Cornel West interview in conversation with Terence Blanchard about the Black aesthetic in jazz. This interview is woven throughout the composition in a conflation of verbal and musical Black texts. See Terence Blanchard, "Winding Roads," *Choices* (Concord Jazz, 2009).

14. Katherine McKittrick and Clyde Adrian Woods, *Black Geographies and the Politics of Place* (Cambridge, MA: Between the Lines, 2007), 6.

15. Camilla Hawthorne, "Black Matters are Spatial Matters: Black Geographies for the Twenty-first Century," *Geography Compass* (2019): 5.

16. McKittrick, *Demonic Grounds*, xix.

17. McKittrick, *Demonic Grounds*, xix.

18. Katherine McKittrick, "On Plantations, Prisons, and a Black Sense of Place," *Social & Cultural Geography* 12, no. 8 (2011): 949.

19. McKittrick, "On Plantations, Prisons, and a Black Sense of Place," 948.

20. McKittrick, "On Plantations, Prisons, and a Black Sense of Place," 949.

21. McKittrick, "On Plantations, Prisons, and a Black Sense of Place," 949.

22. McKittrick, "On Plantations, Prisons, and a Black Sense of Place," 949.

23. McKittrick, *Demonic Grounds*, xiv.

24. See George Lewis, *A Power Stronger than Itself: The AACM and American Experimental Music* (Chicago: University of Chicago Press, 2008); and Daniel Fischlin, Ajay Heble, and George Lipsitz, *The Fierce Urgency of Now: Improvisation, Rights, and the Ethics of Cocreation* (Durham, NC: Duke University Press, 2013).

25. Susan J. Smith, "Beyond Geography's Visible Worlds: A Cultural Politics of Music," *Progress in Human Geography* 21, no. 4 (1997): 502–29, 524.

26. Susan J. Smith, "Beyond Geography's Visible Worlds," 524.

27. Susan J. Smith, "Beyond Geography's Visible Worlds," 523.

28. Black scholars have long made these claims about Black music and positionality. For some examples, see W. E. B. du Bois, *The Souls of Black Folk,* Bantam classic ed. (New York: Bantam Books, 1989); Amiri Baraka, *Blues People: Negro Music in White America* (New York: W. Morrow, 1963); Amiri Baraka, *Black Music* (New York: Morrow, 1968); bell hooks, *Yearning: Race, Gender, and Cultural Politics* (Boston: South End Press, 1990). More contemporary Black scholars continue to discuss these issues of positionality today; see Fred Moten, *In the Break: The Aesthetics of the Black Radical Tradition* (Minneapolis: University of Minnesota Press, 2003); Ingrid T. Monson, *Freedom Sounds: Civil Rights Call Out to Jazz and Africa*

(New York: Oxford University Press, 2007); Rashida K. Braggs, *Jazz Diasporas: Race, Music, and Migration in Post–World War II Paris* (Oakland: University of California Press, 2016).

29. Susan J. Smith, "Beyond Geography's Visible Worlds," 519.

30. See Frank Kofsky, *Black Nationalism and the Revolution in Music* (New York: Pathfinder Press, 1970).

31. Susan J. Smith, "Beyond Geography's Visible Worlds," 518.

32. Susan J. Smith, "Beyond Geography's Visible Worlds," 517.

33. Robin D. G. Kelley, "Black Study, Black Struggle," *Boston Review* 41, no. 2 (2016): 1, 14.

34. Clyde Woods, "'Sittin' on Top of the World': The Challenges of Blues and Hip Hop Geography," in McKittrick and Woods, *Black Geographies and the Politics of Place*, 75.

35. McKittrick, "Rebellion/Invention/Groove," 89.

36. John Shepherd and Peter Wicke, *Music and Cultural Theory* (Malden, MA: Polity Press, 1997), 83.

37. See Nina Sun Eidsheim, *The Race of Sound: Listening, Timbre, and Vocality in African American Music* (Refiguring American Music) (Durham, NC: Duke University Press, 2019); Jennifer Stoever, *The Sonic Color Line: Race and the Cultural Politics of Listening* (New York: New York University Press, 2016).

38. David Ake, *Jazz Matters: Sound, Place, and Time since Bebop* (Berkeley: University of California Press, 2010), 35.

39. E. Patrick Johnson, *Appropriating Blackness: Performance and the Politics of Authenticity* (Durham, NC: Duke University Press, 2003), 19.

40. Henry Threadgill, phone interview by author, April 20, 2009.

41. Threadgill, phone interview.

42. George E. Lewis, Rio Negro II conference, Buffalo, NY, September 6, 2019.

43. Lewis, Rio Negro II conference.

44. Douglas Ewart, Rio Negro II conference, Buffalo, NY, September 6, 2019.

45. Threadgill, phone interview. Abbey Lincoln's "People in Me" appears on her album *Devil's Got Your Tongue* (Verve CD 314 513 574-2, 1992). Backed by a children's choir, Lincoln sings about all the people—she claims Jewish, Chinese, Burundi, Sierra Leone, Japanese, and Mexican—in her. She sermonizes through song about having French blood, Egyptian blood, and encapsulates it in the repeated phrase quoted by Threadgill: "I Got Some People in Me." Lincoln's "People in Me" also includes these lyrics: "Some say the world is hard and cold / and that it's hard to find a friend / but every time you're down and out / somebody takes us in." In the first scene of the music video for "People in Me," a young African American teacher is implementing a lesson plan on ethnic diversity in a noisy, diverse class of middle-school children. It is these children who become Lincoln's chorus. The teacher has "Ethnic Diversity" written on the blackboard, which foreshadows Lincoln's message of human inclusion. The video includes several images of a baby of color among foregrounded multicolored globes. https://youtu.be/wnX9PYQccOs, accessed March 3, 2019.

46. Eidsheim, *The Race of Sound*, 19.

47. Eidsheim, *The Race of Sound*, 19. For Eidsheim, the voice is not formed from unique, essential racial traits but from musical training over many years. Vocal performance is a multivalent performance of race, not race itself. It follows that the performances and compositions of improvisers I discuss in this study should not be viewed through a prism of essentialized racial characteristics that refracts their performances as Black.

48. Horne argues that part of the political economy of jazz is based in white improvisers and composers who continually try to erase Black innovations in regard to the music, while

claiming that they were the ones who could elevate the musical form to a higher standard. See Gerald Horne, *Jazz and Justice: Racism and the Political Economy of the Music* (New York: Monthly Review Press, 2019); Kofsky, *Black Nationalism and the Revolution in Music*.

49. Stoever, *The Sonic Color Line*.

50. Stoever, *The Sonic Color Line*, 7, 6.

51. Walser argues that analyzing jazz from a modernist's point of view is the wrong aesthetic approach for understanding how jazz is created and performed. Henry Louis Gates Jr.'s theory of "Signifyin(g)" is an analytical language that can more adequately address African American improvised performances. For more on musical signifyin', see Robert Walser, "Out of Notes: Signification, Interpretation, and the Problem of Miles Davis," *Musical Quarterly* 77, no. 2 (1993): 343–65. For the original discussion in the context of literary theory, see Henry Louis Gates Jr., *The Signifying Monkey: A Theory of Afro-American Literary Criticism* (New York: Oxford University Press, 1988). For the discussion on Eurological vs. Afrological approaches to music, see George E. Lewis, "Improvised Music after 1950: Afrological and Eurological Perspectives" [1996], *Black Music Research Journal* 22, Supplement: *Best of BMRJ* (2002): 215–46.

52. Leo Smith, *Notes (8 Pieces) Source, a New World Music: Creative Music* (New Haven, CT: Kiom Press, 1973), n.p.

53. Amiri Baraka, "Abbey Lincoln: Straight Ahead," *JazzTimes*, January 1, 2001. https://jazztimes.com/features/abbey-lincoln-straight-ahead/, accessed March 3, 2019.

54. Moten, *In the Break*, 39.

55. Moten, *In the Break*, 39.

56. Moten, *In the Break*, 39.

57. Fumi Okiji, *Jazz As Critique: Adorno and Black Expression Revisited* (Stanford, CA: Stanford University Press, 2018), 64. See also Fred Moten, "Blackness and Poetry," *Evening Will Come* 55 (July 1, 2015). https://arcade.stanford.edu/content/blackness-and-poetry-0, accessed March 3, 2019.

58. Okiji, *Jazz as Critique*, 68.

59. Sara Ahmed, "A Phenomenology of Whiteness," *Feminist Theory* 8, no. 2 (2007): 157.

60. Donald Jay Grout, *A History of Western Music* (New York: W. W. Norton, 1960); Amiri Baraka, *Blues People: Negro Music in White America* (New York: William Morrow, 1963).

61. Crossing bar lines can be seen on sheet music when a musical phrase is long enough to stretch beyond one measure and into another, and so literally cross a bar line. A musician, however, does not need to see notation to know when music crosses the bar lines: one can hear crossing at various gradations of intensity. In traditional Western music notation, the function of bar lines on a musical staff is to separate groupings of beats by measures in order to facilitate sight reading. Music crosses the bar lines when the phrase, generally asymmetrical, extends beyond one measure or bar. This off-the-beat phenomenon is typically called "syncopation," a word rooted in the Latin verb *syncopare*, which describes swooning or a fainting spell. Although bar lines were introduced so musicians could more easily read scores—compartmentalizing units of musical time within a single bar—bar lines represent musical values aesthetically incongruent with non-Western cultural spaces and communities (although music of all types crosses bar lines). In the same way that Google Maps is just one topographical representation of various cities, states, countries, and continents, traditional Western music notation is only one representation of music values.

62. Despite the global domination of Black music, Black innovators of the music continue to be seen as the Other. In fact, the aesthetic Otherness of Blacks had been reasserted

by white, male twentieth-century ethnomusicologists of African music who prioritized rhythm as its most important feature, codifying Black rhythmic Otherness by creating notational systems specifically for transcribing African rhythms. For more on this idea, see Kofi Agawu, "The Invention of 'African Rhythm,'" *Journal of the American Musicological Society* 48, no. 3 (1995): 380–95.

63. Charles W. Mills, *Blackness Visible: Essays on Philosophy and Race* (Ithaca, NY: Cornell University Press, 1998), 5.

64. Okiji, *Jazz as Critique*, 40.

65. Frank Wilderson defines African Americans as a "paradigmatic impossibility" in the West, and the inverse of what the West defines as a human subject. Frank B. Wilderson III, *Red, White and Black: Cinema and the Structure of U.S. Antagonisms* (Durham, NC: Duke University Press, 2010), 9. Despite the gains of the civil rights movement that culminated in the election of the first African American US president, the continued legacy of Black slavery as Black social death is evinced at present in the high rates of HIV infection, police violence in Black communities, and mass incarceration that has led to mass disenfranchisement. Modern forms of institutional slavery continue to function in "the convergence of the private property regime and the invention of racial blackness (which is to say the invention of antiblackness in the invention of whiteness . . .)." Jared Sexton, "The Social Life of Social Death: On Afro-Pessimism and Black Optimism," *InTensions* 5 (Fall/Winter 2011): 17, note 15. http://www.yorku.ca/intent/issue5/articles/jaredsexton.php, accessed March 3, 2019.

66. Frank B. Wilderson III, "Grammar and Ghosts: The Performative Limits of African Freedom," *Theatre Survey* 50, no. 1 (2009): 121.

67. Moten, *In the Break*, 99.

68. Moten, *In the Break*, 99.

69. For an excellent discussion of Thelonious Monk's struggles with adversity, see Robin D. G. Kelley, *Thelonious Monk: The Life and Times of an American Original* (New York: Free Press, 2009).

70. Samuel A. Floyd Jr., *The Transformation of Black Music: The Rhythms, the Songs, and the Ships of the African Diaspora* (New York: Oxford University Press, 2017), xxiv.

71. Floyd, *The Transformation of Black Music*, xxiv.

72. Portia K. Maultsby, "Africanisms in African American Music," in *Africanisms in American Culture*, 2nd ed., ed. Joseph E. Holloway (Bloomington: Indiana University Press, 2005), 330.

73. Aimé Césaire, "Poetry and Knowledge" [1945], trans. A. James Arnold, *Sulfur* 5.5 (1982): 17–32.

74. Two recent incidents come to mind: I was harassed when I was picking up my son from kindergarten in Torrance, California, in 2014, and by New Haven police while walking the streets of New Haven between presentations at a Yale University conference in 2012.

75. Sherrie Tucker, *Swing Shift: "All-Girl" Bands of the 1940s* (Durham, NC: Duke University Press, 2000), 136.

76. Sonny Rollins, *Freedom Suite* (Riverside Records RLP 12-258, 1958). Recorded February 11 and March 7, 1958.

77. Thomas Owens, *Bebop: The Music and Its Players* (New York: Oxford University Press, 1996), 87.

78. Fernando Orejuela and Stephanie Shonekan, eds., *Black Lives Matter and Music: Protest, Intervention, Reflection* (Bloomington: Indiana University Press, 2018). I have also written about the interface of popular music practices with the Black Lives Matter

movement: James Gordon Williams, "Black Muse 4 U: Liminality, Self-Determination, and Racial Uplift in the Music of Prince," *Journal of African American Studies* 21, no. 3 (2017): 296–319.

79. Charles M. Bernstein, "The Traditional Roots of Billy Higgins," *Modern Drummer* 7, no. 2 (February 1983): 20–23, 74–75.

80. Ashon T. Crawley, *Blackpentecostal Breath: The Aesthetics of Possibility* (New York: Fordham University Press, 2017), 40.

Chapter 1: Terence Blanchard and the Politics of Breathing

1. Nathaniel Mackey, "Breath and Precarity," in Myung Mi Kim and Cristanne Miller, eds., *Poetics and Precarity* (Albany: State University of New York Press, 2018), 18.

2. Claudia Rankine, *Citizen: An American Lyric* (Minneapolis: Graywolf Press, 2014), 60.

3. *Malcolm X Jazz Suite* (Columbia CK-53599, 1993); *A Tale of God's Will (A Requiem for Katrina)* (Blue Note 3915322, 2007).

4. Phone interview with Terence Blanchard, September 30, 2019.

5. Phone interview with Terence Blanchard, September 30, 2019.

6. Phone interview with Terence Blanchard, September 30, 2019.

7. Phone interview with Terence Blanchard, September 30, 2019.

8. Aretha Franklin, "Amazing Grace" (1972).

9. "President Obama Makes a Statement on the Shooting in Newtown, Connecticut." December 14, 2012. https://www.youtube.com/watch?v=mIA0W69U2_Y, accessed November 8, 2019.

10. Phone interview with Terence Blanchard, September 30, 2019.

11. Phone interview with Terence Blanchard, September 30, 2019.

12. "#InnovateYourCool: Terence Blanchard on Making Political Music in These Times," posted November 27, 2016. https://www.youtube.com/watch?v=yJaVzqPQp3g, accessed March 7, 2019.

13. Phone interview with Terence Blanchard, September 30, 2019.

14. Matt Taibbi, *I Can't Breathe: A Killing on Bay Street* (New York: Spiegel & Grau, 2017), 303.

15. NBC Nightly News, "Eric Garner Chokehold Death: No Indictment," December 4, 2014. https://www.youtube.com/watch?v=UoY3FH9Nb3I, accessed February 3, 2018.

16. Orta claims he was harassed on Twitter and targeted by the police, and that rat poison was put in his food while in prison at Rikers. The Department of Health proved there was rat poison in his food. Democracy Now!, "Why Is Ramsey Orta, Man Who Filmed Police Killing of Eric Garner, the Only One Criminally Charged?" January 12, 2016. https://www.youtube.com/watch?v=aBZmT7W3aXU, accessed March 7, 2019.

17. Taibbi, *I Can't Breathe*, 297.

18. Robin D. G. Kelley, "Births of a Nation: Surveying Trumpland with Cedric Robinson," in "Race, Capitalism, Justice," ed. Walter Johnson with Robin D. G. Kelley, special issue, *Boston Review/Forum* (October 2017): 117–36, at 126.

19. Taibbi, *I Can't Breathe*, 303.

20. The fear I read on the faces of some white people, avoiding eye contact as they cross the street to avoid me, is a product of the historical stigmas attached to Black males and the currency of media images that support those archetypes. When people follow me in

the store to see if I am stealing, when the nurse in my doctor's office makes a joke about me probably having lots of children, they see their own mental formations; they don't see me as I am. This type of surveillance doesn't allow Black people to breathe freely in the world, and this systemic chokehold is part of the social compact we are all required to uphold, even when that social compact does not protect us all.

21. Taibbi, *I Can't Breathe*, 300. The ACLU lawsuit, *Floyd* v. *City of New York*, was decided on August 12, 2013.

22. Taibbi, *I Can't Breathe*, 30.

23. The so-called broken-windows policy, in a nutshell, is citing minor offenses in order to prevent (the theory goes) the bigger offenses from happening. Taibbi explains, "Kelling believed strongly that the best way to reduce fear was to conquer the external symbols of disorder" (*I Can't Breathe*, 61). For "raw materials," see Taibbi, *I Can't Breathe*, 30.

24. Taibbi, *I Can't Breathe*, 29.

25. Taibbi, *I Can't Breathe*, 31. See also "Blank UF-250 Form—Stop, Question and Frisk Report Worksheet, NYPD, 2016," Prison Legal News. https://www.prisonlegalnews. org/news/publications/blank-uf-250-form-stop-question-and-frisk-report-worksheet-nypd-2016/, accessed March 8, 2019.

26. Phone interview with Terence Blanchard, September 30, 2019.

27. Phone interview with Terence Blanchard, September 30, 2019.

28. Phone interview with Terence Blanchard, September 30, 2019.

29. Ashon T. Crawley, *Blackpentecostal Breath: The Aesthetics of Possibility* (New York: Fordham University Press, 2017), 1.

30. L. Kent Wolgamott, "Terence Blanchard to Bring Groove-Oriented, Bitingly Political Music to Jazz in June," *Lincoln Journal Star*, June 17, 2017. http://journalstar.com/entertainment/music/terence-blanchard-to-bring-groove-oriented-bitingly-political-music-to/article_e4761508-d7c2-5c3d-8c29-66d03b63fee2.html, accessed March 7, 2019.

31. Emily Sullivan, "Laura Ingraham Told LeBron James to Shut Up and Dribble; He Went to the Hoop," NPR.org, February 19, 2018. https://www.npr.org/sections/thetwo-way /2018/02/19/587097707/laura-ingraham-told-lebron-james-to-shutup-and-dribble-he-went -to-the-hoop, accessed March 7, 2019.

32. Dan Kubis, "Improvisation as Birthright: An Interview with George Lewis," *Being Human* podcast, University of Pittsburgh Humanities Center, May 6, 2016. https://sound cloud.com/humanities-pitt/george-lewis-interview, accessed March 7, 2019.

33. Kellie Jones and Amiri Baraka, *Eyeminded: Living and Writing Contemporary Art* (Durham, NC: Duke University Press, 2011), 253.

34. Roger Catlin, "Jazz Trumpeter Terence Blanchard Is All About 'Creating Conversations,'" *Washington Post*, October 14, 2016.

35. Phone interview with Terence Blanchard, September 30, 2019.

36. Monson, *Freedom Sounds*, 285. Blanchard was not making a racial comment about white improvisation as cold and abstract and African American improvisation as soulful. However, his comments could be construed as alluding to the idea of the natural Black musician whose talent falls from the sky instead of decades of hard work of practicing, studying composition, and honing the improvisatory craft on stages all over the world.

37. Phone interview with Terence Blanchard, September 30, 2019.

38. I am referring to the culture of the African Trickster God or Esu Elegba, who is the mediator between spirit and human, life and death. This is the sound of tricksterism, which is a practice that has existed in Kongo African culture for centuries.

39. Ashon Crawley, "Breathing Flesh and the Sound of BlackPentecostalism," *Theology and Sexuality* 19, no. 1 (2013): 50.

40. Phone interview with Terence Blanchard, September 30, 2019.

41. Robert Farris Thompson, *Flash of the Spirit: African and Afro-American Art and Philosophy* (New York: Random House, 1983), 222.

42. Samuel A. Floyd Jr., *The Power of Black Music: Interpreting its History from Africa to the United States* (New York and Oxford: Oxford University Press, 1997); online 2011, doi:10.1093/acprof:oso/9780195109757.001.0001.

43. James Arthur Baldwin interview by Yvonne Neverson, "The Artist Has Always Been a Disturber of the Peace," *Africa: International Business, Economics and Political Magazine* 80 (April 1978): 110.

44. Christine Lucia, "Abdullah Ibrahim and the Uses of Memory," *British Journal of Ethnomusicology* 11, no. 2 (2002): 125–43.

45. Phone interview with Terence Blanchard, September 30, 2019.

46. Aceldama, translated literally from Aramaic as "field of blood," is a place in Jerusalem associated with Judas Iscariot. It's a word commonly used to describe a violent and wretched place. W. E. B. Du Bois used the term to describe the physical brutality visited upon convicts in the Lease System. See W. E. B. Du Bois, *Black Reconstruction* [1935], reprint ed. (Millwood, NY: Kraus-Thomson Organization, 1976). These and subsequent spoken lyrics from "Breathless" were transcribed through repeated listening to the composition.

47. For enslaved Africans from the Congo region–the Bakongo people who come from what is now known as the Democratic Republic of Congo– the Kalunga line represented an invisible line on the surface of a body of water that divided their tangible world from the next. Enslaved Africans believed their ancestors were found beneath this line, which is why Stuckey theorizes that water immersion was very significant for enslaved Black people, particularly in Black Christianity baptism ceremonies, because it was a sign of transformation and a way of contacting their ancestors. The Kalunga line is based on the staff cross found in a Bakongo cosmogram. Within this cosmogram is the symbolism of spiritual rebirth and the continuation of culture represented by four movements of sun signs at each of the four endings. Stuckey explains that Bakongo cosmography was the basis for counterclockwise dance known as the Ring Shout. See Sterling Stuckey, *Slave Culture: Nationalist Theory and the Foundations of Black America*, 25th anniversary ed. (New York: Oxford University Press, 2013), 13.

48. Geraldine Wyckoff, "Terence Blanchard Is Breathless with Frustration," *OffBeat*, June 29, 2015. http://www.offbeat.com/articles/terence-blanchard-breathless-frustration/, accessed February 6, 2018.

49. Soyica Diggs Colbert, "Black Movements: Flying Africans in Spaceships," in *Black Performance Theory*, ed. Thomas DeFrantz and Anita Gonzalez (Durham, NC: Duke University Press, 2014), 129–48.

50. Stuckey, *Slave Culture*, 2–4.

51. Wyckoff, "Terence Blanchard Is Breathless with Frustration."

52. Wyckoff, "Terence Blanchard Is Breathless with Frustration."

53. Robert Farris Thompson, "The Grand Atlantic Kongo Tradition: Art Histories of Ecstasy and Law," W. E. B. Du Bois Lecture series, Barker Center, Harvard University, February 2007. http://hutchinscenter.fas.harvard.edu/robert-farris-thompson-w-e-b-du-bois-lecture-series-robert-farris-thompson-0, accessed March 26, 2018.

54. Catlin, "Jazz Trumpeter Terence Blanchard."

55. George Lipsitz, "What Is This Black in the Black Radical Tradition?" in *Futures of Black Radicalism*, ed. Gaye Theresa Johnson and Alex Lubin (London and Brooklyn, NY: Verso, 2017), 108–19.

56. Keeanga-Yamahtta Taylor, *From #BlackLivesMatter to Black Liberation* (Chicago: Haymarket Books, 2016), 194.

Chapter 2: Billy Higgins in the Zone: Brushwork, Breath, and Imagination

1. Kamau Daáood, excerpt from "The Living Waters," *The Language of Saxophones: Selected Poems of Kamau Daáood*, Pocket Poets No. 57 (San Francisco: City Lights, 2005), 112.

2. Crawley, *Blackpentecostal Breath*, 20.

3. Charles Lloyd, *The Water Is Wide* (CD, ECM 1734, 2000), recorded December 1999, Cello Studios, Los Angeles.

4. David Andrew Ake, *Jazz Matters: Sound, Place, and Time since Bebop* (Berkeley: University of California Press, 2010), 53.

5. Ake, *Jazz Matters*, 52.

6. Jean-Christophe Bailly, "The Slightest Breath (on Living)," trans. Matthew H. Anderson, *CR: New Centennial Review* 10, no. 3 (2010): 5.

7. For a definition of Eurological, see Lewis, "Improvised Music after 1950: Afrological and Eurological Perspectives," *Black Music Research Journal* 16, no. 1 (1996): 91–122.

8. For more information on space–times see Michelle M. Wright, "Forces to Be Reckoned with: Michelle M. Wright on the Physics of Black Art," *Artforum International* 53, no. 10 (2015): 155–56.

9. Stewart Lee, "Evan Parker's Musical Utopia," April 22, 2010. https://www.theguardian.com/music/2010/apr/22/stewart-lee-evan-parker, accessed March 11, 2018.

10. Kelley critiques the constant, singular framing of the Black experience through the lens of trauma and notions of pessimistic black fungibility, which is a frame that does not pronounce how Black people sustained their communities and built social institutions that carry America as a whole. See Kelley, "Black Study, Black Struggle," 1, 14.

11. Sonali Kolhatkar, audio interview of Kamau Daáood, "Kamau Daoud [*sic*] Discusses the Life and Legacy of Legendary Jazz Drummer Billy Higgins," *Uprising with Sonali*, April 28, 2011. http://uprisingradio.org/home/2011/04/28/kamau-daoud-discusses-the-life-and-legacy-of-legendary-jazz-drummer-billy-higgins/, accessed November 30, 2017.

12. Heidi Chang, "Billy Higgins: A Tribute to the Legendary Jazz Drummer," PRX. https://beta.prx.org/stories/16094, accessed March 11, 2019.

13. Guthrie P. Ramsey, *Race Music: Black Cultures from Bebop to Hip-Hop* (Berkeley: University of California Press, 2003), 77.

14. Ramsey, *Race Music*, 4.

15. For more on Leimert Park, see Yolanda Yvette Hester, "Leimert Park, an African Village: The Possibility of an Ethnically Branded Cultural District," M.A. diss., African American Studies, UCLA, 2017. https://escholarship.org/uc/item/3tc764cg, accessed March 11, 2019.

16. Kolhatkar, "Kamau Daoud Discusses . . . Billy Higgins."

17. Randy Weston and Willard Jenkins, *African Rhythms: The Autobiography of Randy Weston* (Durham, NC: Duke University Press, 2010), 83. Weston and Higgins performed

together on an album recorded April 14–17, 1995, at the Hit Factory, New York City: Randy Weston, *African Rhythms* (Gitanes Jazz Productions 529 237-2, 1995).

18. Chang, "Billy Higgins: A Tribute."

19. "The World Stage." https://www.theworldstage.org/about.html, accessed March 11, 2019.

20. Robin D. G. Kelley, *Africa Speaks, America Answers: Modern Jazz in Revolutionary Times* (Cambridge, MA: Harvard University Press, 2012), 96; on Jamal, 91–119.

21. Kelley, *Africa Speaks, America Answers*, 95.

22. Ted Panken, "A Drummers Memorial Roundtable on Billy Higgins on WKCR, May 7, 2001." https://tedpanken.wordpress.com/2011/10/11/a-drummers-memorial-roundtable-on-billy-higgins-on-wkcr-may-7-2001/, accessed November 14, 2017.

23. Karen Bennett, "Billy Higgins: Time on His Hands." http://www.jazzhouse.org/library/?read=bennett2, accessed December 12, 2017.

24. Personal conversation with Kamau Daáood at his Los Angeles home, January 29, 2019.

25. Personal conversation with Kamau Daáood.

26. "Billy Higgins interview by Rasul Muhammed," posted December 27, 2008. https://www.youtube.com/watch?v=ngEOx_j4uX8, accessed December 13, 2017.

27. João H. Costa Vargas, "Jazz and Male Blackness: The Politics of Sociability in South Central Los Angeles," *Popular Music and Society* 31, no. 1 (2008): 37–56.

28. Jason C. Bivins, *Spirits Rejoice!: Jazz and American Religion* (New York and Oxford: Oxford University Press, 2015), 40.

29. Costa Vargas, "Jazz and Male Blackness," 52.

30. Costa Vargas, "Jazz and Male Blackness," 52

31. Costa Vargas, "Jazz and Male Blackness," 39.

32. Greg Burk, "Open, Like a Door," *LA Weekly*, December 15, 1999. https://www.laweekly.com/music/red-aunts-say-goodbye-to-bassist-debi-martini-10139754, accessed November 29, 2017.

33. Valerie Wilmer, *Jazz People*, 3rd ed. (London: Allison & Busby, 1977), 57.

34. Kolhatkar, "Kamau Daoud Discusses . . . Billy Higgins."

35. Costa Vargas, "Jazz and Male Blackness," 49.

36. The term "the music" is affectionately used by many improvisers, including myself, to denote a recognition of aesthetic agreement and buttressing of values regarding a certain level of excellence in improvisation as a cultural sphere. The term does not indicate a reified definition of what improvised music is supposed to be; rather, it indicates a political stake in creating music that adds value to one's life and defines one's positionality in contradistinction to a world obsessed with commodifying Black musical lived experiences manifested in musical expression.

37. Wilmer, *Jazz People*, 62.

38. Bernstein, "The Traditional Roots of Billy Higgins." Greer was Duke Ellington's first drummer.

39. Cyrille, quoted in Panken, "A Drummers['] Memorial Roundtable."

40. Bernstein, "The Traditional Roots of Billy Higgins."

41. Personal conversation with Kamau Daáood.

42. Burk, "Open, Like a Door."

43. Nicholas "Africa" Kotei Djanie with Cynthia Cohen, "Drumming and Reconciliation," The International Center for Ethics, Justice, and Public Life, Brandeis University, Waltham, MA (2003–2004), quotes at 2 and 1. https://www.brandeis.edu/ethics/peacebuildingarts/pdfs/peace buildingarts/nicholas%20drumming_and_reconciliation.pdf, accessed November 17, 2017.

44. Bernstein, "The Traditional Roots of Billy Higgins."

45. On interpellation, see the introduction's section on "The non-Utopian Inclusion of Black Musical Space."

46. Cyrille, quoted in Panken, "A Drummers Memorial Roundtable." It is gratifying here that what Cyrille saw when Higgins played provides backup for what I hear in the Higgins–Mehldau musical interaction during "Georgia" on the Lloyd record.

47. Nate Chinen, "Abbey Lincoln's Emancipation Proclamation," *New York Times*, May 20, 2007. https://www.nytimes.com/2007/05/20/arts/music/20chin.html, accessed March 12, 2019. Also see Baraka, "Abbey Lincoln: Straight Ahead."

48. Harold Howland, "Elvin Jones," interview, *Modern Drummer* 3, no. 4 (January–February 1979): 14ff. https://www.moderndrummer.com/article/august-september -1979-elvin-jones/, accessed November 14, 2017.

49. Bennett, "Billy Higgins: Time on His Hands."

50. Bernstein, "The Traditional Roots of Billy Higgins."

51. "Billy Higgins: The Shape of Jazz," November 2011. https://www.moderndrummer.com /2011/11/billy-higgins/, accessed November 17, 2017.

52. Personal conversation with Kamau Daáood.

53. Bailly, "The Slightest Breath (on Living)," 4.

54. Personal conversation with Kamau Daáood.

55. Crawley, *Blackpentecostal Breath*, 40.

56. Jean-Michel Beaudet, "Mystery Instruments," in *Burst of Breath: Indigenous Ritual Wind Instruments in Lowland South America*, ed. Jonathan D. Hill and Jean-Pierre Chaumeil (Lincoln: University of Nebraska Press, 2011), 379.

57. Hill and Chaumeil, "Overture," in *Burst of Breath*, 1–46, esp. 6–8, quote at 19.

58. Hill and Chaumeil, "Overture," 19.

59. Hill and Chaumeil, "Overture," 20–21, quote at 20.

60. Hill and Chaumeil, "Overture," 22.

61. Bernstein, "The Traditional Roots of Billy Higgins."

62. Billy Hart, in Panken, "A Drummers Memorial Roundtable."

63. Charles Lloyd and Billy Higgins, *Which Way Is East* (ECM Records ECM 1878/79, 2004).

64. Larry Blumenfeld, "When Charles Met Billy," *Jazziz* 21, no. 10 (2004): 52. https:// search.proquest.com/docview/194503605?accountid=14214, accessed February 17, 2018.

65. Gaston Bachelard, *The Poetics of Space* [French, 1958], trans. Maria Jolas, new ed. (New York: Penguin Books, 2014), 231–32.

66. Howland, "Elvin Jones."

67. According to his friend Dorothy Darr, he died of both kidney and liver failure. Ben Ratliff, "Billy Higgins, 64, Jazz Drummer with Melodic and Subtle Swing," *New York Times*, May 4, 2001. https://www.nytimes.com/2001/05/04/arts/billy-higgins-64-jazz-drummer -with-melodic-and-subtle-swing.html, accessed March 12, 2019.

68. Blumenfeld, "When Charles Met Billy," 53.

69. Blumenfeld, "When Charles Met Billy," 53.

70. My transcription of Higgins's sung lyrics from "Blues Tinge" on Charles Lloyd and Billy Higgins, *Which Way Is East* (CD, ECM, 2004).

71. My transcription of Higgins's sung lyrics from "Blues Tinge."

72. This is not a linear or chronological analysis but an examination that highlights where Higgins's breathing strategies aid his improvisation and influence that of Brad Mehldau.

73. "Georgia (On My Mind)," composed by Hoagy Carmichael with lyrics by Stuart Gorell, is an American Songbook standard in AABA form, recorded by musicians across genres over the years. It remains a popular vehicle for improvisation today.

74. For more on Signifyin(g), see Floyd Jr., *The Power of Black Music*, 87–99; and see the section "Black Sound and the Performance of Black Musical Space" in my introduction.

75. Robyn Flans, "A Different View: Kevin Eubanks—*Tonight Show* Bandleader," *Modern Drummer* 24, no. 4 (April 2000): 112. https://search.proquest.com/docview/1316400?account tid=14214, accessed March 27, 2018.

76. Butch Morris, "Conduction," https://vimeo.com/91050770, accessed January 19, 2017. I should point out that Morris understood he was "leading the ensemble," but he based his decisions on the information given to him by his musicians.

77. Personal conversation with Kamau Daáood.

78. Wilmer, *Jazz People*, 62.

79. Blumenfeld, "When Charles Met Billy," 53.

80. Personal conversation with Louis Hayes in New York City after a performance at Sweet Basil in the 1990s.

81. Kevin Eubanks, in Ashley Kahn, "Charles Lloyd and Billy Higgins: The Seekers," *Jazz-Times*, June 1, 2004. https://jazztimes.com/features/charles-lloyd-and-billy-higgins-the-seekers/, accessed March 12, 2019.

82. Brad Mehldau, in Kahn, "Charles Lloyd and Billy Higgins."

83. Eubanks, in Kahn, "Charles Lloyd and Billy Higgins."

84. Mehldau, in Kahn, "Charles Lloyd and Billy Higgins."

85. Mehldau, in Kahn, "Charles Lloyd and Billy Higgins."

86. A sizzle cymbal has rivets hanging loosely in drilled holes, vibrating against the cymbal when struck.

87. Higgins, from an August 6, 1990, interview with Ingrid Monson in New York City; cited in Ingrid Monson, *Saying Something: Jazz Improvisation and Interaction* (Chicago: University of Chicago Press, 1996), 63.

88. Chip Stern, "Shop Talk: Billy Higgins," *JazzTimes*, November 1, 2000. https://jazztimes.com/reviews/gearhead/shop-talk-billy-higgins/, accessed March 12, 2019.

89. Personal conversation with Kamau Daáood.

90. Daáood, excerpt from "The Last Psalms," *The Language of Saxophones*, 45.

Chapter 3: The Social Science Music of Terri Lyne Carrington

1. For more information on Carrington's accolades, see Leslie Gourse, *Madame Jazz: Contemporary Women Instrumentalists* (New York: Oxford University Press, 1996).

2. Sherrie Tucker, "Jazz History Remix: Black Women from 'Enter' to 'Center,'" in Portia K. Maultsby and Mellonee V. Burnim, eds., *Issues in African American Music: Power, Gender, Race, Representation* (New York: Routledge, Taylor & Francis Group, 2017), 264.

3. Julie Dawn Smith, "Playing Like a Girl," in Rebecca Caines and Ajay Heble Routledge, eds., *Improvisation Studies Reader: Spontaneous Acts* (New York: Routledge, 2015), 265.

4. Smith, "Playing Like a Girl," 265.

5. Robin D. G. Kelley, "Introduction to Black Radicalism," in Keisha N. Blain, Christopher Cameron, and Ashley D. Farmer, eds., *New Perspectives on the Black Intellectual Tradition* (Evanston, IL: Northwestern University Press, 2018), 195.

6. Tucker, *Swing Shift*, 7.

7. Tucker, *Swing Shift*, 7.

8. Tucker, *Swing Shift*, 7.

9. Phone conversation with Terri Lyne Carrington, November 10, 2019.

10. Bob Blumenthal, "Terri Lyne Carrington: Sophisticated Lady," *Jazz Times*, January 27, 2020. https://jazztimes.com/features/profiles/terri-lyne-carrington-sophisticated-lady/, accessed April 23, 2020.

11. Phone conversation with Terri Lyne Carrington, November 11, 2019.

12. Phone conversation with Terri Lyne Carrington, November 11, 2019.

13. Isabelle Pitman, "An Interview with Terri Lyne Carrington: 'I Try to Paint as I Play,'" Culture Trip, December 11, 2015. https://theculturetrip.com/north-america/usa/massachusetts/articles/interview-with-terri-lyne-carrington-i-try-to-paint-as-i-play/, accessed July 15, 2019.

14. For more on the history of M-Base, see Matthew Daniel Clayton II, "M-Base: Envisioning Change for Jazz in the 1980s and Beyond," diss., Harvard University (ProQuest Dissertations Publishing, 2009).

15. Gourse, *Madame Jazz*, 135.

16. Blumenthal, "Terry Lyne Carrington: Sophisticated Lady."

17. Phone conversation with Terri Lyne Carrington on November 11, 2019.

18. Gourse, *Madame Jazz*, 135.

19. Gourse, *Madame Jazz*, 135.

20. Patricia Hill Collins, *Black Feminist Thought: Knowledge, Consciousness, and the Politics of Empowerment*, 2nd ed. (London: Harper Collins Academic, 1991), 17.

21. This information was taken from International Music Network's Terri Lyne Carrington page. http://www.imnworld.com/artists/detail/170/Terri-Lyne-Carrington, accessed June 15, 2019.

22. Phone conversation with Terri Lyne Carrington, November 10, 2019.

23. Phone conversation with Terri Lyne Carrington, November 11, 2019.

24. Personal interview with Terri Lyne Carrington in Ottawa, Canada, June 27, 2019.

25. Tucker, *Swing Shift*, 261.

26. Tammy L. Kernodle, *Soul on Soul: The Life and Music of Mary Lou Williams* (Boston: Northeastern University Press, 2004), 2.

27. Personal interview with Terri Lyne Carrington in Ottawa, Canada, June 27, 2019.

28. Personal interview with Terri Lyne Carrington in Ottawa, Canada, June 27, 2019.

29. Personal interview with Terri Lyne Carrington in Ottawa, Canada, June 27, 2019.

30. Berklee Institute of Jazz and Gender Justice promotional video. https://www.youtube.com/watch?time_continue=3&v=w1rW5ZUAPL0, accessed July 15, 2019.

31. Angela Y. Davis, *Blues Legacies and Black Feminism: Gertrude "Ma" Rainey, Bessie Smith and Billie Holiday* (New York: Vintage, 1999).

32. Personal interview with Terri Lyne Carrington in Ottawa, Canada, June 27, 2019.

33. Personal interview with Terri Lyne Carrington in Ottawa, Canada, June 27, 2019.

34. Kathleen M. McKeage, "Gender and Participation in High School and College Instrumental Jazz Ensembles," *Journal of Research in Music Education* 52, no. 4 (2004): 343–56.

35. Personal interview with Terri Lyne Carrington in Ottawa, Canada, June 27, 2019.

36. McKeage, "Gender and Participation," 347.

37. Sherrie Tucker, "Women in Jazz," Grove Music Online, 2003. https://www.oxfordmusiconline.com/grovemusic/view/10.1093/gmo/9781561592630.001.0001/omo-9781561592630-e-2000730100, accessed July 23, 2019.

38. McKeage, "Gender and Participation," 346.

39. The Berklee Institute of Jazz and Gender Justice Library Guide identifies an Essential Reading list that consists of PDF copies of articles and ebooks. https://guides.library.berklee.edu/BIJGJ/books, accessed July 14, 2019.

  Muller, Carol Ann and Sathima Bea Benjamin. *Musical Echoes: South African Women Thinking in Jazz.* Durham: Duke University Press, 2011, Rustin-Paschal, Nichole and Sherrie Tucker. *Big Ears: Listening for Gender in Jazz Studies.* Durham: Duke University Press, 2008, Lorde, Audre. Sister Outsider: Essays and Speeches. Trumansburg, NY: Crossing Press, 1984, Hayes, Eileen M. and Williams, Linda F. (Linda Faye). *Black Women and Music: More than the Blues.* Urbana: University of Illinois Press, 2007, hooks, bell. *Teaching to Transgress: Education as the Practice of Freedom.* New York: Routledge, 1994, Johnson, Allan G. *Privilege, Power, and Difference.* Third ed. New York, NY: McGraw-Hill Education, 2018.

40. Audre Lorde, *Sister Outsider: Essays and Speeches* (Trumansburg, NY: Crossing Press, 1984), 112.

41. Personal interview with Terri Lyne Carrington in Ottawa, Canada, June 27, 2019.

42. Personal interview with Terri Lyne Carrington in Ottawa, Canada, June 27, 2019.

43. Ivette Feliciano, "Female Jazz Musicians Raise Their Voices Against Sexism," *PBS NewsHour*, March 3, 2018. https://www.pbs.org/newshour/show/female-jazz-musicians-raise-their-voices-against-sexism, accessed April 23, 2020.

44. See Tammy L. Kernodle, "Black Women Working Together: Jazz, Gender, and the Politics of Validation," *Black Music Research Journal* 34, no. 1 (2014): 36.

45. Kernodle, "Black Women Working Together," 36.

46. Abigail Jones, "Sisters of Swing," *Vanity Fair*, July 9, 2019. https://www.vanityfair.com/style/2019/07/women-in-jazz-sisterhood, accessed July 27, 2019.

47. bell hooks, *Feminism Is for Everybody: Passionate Politics* (Cambridge, MA: South End Press, 2000), 117.

48. hooks, *Feminism is for Everybody*, 117.

49. Interview comments made by founder and artistic director Terri Lyne Carrington in Berklee Institute of Jazz and Gender Justice promotional video. https://www.youtube.com/watch?time_continue=1&v=w1rW5ZUAPLo, accessed July 14, 2019.

50. Berklee Institute of Jazz and Gender Justice promotional video.

51. Interview comments made by feminist studies scholar Gina Dent in Berklee Institute of Jazz and Gender Justice promotional video.

52. Collins, *Black Feminist Thought*, 204.

53. Bernice Johnson Reagon, "Coalition Politics: Turning the Century," in Barbara Smith, ed., *Home Girls: A Black Feminist Anthology* (New Brunswick, NJ: Rutgers University Press, 2000), 358.

54. Kernodle, "Black Women Working Together," 53.

55. Terri Lyne Carrington, "I Am the Drums," TedX Talk, February 4, 2016. https://www.youtube.com/watch?v=jfS19b7pF8o, accessed July 17, 2019.

56. Carrington, "I Am the Drums."

57. Collins, *Black Feminist Thought*, 9.

58. Tucker, *Swing Shift*.

59. Eileen M. Hayes, "The Reception of Blackness in 'Women's Music,'" in Maultsby and Burnim, *Issues in African American Music*, 270.

60. Barbara Ransby, *Making All Black Lives Matter: Reimagining Freedom in the Twenty-First Century* (Oakland: University of California Press, 2018), 149.

61. "Drummer/Producer Terri Lyne Carrington Creates a Brilliant Jazz Picture from Many Fascinating Pieces," Concord Records promotional video for Terri Lyne Carrington's *The Mosaic Project*, June 1, 2011. https://www.youtube.com/watch?v=zRhG6RwLpEU, accessed July 5, 2019.

62. Personal interview with Terri Lyne Carrington in Ottawa, Canada, June 27, 2019.

63. Personal interview with Terri Lyne Carrington in Ottawa, Canada, June 27, 2019.

64. Personal interview with Terri Lyne Carrington in Ottawa, Canada, June 27, 2019.

65. Personal interview with Terri Lyne Carrington in Ottawa, Canada, June 27, 2019.

66. Phone interview with Carrington, November 10, 2019.

67. See, for example, Angela Y. Davis, *Are Prisons Obsolete?* (New York: Seven Stories Press, 2003); and Angela Y. Davis, *Abolition Democracy: Beyond Empire, Prisons, and Torture* (New York: Seven Stories Press, 2011).

68. Comments from promotional video for *The Mosaic Project* (2011).

69. From the liner notes to Terri Lyne Carrington's *Jazz Is a Spirit* (Act Music + Vision, 2002).

70. Angela Davis, introduction to "Echo," *The Mosaic Project.*

71. Personal interview with Terri Lyne Carrington in Ottawa, Canada, June 27, 2019.

72. Personal interview with Terri Lyne Carrington in Ottawa, Canada, June 27, 2019.

73. Personal interview with Terri Lyne Carrington in Ottawa, Canada, June 27, 2019.

74. Personal interview with Terri Lyne Carrington in Ottawa, Canada, June 27, 2019.

75. Kenneth Robert Janken, *The Wilmington Ten: Violence, Injustice, and the Rise of Black Politics in the 1970s* (Chapel Hill: University of North Carolina Press, 2015).

76. Last stanza to the lyrics of "Echo," *The Mosaic Project* (2011).

77. A statement by Terri Lyne Carrington, pianist Aaron Parks, and guitarist Matthew Stevens from the liner notes, Terri Lyne Carrington and Social Science, *Waiting Game* (2019).

78. Kimberlé Crenshaw, "Demarginalizing the Intersection of Race and Sex: A Black Feminist Critique of Antidiscrimination Doctrine, Feminist Theory and Antiracist Politics," *University of Chicago Legal Forum* Vol. 1989, Issue 1.

79. Vivian M. May, *Pursuing Intersectionality, Unsettling Dominant Imaginaries* (New York: Routledge, Taylor & Francis Group, 2015), xi.

80. Patricia Hill Collins and Sirma Bilge, *Intersectionality* (Malden, MA: Polity Press, 2016).

81. Terri Lyne Carrington and Social Science, Tiny Desk Concert, NPR, March 4, 2020. https://www.youtube.com/watch?v=qreeSgvYH3M.

82. Lyrics by Kokayi from Terri Lyne Carrington and Social Science, "Purple Mountains," *Waiting Game* (2019).

83. "Terri Lyne Carrington's Social Science Raises Its Voice," Afropunk, October 2, 2019. https://afropunk.com/2019/10/terri-lyne-carrington-social-science-kassa-overall-trapped-in-the-american-dream/, accessed April 19, 2020.

84. I quote the first verse of "Lift Ev'ry Voice and Sing" (1905), the so-called "Negro National Anthem" composed by James Weldon Johnson and John Rosamond Johnson, to contrast the chasm between the nations ideals and the realities for Black people and other marginalized groups.

85. Personal conversation with pianist Aaron Parks backstage after a Social Science concert at Cornell University's Bailey Hall on September 13, 2019.

Chapter 4: Ambrose Akinmusire's Satchel of Origami

1. Lyrics from vocalist Abbey Lincoln, "Wholly Earth," *Wholly Earth* (Verve Records, 1998). This song relates to ideas of a Black sense of place in McKittrick's Black geographies as I connect it to the production of Black musical space. It is about cultural memory and the interruption of common time cycles that have displaced Black people. Most importantly, it is the lyrical representation of how both Lincoln and Akinmusire both believe how the ancestors live within us, and how they help us carry the tradition forward.

2. See Stoever, *The Sonic Color Line*; Nina Sun Eidsheim, "The Micropolitics of Listening to Vocal Timbre," *Postmodern Culture* 24, no. 3 (2014), doi:10.1353/pmc.2014.0014; and Ake, *Jazz Matters*, 50–53.

3. The Black Lives Matter movement was spearheaded by feminists Alicia Garza, Patrisse Cullors, and Opal Tometi. For more information on the genesis of the #BlackLivesMatter hashtag, see Alicia Garza, "A Herstory of the #BlackLivesMatter Movement," *Feminist Wire,* October 7, 2014. http://www.thefeministwire.com/2014/10/blacklivesmatter-2/, accessed March 14, 2018.

4. Robin D. G. Kelley, "The U.S. v. Trayvon Martin: How the System Worked," Huffington Post, July 13, 2013. http://www.huffingtonpost.com/robin-d-g-kelley/nra-stand-your-ground -trayvon-martin_b_3599843.html, accessed March 23, 2014.

5. Jesse McKinley, "In California, Protests after Man Dies at Hands of Transit Police," *New York Times,* January 8, 2009. http://www.nytimes.com/2009/01/09/us/09oakland.html?_r=0, accessed March 21, 2014.

6. Christine Joy Ferrer, "Oscar Grant Memorial Arts Project," Media Alliance, April 13, 2009. http://www.media-alliance.org/article.php?list=class&class=20&offset=176, accessed March 22, 2014; now at Reimagine, http://www.reimaginerpe.org/rpe/oscar, accessed March 14, 2019.

7. *Fruitvale Station*, dir. Ryan Coogler (Forest Whitaker's Significant Productions/OG Project, 2013).

8. Ambrose Akinmusire, "My Name Is Oscar," *When the Heart Emerges Glistening* (Blue Note 509990 70612 2 9, 2011); album recorded September 20–22, 2010, at Brooklyn Studios, Hollywood, CA.

9. Personal conversation with Ambrose Akinmusire in New York City, March 9, 2019. Akinmusire is quoting "'There's No Place to Go but Up': bell hooks and Maya Angelou in Conversation," mod. Melvin McLeod, *Shambhala Sun*, January 1, 1998. https://www.lionsroar .com/theres-no-place-to-go-but-up/, accessed March 14, 2019; also available as "Angelou," http://www.hartford-hwp.com/archives/45a/249.html, accessed July 1, 2016.

10. Personal conversation with Ambrose Akinmusire in New York City, March 9, 2019.

11. Siddhartha Mitter, "Trumpeter Ambrose Akinmusire Makes a Jazz Life on His Own Terms," *Boston Globe*, May 4, 2002. https://siddharthamitter.com/2012/05/04/trumpeter -ambrose-akinmusire-makes-a-jazz-life-on-his-own-terms/, accessed March 15, 2019.

12. Donna Murch, "The Campus and the Street: Race, Migration, and the Origins of the Black Panther Party in Oakland, CA," *Souls: A Critical Journal of Black Politics, Culture, and Society* 9, no. 4 (2007): 333–45.

13. Personal conversation with Akinmusire in New York City, March 9, 2019.

14. Personal conversation with Akinmusire in New York City, March 9, 2019.

15. Personal conversation with Akinmusire in New York City, March 9, 2019.

16. Personal conversation with Akinmusire in New York City, March 9, 2019.

17. Avery Gordon, *Ghostly Matters: Haunting and the Sociological Imagination*, 2nd ed. (Minneapolis: University of Minnesota Press, 2008), 22.

18. N.W.A, *Straight Outta Compton: 20th Anniversary Edition* (Ruthless Records 509995-11239-1-8, 2007).

19. "Ambrose Akinmusire: When the Heart Emerges Glistening," *Anteprima*. http://www.anteprimaproductions.com/Ambrose-Akinmusire,72?lang=fr, accessed April 5, 2014.

20. Ambrose Akinmusire, *The Imagined Savior Is Far Easier to Paint* (Blue Note B001972602, 2014).

21. "The Imagined Savior Is Far Easier to Paint," AmbroseAkinmusire.com. https://www.ambroseakinmusire.com/the-imagined-savior, accessed March 15, 2019.

22. I want to thank Robin D. G. Kelley for bringing "Quiet Dawn" to my attention.

23. African American women were lynched as well, of course, and they continue to be killed by police, in addition to suffering other forms of violence, such as rape. Crenshaw believes new frameworks are needed for understanding how African American women experience police violence, so as to provide new information to inform policy, media representations, and stories of survival. "Rollcall for Those Absent" rightfully calls attention to police killings of African American males; yet the composition would be more complete had it included names such as Shelly Frey, Alberta Spruil, and Rekia Boyd. See "#Say Her Name: Resisting Police Brutality against Black Women." http://www.aapf.org/sayher namereport/, accessed July 30, 2015. Janelle Monáe's "Hell You Talmbout" (2013) is an example of a musical piece that strikes a balance in acknowledging the lives of both Black women and men.

24. "The Imagined Savior Is Far Easier to Paint."

25. See "The Rise and Fall of an All-American Catchphrase: 'Free, White, and 21,'" Jezebel, September 9, 2015. https://pictorial.jezebel.com/the-rise-and-fall-of-an-all-american -catchphrase-free-1729621311, accessed April 20, 2020.

26. Personal conversation with Akinmusire in New York City, March 9, 2019.

27. Personal conversation with Akinmusire in New York City, March 9, 2019.

28. Ambrose Akinmusire, "Free, White and 21," *Origami Harvest* (Blue Note B002866202, 2018).

29. Email communication with Ambrose Akinmusire, March 26, 2019.

30. Cormac Larkin, "Ambrose Akinmusire: 'Ugly things aren't valued any more,'" *Irish Times*, April 30, 2015. https://www.irishtimes.com/culture/music/ambrose-akinmusire-ugly -things-aren-t-valued-any-more-1.2193680, accessed March 15, 2019.

31. Lewis, "Improvised Music after 1950."

32. See my discussion of this effect in James Gordon Williams, "Crossing Cinematic and Sonic Bar Lines: T-Pain's 'Can't Believe It,'" *Ethnomusicology Review* 19 (2014).

33. Personal conversation with Akinmusire in New York City, March 9, 2019.

34. Similar performance strategies of staggering, melodic, collective improvisation is found in Ornette Coleman's "Lonely Woman" (1959), Don Cherry's album *Where Is Brooklyn?* (1969), and Andrew Hill's *Time Lines* (2006).

35. Geoffrey Himes, "Ambrose Akinmusire: The Storyteller," *JazzTimes*, April 30, 2011. https://jazztimes.com/features/ambrose-akinmusire-the-storyteller/, accessed March 15, 2019.

36. Akinmusire's approach is similar to the improvisational approaches of bassist Charles Mingus, saxophonists John Coltrane, Pharaoh Sanders, Anthony Braxton, and Kenny Garrett, and many other musicians.

37. Frank J. Oteri, "Henry Threadgill: No Compromise," conversation August 26, 2010, in New York City's East Village, posted October 1, 2010. https://nmbx.newmusicusa.org/henry -threadgill-no-compromise/, accessed March 15, 2019.

38. "Ambrose Akinmusire—Origami Harvest (Album Trailer)," posted October 10, 2018. https://www.youtube.com/watch?v=swcSU71gixw, accessed March 15, 2019.

39. Personal conversation with Ambrose Akinmusire in New York City, March 9, 2019.

40. Personal conversation with Ambrose Akinmusire in New York City, March 9, 2019.

41. Akinmusire's wide intervals are similar in their idiosyncratic nature to multi-reedist Eric Dolphy's wide registral leaps in his flute improvisations on "Like Someone in Love," on his album *At the Five Spot, Volume 2* (1964).

42. Du Bois's theory of double consciousness is discussed briefly in the introduction ("Black Musical Space and Inclusion").

43. Angelika Beener, "Ambrose Akinmusire: An Emergence of Truth," https://alternate -takes.org/2011/09/07/ambrose-akinmusire-an-emergence-of-truth/, accessed March 15, 2019.

44. George E. Lewis, "The Timeless Blues," in *Blues for Smoke*, ed. Bennett Simpson (London and New York: Prestel, 2012), 90.

Chapter 5: Unified Fragmentation: Andrew Hill's Street Theory of Black Musical Space

1. Andrew Hill was influenced by concepts espoused by the philosopher Jiddu Krishnamurti. In fact, when I spoke with him in the jazz club Birdland in 2007, he had a copy of a Krishnamurti book in his hand. See Jiddu Krishnamurti, *The Collected Works of J. Krishnamurti (Book 2)* (United States: K Publications, 2012), 99.

2. Richard Iton, *In Search of the Black Fantastic: Politics and Popular Culture in the Post–Civil Rights Era* (New York and Oxford: Oxford University Press, 2008), 200.

3. Ray Comiskey, "Why Black Jazz Died and White Survived," *Irish Times*, April 25, 2006.

4. Please see my discussion of Eidsheim's thesis in the introduction, and see Eidsheim, *The Race of Sound*, 2.

5. This expression is from the preface of his unpublished writings on "Project Acculturation" [1994], located among the Andrew Hill Papers, Music and Audiovisual Recordings collection, at the Institute of Jazz Studies, Rutgers University Libraries, New Brunswick, NJ [hereafter Andrew Hill Papers], Box 1, Folder 4.

6. Two versions of "Malachi" are the first (ensemble) and final (solo piano) tracks on his *Time Lines* (Blue Note 0946-3-351 170 2 8, 2006), respectively recorded June 30 and July 18, 2005, at Bennett Studios in Englewood, NJ.

7. Hill's misleading information about his origins has lasted for generations through the jazz discourse, repeated by critics and historians. See Don Heckman, "Roots, Culture and Economics: An Interview with Avant-garde Pianist-Composer Andrew Hill," *Down Beat*, May 5, 1966, 19.

8. Andrew Hill, *Black Fire* (Blue Note BLP 4151, 1964), recorded November 8–9, 1963, at Van Gelder Studio, Englewood Cliffs, NJ.

9. "Andrew Hill: Blue Note Records" press release, Liberty Records press office, March 6, 1968, Andrew Hill Papers, Box 1, Folder 4.

10. Phil Johnson, "Forty Years On, This Is Your Haitian Divorce," *The Independent* [UK], May 12, 2003. https://www.independent.co.uk/arts-entertainment/music/features/forty-years-on-this-is-your-haitian-divorce-590452.html, accessed March 26, 2018.

11. Johnson, "Forty Years On, This Is Your Haitian Divorce."

12. Amy Absher, *The Black Musician and the White City: Race and Music in Chicago, 1900–1967* (Ann Arbor: University of Michigan Press, 2014), 2.

13. Absher, *The Black Musician and the White City*, 9.

14. For more on this history, see Lewis, *A Power Stronger than Itself*.

15. Amiri Baraka, *Digging: The Afro-American Soul of American Classical Music* (Berkeley: University of California Press, 2009), 156.

16. Jason Robinson, "The Challenge of the Changing Same: The Jazz Avant-Garde of the 1960s, the Black Aesthetic, and the Black Arts Movement," *Critical Studies in Improvisation/Études critiques en improvisation* 1, no. 2 (2005): 20–37. https://www.criticalimprov.com/index.php/csieci/article/view/17/48, accessed March 21, 2019.

17. Monson, *Freedom Sounds*, 27.

18. Monson, *Freedom Sounds*, 27.

19. Personal communication by phone with Michael Cuscuna, February 15, 2018.

20. Eddie S. Meadows, *Bebop to Cool: Context, Ideology, and Musical Identity* (Westport, CT: Greenwood Press), 2003, 35–36.

21. Barnaby Skinner, "Blue Note Jazz King Peddles New York Soul," Beirut *Daily Star*, August 8, 2002. http://www.dailystar.com.lb/Culture/Art/2002/Aug-08/108551-blue-note-jazz-king-peddles-new-york-soul.ashx, accessed March 14, 2018.

22. Philippe Carles and Jean-Louis Comolli, *Free Jazz/Black Power*, trans. and intro. Grégory Pierrot (Jackson: University Press of Mississippi, 2015), 169.

23. Carles and Comolli, *Free Jazz/Black Power*, 180.

24. Darby English, *1971: A Year in the Life of Color* (Chicago: University of Chicago Press, 2016), 96.

25. English, *1971: A Year in the Life of Color*, 98, my emphasis.

26. Ishmael Reed, "The Black Artist: Calling a Spade a Spade," *Arts Magazine* 41 (May 1967): 48–49.

27. Reed, "The Black Artist: Calling a Spade a Spade," 49.

28. English, *1971: A Year in the Life of Color*, 97–98.

29. Raymond Saunders, *Black Is a Color* (n.p., 1967, pamphlet), reprinted as an appendix in English, *1971*, 272.

30. Saunders, *Black Is a Color*; lowercasing per the original.

31. Monson, *Freedom Sounds*, 25.

32. "Andrew Hill on Piano Jazz," *Marian McPartland's Piano Jazz*, NPR, recorded February 24, 2005; aired December 6, 2005. https://www.npr.org/2007/12/21/17460558/andrew-hill-master-of-melody, accessed March 3, 2019.

33. "Andrew Hill on Piano Jazz," at 1:14–1:29.

34. Rosamond C. Rodman, "Naming a Place Nicodemus," *Great Plains Quarterly* 28, no. 1 (2008): 49–62.

35. Rodman, "Naming a Place Nicodemus," 55, 58.

36. Rodman, "Naming a Place Nicodemus," 57.

37. "Andrew Hill on Piano Jazz," at 14:00–14:14.

38. "Andrew Hill on Piano Jazz," at 14:17–14:40.

39. Eitan Y. Wilf, *School for Cool: The Academic Jazz Program and the Paradox of Institutionalized Creativity* (Chicago: University of Chicago Press, 2014), 105.

40. Ken Prouty, *Knowing Jazz: Community, Pedagogy, and Canon in the Information Age* (Jackson: University Press of Mississippi, 2012), 52.

41. Herman Gray, *Cultural Moves: African Americans and the Politics of Representation* (Berkeley: University of California Press, 2005), 48.

42. Andrew Hill Papers, Box 1, Folder 4.

43. Comiskey, "Why Black Jazz Died and White Survived."

44. Comiskey, "Why Black Jazz Died and White Survived."

45. Comiskey, "Why Black Jazz Died and White Survived."

46. Andrew Hill Papers, Box 1, Folder 4.

47. Andrew Hill Papers, Box 1, Folder 4.

48. Monson, *Freedom Sounds*, 284.

49. Heckman, "Roots, Culture and Economics," 19–20.

50. Undated "Curriculum Vitae" document with a short mission statement by Andrew Hill, Andrew Hill Papers, Box 3, Folder 4.

51. Personal communication by email with Charley Gray, April 2, 2018. Gray was director of jazz studies at Portland State University for twenty-seven years and co-founder and director of the Portland Jazz Orchestra.

52. Personal communication by phone with Charley Gray, April 2, 2018.

53. Paul Steinbeck, *Message to Our Folks: The Art Ensemble of Chicago* (Chicago: University of Chicago Press, 2017), 17, 45.

54. "Andrew Hill on Piano Jazz," at 7:18–7:29, 7:40–7:47; here, he was discussing his performance of "Nicodemus."

55. Roger T. Dean, *New Structures in Jazz and Improvised Music since 1960* (Philadelphia and Milton Keynes, UK: Open University Press, 1992), 118.

56. Ben Ratliff, "Andrew Hill: One Man's Lifelong Search for the Melody in Rhythm," *New York Times*, February 24, 2006. https://www.nytimes.com/2006/02/24/arts/music/andrew-hill-one-mans-lifelong-search-for-the-melody-in-rhythm.html, accessed March 21, 2019.

57. Personal communication by email with Charley Gray, April 2, 2018.

58. Personal communication by email with Calvin Jones, April 6, 2018.

59. Personal communication by email with Calvin Jones, April 6, 2018.

60. Dean, *New Structures*, 116.

61. Monson, *Freedom Sounds*, 286.

Epilogue: The Sonic Archive of Black Spatiality

1. This is an excerpt from a recorded conversation between trumpeter Christian Scott aTunde Adjuah X and poet Saul Williams in promotion of aTunde Adjuah's *Ancestral Recall* (2019), a recording that features Williams. Williams echoes much of what I have discussed throughout this book, which is the importance of understanding the ontological relationship to musical space and how the power of that understanding shapes musical approaches. See https://www.youtube.com/watch?v=rD6EIlLG3wo, accessed April 22, 2020.

2. This comment was made by multi-instrumentalist, improviser, and fine artist Douglas Ewart at the Rio Negro Conference in Silo City on September 9, 2019, in Buffalo, NY. This

comment expresses his ontological and musical agency beyond any recommendations from a prescriptive, nationalist discourse.

3. David Beard and Kenneth Gloag, *Musicology: The Key Concepts*, 2nd ed. (New York: Routledge, 2016), 15.

4. Joseph Kerman, *Contemplating Music: Challenges to Musicology* (Cambridge, MA: Harvard University Press, 1985), 12.

5. Aimé Césaire, "Poetry and Knowledge," *Sulfur* 5, no. 5 (1982): 17.

6. In a personal conversation in August 2018, Fred Moten asked me whether I was on the inside or the outside of the house in relation to ideas in Gaston Bachelard's *Poetics of Space*.

7. Marina Abramović, Klaus Biesenbach, and Museum of Modern Art, *Marina Abramović: The Artist Is Present* (New York: Museum of Modern Art, 2010), 211.

8. Eidsheim, *The Race of Sound*, 9.

9. Eidsheim, *The Race of Sound*, 9.

10. Personal conversation at the home of Kamau Daáood, January 29, 2019.

11. Eidsheim, *The Race of Sound*, 21.

12. Personal conversation with Andrew Hill at Birdland, 2006. I cannot remember the exact date of the performance.

13. Okiji, *Jazz as Critique*, 86.

14. Ambrose Akinmusire, "My Name Is Oscar," on *When the Heart Emerges Glistening* (Blue Note 509990 70612 2 9, 2011); album recorded September 20–22, 2010, at Brooklyn Studios, Hollywood.

INDEX

References to figures and tables appear in **bold**.

artists: defiance of categorization of, 135; role in society of, 108; true artists, 131. *See also* African American improvisers; women improvisers
Association for the Advancement of Creative Musicians (AACM), 9–10, 76, 134, 146
Attica Blues (Shepp), 114
Auto-Tune, 117
Ayler, Albert, 134, 135

Bailly, Jean-Christophe, 47–48
Baldwin, James, 36
Baraka, Amiri (formerly LeRoi Jones): *Blues People*, 87; on release of Hill's albums, 134–35
bar lines, 17, 164n61. *See also* crossing bar lines
basslines, 95–96
Beaudet, Jean-Michel, 60
bebop music, 12
Bell, Sean, 115
bells, symbolism of, 101
Berklee College of Music, 75
Berklee Institute of Jazz and Gender Justice: Carrington's work in, ix–x, 23, 72; core mission and philosophy of, 86–87, 88; motivation for founding of, 82
Black aesthetic: Akinmusire's expression of, 117; asymmetrical equilibrium in, 36; and drumming, 80; infinite deferrals in, 40; as outside of Western music aesthetics, 154
Black art: political positioning of, 32–33; and spatiality, 7–8
Black Artists Group (BAG), 76
Black Arts movement, 135, 137
Black Arts Repertory Theatre/School (BARTS), 134
Black authenticity, 12, 138, 143–44
Black churches: nighttime practices of enslaved Africans, 140; rhetorical pacing of preachers in, 26–27; whooping in, 34, 60
Black civil society, 6, 7, 89, 135
Black feminist coalition politics, 87, 89
Black feminist thought, 72–74, 77–79, 99
Black geographies, 7–10, 176n1. *See also* place-making

Black humanity: affirmations of, 155; artistic articulation of, 4, 5–6, 16, 17; joy in improvising, 157; love and, 43; and survival, 43. *See also* Akinmusire, Ambrose; Blanchard, Terence; breath and breathing; crossing bar lines; gender equity; inclusiveness in Black musical space; marginalization; place-making
Black liberation, 43–44
Black Lives Matter (BLM) movement, 21, 27, 30, 90, 107, 115, 176n3
Black musical space: and affirmation of life, vii–viii, 8, 18; and African cosmology, 95; and all humanity, 19, 156; Black sound and performance of, 13–18; charting of Black life in, 10–11, 20; codification in, 128–29, 155; and community, 56, 134, 142–43, 155; concept of, vii–viii, ix, 5–6, 12, 19, 20; as conceptual and experiential, 131; education about culture of, 53–54; ensemble as community in, 120; as force of resistance and regeneration, viii–ix, 32; and improvisational culture, 3–4; inclusiveness of, x; liminality of, 106, 156; from lived experience, 6, 17–18, 59, 110, 131, 154–55, 156; music critics on Black music, 32; parameters of, 9; as space of joy, ix, 20, 155. *See also* African American improvisation; African American improvisers; Akinmusire, Ambrose; Blanchard, Terence; breath and breathing; Carrington, Terri Lyne; Higgins, Billy; Hill, Andrew; improvisation; place-making
Black nationalism, 24, 32, 87, 136
Blackness: and Black art, 137–38; and experience of fear and prejudice, 27–28; as fluid expressive space, 154; illusion of tangible Blackness, 128; improvisation and luminescence of, 153; measurement in improvisation of, 12; patriarchal views of, 52–53; and spatiality, 7–8; uncontainability of, 45
Black Panther Party (BPP), 109
"black pneuma" hermeneutic, 22, 34
Black popular music, 11
Black spirituality, 21

ABOUT THE AUTHOR

Photo credit: Amy Manley

James Gordon Williams is a transdisciplinary American pianist, composer, and improviser who has worked with poets and experimental filmmakers and video artists. He is also a critical musicologist. His research is in the burgeoning field of Critical Improvisation Studies and African American popular music studies. Williams has performed around the world, including such places as the Village Vanguard, Birdland, and music festivals in the United States, Malta, Switzerland, France, and Italy. Williams is assistant professor at Syracuse University.

CPSIA information can be obtained
at www.ICGtesting.com
Printed in the USA
JSHW022136161121
20520JS00001B/7

9 781496 832108